Calculating
Human Resource
Costs and Benefits

Calculating Human Resource Costs and Benefits

CUTTING COSTS AND IMPROVING PRODUCTIVITY

Lyle M. Spencer, Jr.

McBer and Company

A Wiley-Interscience Publication

JOHN WILEY & SONS

New York   Chichester   Brisbane   Toronto   Singapore

This publication is designed to provide accurate and
authoritative information in regard to the subject
matter covered. It is sold with the understanding that
the publisher is not engaged in rendering legal, accounting,
or other professional service. If legal advice or other
expert assistance is required, the services of a competent
professional person should be sought. *From a Declaration
of Principles jointly adopted by a Committee of the
American Bar Association and a Committee of Publishers.*

Library of Congress Cataloging-in-Publication Data:

Spencer, Lyle M.
    Calculating human resource costs and benefits.

    "A Wiley-Interscience publication."
    Bibliography: p.
    Includes index.
    1. Personnel management. 2. Employees, Training of—
Cost effectiveness. 3. Labor costs. I. Title.

HF5549.S84133   1986   658.3   85-26644
ISBN 0-471-81040-1

Printed in the United States of America

10 9 8 7 6 5 4 3 2 1

Preface

WHY THIS BOOK?

The purpose of this book is to show you how to give "hard" dollar numbers to "soft" human resource projects and programs. It summarizes the lessons of a course I have taught for 10 years on cost-benefit evaluation. At first the course attracted trainers, consultants, and personnel administrators. Recently, more participants are managers of "knowledge workers," for example, sales people, engineers, computer programmers, market researchers, strategic planners, corporate legal staff, and health care professionals.

These people expressed a common need that: "There are many academic references on cost-benefit analysis and productivity improvement, but no simple, practical guide that shows me exactly how to do it in my own job."

My objective is to provide this simple, how-to-do-it guide. You will find many worksheets with very specific instructions, for example: "Add lines 1 to 5. Divide line 6 by line 7."

Math used is deliberately limited to fifth grade arithmetic. If you can add, subtract, multiply, and divide, you can follow any example in the book.

An appendix provides a Lotus 1–2–3 (or other spreadsheet) template and a BASIC program for key worksheets.

All methods described can be applied to any administrative or professional "knowledge" worker group. Case examples from industry, military, government, and health care organizations provide models you can follow.

PLAN OF THE BOOK

Chapter 1, "Why Evaluate?," describes business and productivity trends that make cost-benefit evaluation particularly important at the present time.

Chapter 2, "Developing Measures," shows you how to develop efficiency, effectiveness, and productivity measures for any "knowledge worker," job, or work group.

Chapter 3, "Calculating Costs," shows you how to find the cost of any human resource or staff program, function, or project.

Chapter 4, "Calculating Benefits Basic Strategies" describes ways of documenting the dollar benefits of human resource people, projects, and services.

Chapter 5, "Calculating Benefits Applications," provides a reference list of benefits for many human resource services.

Chapter 6, "Increasing Productivity," describes, with practical business examples, proven methods that can increase productivity 30 to 50%.

Chapter 7, "Evaluation Designs Proving You Made the Difference," shows you how to design evaluations to document the effects of your projects and efforts.

Chapter 8, "Designing Projects and Programs to Get Results," shows you how to set up your projects and programs in ways that all but guarantee they will show benefit results measurable in dollar terms.

A postscript, "Cost-Benefit Analysis: Science or Political Science?," discusses the uses and abuses of cost-benefit approaches and shows you how to use numerical data for maximum impact.

LYLE M. SPENCER

Boston, Massachusetts
April 1986

Acknowledgments

Case examples in the book are drawn from my own consulting and work done by my students and clients. (Names and some numbers have been disguised to protect innocent and guilty.)

I cannot begin to acknowledge all the people who have contributed to this effort, but I would particularly like to thank:

Military and Government: Doctors Owen Jacobs, Laurel Oliver, and Paul Duffey of the Army Research Institute, who funded much of my original research; Lieutenant Colonels Robert Jackson and Robert Robertson, and Majors Robert Begland, Ph.D., Warren Klein, Eddie Mitchell, and Walter Stewart, who provided examples from their cost-benefit evaluations of consulting projects.

Commander Ulysses S. James, U.S. Navy (ret.), with whom I have worked on cost-benefit analyses since 1974.

Mr. Brian Gillespie, U.S. Postal Service.

Industry: Keith Bolte, Corporate Manager of Productivity, Intel Corporation. Dr. Carl Thor, American Productivity Center. Dr. June Mall, AT&T. Jerry Wowk, Robert Daniels, and John O'Brien, Digital Equipment Company. Dr. David Miron, Vice President of Human Resources, Owens-Illinois, now at Temple Barker Sloan. Mr. David Morena, Wickes Corporation.

Health Care: Mr. Greg Finnegan, Little Company of Navy Hospital. Dr. Ronald Galbraith, Hospital Corporation of America and Dr. Nancy Richardson, Cambridge Management Institute.

I would also like to thank the following companies for use of their materials:

Figures 3.1 and 8.2 and Tables 3.6, 3.10, 4.1, 4.2, and 5.7 reprinted by permission of the publisher, from "Calculating Costs and Benefits," by Lyle M. Spencer, Jr., in *Human Resources Management and Development Handbook*, edited by William R. Tracy, pp. 1489, 1491, 1496–7, 1500–1, 1504–5, 1509, © 1985 AMACOM, a division of American Management Association, New York. All rights reserved.

Figure 8.1 reprinted with permission from the July 1984 issue of *Training, The Magazine of Human Resources Development*. © 1984, Lakewood Publications, Inc., Minneapolis, MN (612) 333–0471. All rights reserved.

Table 5.10 reprinted with permission of the author, from J. F. Follman, Jr., ALCOHOLISM AND BUSINESS, New York, AMACOM, 1976, p. 86.

Figure 6.9 reprinted with permission of the author, Jeremy Main, Fortune, © 1981 Time, Inc. All Rights Reserved.

Figure 6.3 reprinted by permission of the *Harvard Business Review*. An exhibit from "Cost Effectiveness Comes to the Personal Personnel Function" by Logan M. Creek (May/June 1973). Copyright 1973 by the President and Fellows of Harvard College; all rights reserved.

Figures 5.4, 5.6, 6.2, 6.5, 6.8, and 7.6, and Table 5.8. © 1985, McBer & Company, Boston, Massachusetts.

Table 5.9, reprinted by permission from W. Cascio, "Costing Human Resources," Kent Publishing Co., Boston, MA, 1982.

Text quote "Boom in Worker Leasing" by Eric Gelman and Richard Sandza reprinted by permission of the publisher. © 1984 by Newsweek, Inc. All Rights Reserved.

Michael Hamilton, John Wiley and Sons, my editor.

Kim Welch, who helped write and de-bug the BASIC program in Appendix A, my wife Signe Magnuson Spencer, who provided examples from her own work, editorial suggestions, and deeply appreciated moral support.

I have learned most from my clients and colleagues. Many of the ideas expressed in this book were developed with their help. Benefits of the present effort are to the credit of all; any errors or omissions are my responsibility.

L. M. S.

Contents

List of Figures

List of Tables

Calculating
Human Resource
Costs and Benefits

Determining the costs and benefits of HRD programs . . . [will be] one of the five top issues facing HRD professionals in the 1980s.

JAN MARGOLIS, PRESIDENT, AMERICAN SOCIETY
OF TRAINING AND DEVELOPMENT, 1980

We've moved to a period where the major criterion for judging things is cost effectiveness. In the 40's and 50's it was growth. In the 60's and 70's it was morality. Now there is no set of objective ideals except cost benefit. Business is moving to reexamine basic assumptions; the services they use, their portfolios, bank, lawyers, consultants, agencies, philosophy, employee benefits. Companies will be a lot more candid about certain operations that are not working, a lot more willing to say that the Emperor has no clothes. This affects service businesses. The issue of cost effectiveness will be critical. . . . You'll have to explain everything (in cost-benefit terms).

FLORENCE SKELLEY, PRESIDENT,
YANKELOVICH, SKELLY AND WHITE,
ADWEEK, AUGUST 1983

CHAPTER 1

Why Evaluation?

To make sure that staff is helping rather than hindering the line, staff departments must justify their budgets to the operational units, on the theory that operations pay for them. Cuts in middle management staffs are ranging from 20% to 40% . . . to improve efficiency 30% to 50%.

"THE SHRINKING OF MIDDLE MANAGEMENT,"
BUSINESS WEEK, APRIL 25, 1983

I invest in training the way I invest in a machine tool. If you can't show me an ROI equal to this firm's cost of capital, I'm not buying—and your budget is going to be cut.

FORTUNE 100 FINANCIAL VP TO
DIRECTOR OF HRD

Why cost-benefit evaluation? Four reasons:

Improve Practice.   Cost benefit methods can increase the productivity of human resource people and programs 30 to 50%.

Survival.   The times and economy demand it.

Credibility   with "bottom-line"-minded clients: Use of dollars—"the language of business"—can increase your clout.

Professional Development and Satisfaction.   Showing results can increase your own morale and professionalism.

IMPROVING PRACTICE

The best reason to use cost-benefit analysis (CBA) is its great power to increase the efficiency and effectiveness of human resource services. Cost-benefit methods have a double impact:

1. *Efficiency.*   Cost-benefit analysis results in better use of resources: people, projects, and the entire personnel program. You can provide the same services with fewer people, or more service with the same number of people.

2. *Effectiveness.*   Cost-benefit analysis leads you to focus on the *right* problems—those with the greatest dollar value to the firm—and to *focus* your services to produce maximum dollar benefits in fixing these problems.

Efficiency and effectiveness savings and benefits can increase human resource productivity 30 to 50% immediately and 10 to 15% a year afterwards *indefinitely*.

SURVIVAL

As the gloomy quotes at the beginning of this chapter suggest, increased worldwide competition and major changes in the U.S. economy require everyone to be more productive. The good news is that these pressures represent a major opportunity for human resource people.

The United States is now a 70% service economy, and the trend is to 85% service by 1990. In 1960 there were two workers (blue-collar people who made products) for every one staff person (white-collar managers, professional "knowledge workers," secretaries, and clerks). A short 20 years later there are two staff for every one worker. From 1973 to 1983, manufacturing worker productivity increased 22%. Office worker productivity increased less than 2%, 11 times less (Department of Labor, 1984).

An important implication of these figures is often overlooked. Service *people* are the major cost in most organizations. Observers awed by robot-automated assembly lines the length of a football field operated by two workers forget that somewhere nearby there is an office with 80 software engineers maintaining several million lines of code. Whatever the hopes for increased productivity from capital investment in high technology, computers, robots, and the like, *"most productivity increases will have to come from better use of these people."* (Business Week Magazine, Oct. 8, 1984, 124–125). *Business Week* went on to say: "Secretaries and typists represent only 8.7% of salary costs, while professionals account for 68%. . . . While word processing systems could eliminate 3.8% of all office costs if they replaced every typewriter, savings from professionals and managers could be much higher (because) interpersonal communication, analysis and decision-making—all primary managerial functions—make up a hefty 47.2% of all office expenses."

People problems and the need to make people more productive will not go away. Both will increase as organizations become more complex and service oriented. It follows that astute human resource people will always have jobs—and major opportunities to help their firms increase productivity.

CREDIBILITY

Human resource people everywhere are under pressure to become "business partners," (people who *make* money) rather than "overhead," (people who *cost* money). Becoming a business partner requires being able to speak the language of business: dollars. Personnel staff receive a very different reception when they come to the management table with figures that show dollar benefits. Selling personnel services in bottom line revenue or cost-savings terms can greatly increase your acceptance and clout. You join those who make money, as opposed to those who are costs.

PROFESSIONAL DEVELOPMENT SATISFACTION

The most often cited frustration of human resource people is lack of feedback: "I never get any information to show my programs make a difference, or really benefit my firm." Cost-benefit evaluation can show you the difference you make. Because feedback on outcome results motivates people to improve practice, cost-benefit methods promote professional development.

Why Don't People Evaluate?

Evaluation is like Mark Twain's weather: "Everyone talks about it, but nobody does anything about it." Managers agree it's a good thing, it should be done; they even pound on the table and demand it. The sad truth is that most organizations do little, if any evaluation. Why? Because of the following five reasons:

1. *People Do Not Know How.*   This book will address this problem. It will show you simple ways to cost and evaluate many types of programs.

2. *Fear That Evaluation Will Show That Programs Do Not Work, Are Not Worth Their Cost.*   This fear is realistic. Skillfully used, however, cost-benefit methods can be a no-lose game. If your program works, claim the benefits. If your program doesn't work, kill it and claim the benefits—either resource savings or increased benefits from replacing the old program with a new improved version. Use of evaluation results for maximum impact is a "political-science" issue discussed in the postscript.

3. *Belief That Cost-Benefit Figures Are Phony, "Funny Money."*   This too is a realistic fear; they can be. Healthy skepticism is always advisable when dealing with numbers. But CBA puts everything

in common language—numbers and dollars—in a way that makes underlying assumptions clear and explicit. The language and methods of CBA can be used to smoke out the phony numbers and isolate the truth from the smoke.

4. *Evaluation Is Not Worth It.* It takes too much time, costs too much. The value of CBA is itself a CBA question, technically called a "sensitivity" or "expected value of perfect information" analysis. You invest in getting better data when this investment has a return in making a better decision about a larger investment. Cost-benefit analysis is more likely to prove its worth when its cost is reduced, or the likelihood of benefits is increased. This book shows you methods for getting cost and benefit data quickly, cheaply, and easily. Most analyses shown can be done in less than an hour. With less investment in time and bigger benefits, CBA is a better deal. You will see that a small investment in CBA can produce larger returns than any competing use of your time.

5. *There Is No Real Incentive to Do It.* Sadly, in many organizations, there are few rewards for providing human resource services efficiently and effectively. Often people do not know the difference. Cost-benefit analysis cannot make people care about efficiency, quality, or effectiveness. It *can* show the stark, shocking dollar costs of inefficiency and ineffectiveness—and the dollar benefits from doing things better. Simply having these figures can raise the level of the debate and increase awareness and appreciation of human resource programs. With greater awareness and appreciation come rewards. Staff people who can show the dollar value of their services increase their visibility and influence and are better able to compete for bonuses and promotions.

It Can Be Done

Adding simple cost-benefit steps to every human resource task or program you undertake can ensure that you will always be able to evaluate your efforts in "hard" cost-benefit terms. These steps are:

1. *Value the Problem.* Calculate how much in dollars the task or problem situation you are asked to address costs your client or

firm now. Cost-benefit analysis will highlight the *right* problems—those which cost the most or offer the most savings if solved. Chapter 3 will show you how to do this.

2. *Value the Solution.* Calculate the difference in dollars you have to make in the problem to pay for your program. This will lead you to focus your program to have the best chance of showing dollar savings. Chapters 4 and 5 will show you how to do this.

3. *Value the Result.* Follow up and compare the cost of the problem after your program with its "before" baseline cost. Claim the savings!

For example, a request to a director of training by a plant manager might be, "Joe, you gotta get us some first-level supervisory training. My first-level folk don't know anything about management." Typically, the training director will take this request at face value and develop or buy off-the-shelf a first-level supervisory training program.

Following the advice to "value the problem" before intervening, the conversation might go a few steps further.

Training director:	How do you know they need management training? What aren't they doing now that management training would get them to do?
Plant manager:	They don't communicate too good.
Training director:	(Thinking "so what?") Really! Who doesn't communicate too well with whom? What communication problems have you seen?
Plant manager:	Well, the number one complaint we're getting from their subordinates is that they never get any feedback or any advice about how they can advance in this place.
Training director:	(Still thinking, "So what?") Well, is that causing any problem that you can see?
Plant manager:	Damn straight! I've lost four critical skills engineers out of 20 in the last three months!
Training director:	(Thinks, "Aha, turnover!") How much does an engineer make when he or she leaves?

Plant manager:	Thirty thousand bucks.
Training director:	You know, studies show that replacing professionals costs at minimum the salary they are making when they leave. If you've lost four of them, that has cost the organization $120,000, and if you keep losing them at the same rate, that will cost us $480,000 this year.
Plant manager:	(Expletive deleted)!

At this point, the training director has established a baseline cost for a problem that might be helped by management training: turnover due to lack of performance appraisal feedback and career planning discussions with subordinates. More important, he knows how to focus his training to impact on this specific problem: how to conduct performance appraisal/career planning discussions with junior engineers to motivate them to stay with the firm, as opposed to "general first-level supervisory training," which might include Maslow's hierarchy, functions of management, and so forth.

Further, the training director can easily figure out how big a difference in turnover would be needed to justify the training program. For example, if a training program for 20 first-level managers costs approximately $50,000, a saving of just two engineers, worth $60,000—a reduction in turnover of 12.5%—would not only pay for the training, but produce a $10,000/$50,000 = 20% return on investment. These figures should make the $50,000 training effort an easy sell to the plant manager.

Establishing the baseline data for turnover costs makes valuing the result of the training very easy because you know exactly what to look for. The training director can track turnover and calculate the dollar value of the training. Any saving in "before" versus "after" turnover costs can be claimed by the training department. Human resource people should always document and circulate a one-page "final report" of results they achieve. Such reports have great power to change the way the value of human resources groups is perceived.

Cost-benefit analyses—valuing the problem, valuing the solution, and valuing the result—can be a valuable marketing tool for human resources people. Understanding the dollar value of people—problems at the beginning gets managers' attention. Showing in dollars the outcomes needed to justify the cost of a program and its potential return on investment is a very effective way of selling it. Finally, documenting the dollar benefits of interventions proclaims to all the worth of human resource or other knowledge workers' services.

This book may appear to be about accounting. It is not—you need only the bare minimum of accounting necessary to state problems and program outcomes in dollars. It is really about outcomes.

My purpose is to give you an intellectual tool—a way of looking at and thinking about what you do—that can help you to clarify priorities and make *effective* choices. As you endure the discussion of costs in Chapter 3 keep in mind that the point is, as simply as possible, to translate problems, activities, and results into dollars so that they can be compared and evaluated. The true value of cost-benefit analysis lies in the *decisions* you and your company will make, based on your analyses. In most cases the final cost-to-benefit ratio or return on investments will be so clear and the differences between your options so dramatic that which method you use to account for overhead won't affect your final decision. So, don't let yourself be intimidated or bogged down by the math.

CHAPTER 2

Developing Measures

This chapter shows you how to identify "hard" dollar results measures for "soft" human resource programs.

EVALUATION

Evaluation means measuring something to make a decision about it, for example, to stop, modify, or expand it to increase its benefits. This implies:

Knowing what decision the evaluation data will help you make.

Measuring "scientifically," using data collection methods and research designs that separate the effects your program is having from all other influences on your outcome variables (the topic of Chapter 7, Proving You Made the Difference).

Choosing the right measures for what your program is really trying to accomplish.

Evaluation efforts are described as "formative" or "summative." "Formative" means evaluation data are used to see how a program is doing, to modify or improve it. "Summative" means data are used to make a final judgment on a program: it worked or didn't, was or was not worth its cost, should be continued or dropped. (Summative evaluations that fail to prove a program's worth are often retitled "formative"—if program staff can get away with it.)

TYPES OF MEASURES

It is useful first to distinguish results measures from other types of measures commonly used to evaluate human resource programs. In a famous article, Kirkpatrick (1975) observed that training and other programs could be evaluated at one of four levels:

1. Reactions: How people *feel* about a program.
2. Learning: Whether people *know* anything as a result of a program.

3. Behavior: Whether people *do* anything differently after the program.

4. Results: Hard *outcome* measures of individual or organizational effectiveness produced by the program.

REACTIONS

Measures of how people feel about a program include overheard comments, postcourse evaluation questionnaires and judgments of external observers.

FIGURE 2.1
Reactions Evaluation Form

1. I liked the Career Planning Program:

   very little   a little   so-so   a lot   very much

2. I think the Career Planning Program will help me be more successful in my career:

   very little   a little   so-so   a lot   very much

Reactions measures are useful for marketing, ''quick-fix'' formative redesign, quality control, and positive personal feedback.

Marketing. If trainees strongly dislike a program, you may have problems attracting people to the next course. Conversely, in the absence of cost-benefit data, most services are sold on reactions. Management often funds programs on the basis that "everyone loves it."

Fixing. Reactions data can alert you to a problem in time to fix it. If you can identify specifically what participants like or dislike about the program, you can delete or modify unpopular parts and expand popular parts.

Quality Control. Reactions surveys can be used as a "quality control" indicator for services. For example, if you cut an employee newsletter from weekly to monthly to reduce costs, employee response to reactions questions about whether the firm "cares about us" or "communicates with us" can tell you if people care about or even notice the change. If one of your trainers consistently gets lower ratings than the rest, you are alerted to find out why his or her delivery quality is lower.

Positive Feedback from participants can reinforce and reward the people conducting the program.

The problem with reactions measures is that most do not predict anything—not results, not behavior, not even how much people learn. As a result, reactions data are useless for making cost-effectiveness decisions about human resource programs.[1]

Method Guidelines

If you are going to use reactions measures, the following guidelines have been found to increase the usefulness of the data you collect.

Use Written Data Collection Forms. This may seem obvious, but think of the number of programs you have seen sold on the basis of anecdotal "Gee, that was the best thing I've attended this year" statements. Written forms at minimum provide a standardized format for data collection and a permanent record of data collected.

Design Question Items for Easy Numerical Tabulation.

[1]Validated organizational climate surveys may be an exception to this rule. See Chapter 5, for a description of ways to relate reactions data to results measures.

Be Specific About the Element of the Program People Are Reacting to. For example, the global response "I liked/disliked the cost-benefit seminar" does not provide useful feedback. If you ask, "I was/wasn't able to use Costing Worksheet 2.1," you get feedback about what specifically to drop, fix, or keep.

Ask About Expected Use and Value on the Job as Opposed to Feelings. "I will/will not be able to apply what I've learned in this course back on the job" is a better question than "I liked/did not like the program."

Have Independent Observers as Well as Participants Complete the Reactions Form. Training and consulting efforts create a "group-dynamics" effect. Just being together and sharing an experience causes people in a group to feel unrealistically high or low about a program. Independent "fly-on-the-wall" observers who are not a part of the group process can make more objective observations.

Get Reactions Data Three Months After the Program. This will minimize the immediate group dynamics effect. More important, participants will have been back in their real job situations and much better able to judge whether in fact the experience was useful to them.

LEARNING

Learning outcomes include change in knowledge about a subject and also change in attitudes or motivation. Learning is usually measured by postcourse tests on knowledge content, attitude surveys, or personality tests.

Learning measures are somewhat stronger if the knowledge, attitude, or motivation taught has been shown to predict behavior on the job needed to get hard results.

The problem with learning tests is that very often they do *not* predict either behavior or results. What people know at best predicts what they *can* do, not what they *will* do. Knowledge may be necessary to perform a task, but it may not change job behavior.

One of the oldest findings in behavioral science is that changing people's attitudes does not change their behavior (Allport, 1954; Cohen, 1964). In fact, the exact opposite is true. If you change people's behavior, they change their attitudes to be consistent with their behavior. This has led to the replacement of most race and gender awareness programs by affirmative action goals to change behavior and results.

Personality measures may or may not predict behavior and results. Changing people's minds is more difficult, time consuming, expensive, and politically sensitive than changing their behavior. Learning outcomes must be directly related to behavior changes and to end-results or bottom-line measures to be meaningful.

Method Guidelines

Use Operant Instead of Respondent Measures.   Operant tests require a person to demonstrate a behavior. Respondent tests ask people to respond to abstract questions, for example, "List the five rules of effective feedback" or "Which of the following is an example of persuasive argument: a, b, c, d, or e?"

It is easy to see that the *respondent* ability to list knowledge of rules for giving feedback, or selecting someone else's persuasive argument is very different from the *operant* ability to give feedback effectively or stand on one's feet and argue persuasively.

An operant test, for example, a role play or simulation that requires participants to conduct a performance appraisal or to make a persuasive presentation and then codes them on their ability to do so is a better predictor of on-the-job behavior. Operant learning tests should be as similar as possible to actual on-the-job situations and to the behaviors you are teaching, that is, as close to "behavior measures" as can be simulated in a class.

BEHAVIOR

Whether people *do* anything differently as the result of a program can be measured in many ways, for example:

Documented completion of goals or action steps stated in the workshop

Development of a written affirmative action plan

Introduction of staff meetings or of an education program

Observed use of a new managerial style

Behavior measures provide much better evaluation data *if* the behaviors measured actually lead to desired results for the organization. An example would be setting goals or creating an action plan. Goal setting has been shown to increase the probability of goal attainment from 5% to between 60 and 70% and increase productivity an average of 19% (French, Kay, and Meyer, 1957; Kolb and Boyatzis, 1970; Latham and Locke, 1979).

The problem with behavior measures is that behaviors taught may *not* produce desired results. The best example is the T-group, the rage of the late 1960s. Managers were sent off to T-groups and returned with changed behaviors: hugging fellow employees, volunteering intimate personal feelings in meetings, and the like. The only problem was that subsequent evaluation studies showed that T-groups produced lower performance and lower morale in all organizations—industry, military, and government (Bowers, 1973). The human resources field is lamentably prone to "program of the month" fads (transactional analysis, EST, and neuro-linguistic programming, to mention a few recent offerings), few of which come with any data to show that the behaviors they teach in fact produce bottom-line benefits for an organization.

Method Guidelines

Behavior data can be collected from a variety of sources (participants or their bosses, peers, subordinates, clients, observers), using one of four techniques: interviews, questionnaires and surveys, direct observation, and organizational record sources. Method guidelines include:

Use Multiple Sources.   Self-reports from participants are the least accurate and reliable. A manager's self-perception of whether he or she is behaving more or less "democratic participatively" will be less accurate than subordinates' rating of "My boss is more/less likely to discuss with me important changes concerning my job." Data from trained observers are most reliable (but very expensive), followed by data collected from subordinates, peers, and superiors (Lewin and Zwaney, 1976; Kane and Lawler, 1979).

Get Good Baseline Data Before the Program and Collect "After" Data Three Months Following. This will enable you to measure the difference made by the program and to see whether or not the behavior persists in a meaningful way on the job.

Use Organizational Record Data where possible, as opposed to hearsay interview data. Useful organization records might include sales calls or speeches actually made, management-by-objective forms filled out, performance appraisals completed and signed by both manager and subordinate. In general, organizational data provide the best measures of behavior. The next best method is survey data collected from persons other than the participant (enough to get statistical averages and confidence intervals), and after that, judgments of trained observers, and participant interviews.

Check Measure Reliability. Reliability means that the measure is not a rubber yardstick, that any change in the variable being measured is due to change in what is being measured, not in the method used to measure it. Reliable measures are resistent to bias, outright lying, and "cooking" of data.

Ways to check the reliability of measures are: (1) get two or more observers' data on the same event (inter-rater reliability); (2) get measures of the same event at two points in time; (time$_1$-time$_2$ reliability).

If you have more than one observation for a measure, you can find the average and the "standard deviation," a statistical measure of whether the people observing the event agree or if repeated measures of a variable produce more or less the same value. (See any elementary statistics book.)

Use Unobtrusive Measures. An unobtrusive measure is one where people do not know data is being collected on them. Examples are bosses' ratings of subordinates when the subordinates do not know that their behavior or performance is being rated, or observations of employee behavior through one-way mirrors.

Obtrusive measures are ones where people do know you are measuring them, for example, giving trainees a reactions form or interviewing them after a training course. The problem with obtrusive measures is that people tend to tell you what makes them look good (social desirability) or what you want to hear. You can reduce this bias by asking for data anonymously, but people's responses will still be affected by questions being asked.

You can actually use obtrusive evaluation questions as part of your intervention to get behavior change. For example, knowing that they will be asked pointed evaluation questions (e.g., ''How are you doing on your affirmative action goals?'') will encourage people to work on these goals.

As an example, an *obtrusive* measure to evaluate salespeople's behavior after a training program would be an interview that asked salespeople how they spent their time: who they called on, how much time they spent with each prospect, and the like. An *unobtrusive* measure for getting similar data would be to look at sales people's desk calendars, schedule books, travel and expense documents, and phone bills.

Many kinds of organizational record data—for example, sales, turnover, absenteeism, and grievances—are unobtrusive in the sense that they are routinely collected by people unrelated to the employees for whom these may be measures of performance. Collecting results data unobtrusively reduces the chances that data will be biased by respondents' tendency to tell you what they think you want to hear. (Webb, Campbell, Schwartz, & Sechrest, 1966)

RESULTS

Hard outcome measures of individual and organizational effectiveness include sales, profits, productivity, quality, costs, scrappage losses, combat-preparedness inspection scores, and all personnel outcomes that can be measured in dollars: for example, turnover, grievances, and accidents.

The use of results data is obvious. Bottom-line costs and benefits are the real measure of any human resources program.

The difficulty with results measures is that most people believe these data are hard, expensive, and take a long time to get. Rated on a continuum, more valuable measures may require more resources: you get what you pay for. (See Figure 2.2.)

FIGURE 2.2

Evaluation Variable Continuum: Reactions - Results

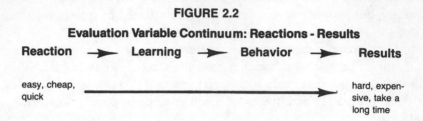

In fact results measures *can* be gotten quickly, cheaply, and easily using methods described in Chapters 3 and 4.

Developing Meaningful Results Measures

Developing good results measures is crucial. People and organizations become what they measure. Measures drive behavior because feedback, rewards, and punishments are based on what is measured. It is therefore very important to define the right measures: what the organization really wants people to do and achieve. Cost and benefit calculations are useless or can be destructive if the wrong measures are used.

The basic results measure is *productivity*. Productivity is defined as outputs divided by inputs, or benefits divided by costs. For human resource and knowledge workers, whose principal input is professional time, this translates as "whatever you produce (output) divided by the time (input) it takes you to produce it."

The reciprocal of the productivity equation is also commonly used, for example, as a ratio of the inputs to outputs (75 "input" hours of development time to produce one "output" hour of training), or "input" cost per unit "output," for example, $7000 cost per wage and compensation plan.

Three common definitions of the basic output/input productivity equation are:

1. *Efficiency:* The same output benefits with lower costs, smaller inputs, for example, a training module prepared with fewer hours of developer's time. Efficiency, or "benefit-cost" measures, are often used when the benefit can not be expressed in dollars, for example, "combat preparedness," "good community relations," or "health." (See Figure 2.3.)

FIGURE 2.3

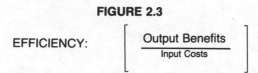

Efficiency measures are usually "immediate" or "first order" benefits: how much it costs to produce something without measurement of whether the thing produced provides the desired result. For this reason efficiency measures should always have a quality control definition, for example, the combat-preparedness inspection score or survey result that defines when an army unit is ready to fight, a firm has "good community relations," or a patient is healthy enough to leave a hospital.

2. *Effectiveness:* Larger outputs, more or better benefits for the same input costs, for example, more sales for the same sales training cost. Benefits in the effectiveness equation usually are expressed in dollars. (See Figure 2.4.)

FIGURE 2.4

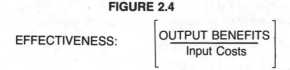

Effectiveness measures tend to be "ultimate" benefits—what the service being measured is really contributing to the organization. For example, the efficiency measure for a wage and compensation specialist is how many person-days (or dollar cost) it took to produce a plan. Effectiveness measures are reduced hiring costs or less turnover of skilled personnel due to good wage and compensation planning.

3. *Productivity:*   Increased output benefits for decreased input costs, "more for less." Productivity measures, both benefits and costs, are expressible in dollars. The productivity equation explicitly relates immediate efficiency and ultimate effectiveness. (See Figure 2.5.)

FIGURE 2.5

$$\text{PRODUCTIVITY:} \qquad \left[\frac{\text{OUTPUT BENEFITS}}{\text{Input Costs}} \right]$$

Although each definition has a somewhat different meaning, the efficiency, effectiveness, and productivity equations are the same. Each can be used to show "cost benefits":

1. *Efficiency.*   Doing what you are doing now (with no loss of quality) for less. The benefit is the "for less" (i.e., dollars saved).

2. *Effectiveness.*   Doing more or better with what you now have. The benefit is the dollar value of the "more or better" results.

3. *Productivity.*   Doing more or better with less than you now have. The benefit is the sum of the "for less" dollars saved and the dollar value of the "more or better" results.

The following steps will help you develop meaningful results measures for any human resource or knowledge worker, product, or service. (See Figure 2.6.)

1. Start by defining an efficiency measure for what you do.

FIGURE 2.6
Measure Development Worksheet

I. EFFICIENCY

II. EFFECTIVENESS

(a) Product/ Service	(b) 1 Unit Output	(c) "Quality Control" Standard	(d) Unit Inputs	(e) $ Cost/Unit	(a) Value/Cost Avoided	(b) Unit Measure/ Value	(c) $ Benefit Value
Examples A. Career Counseling	1 session	Goal and plan signed by boss and employee	Hours to deliver 1 session		- productivity - morale - turnover - grievances	% productivity % turnover # grievances	
B. Wage and Salary Planning	1 plan	Accepted by client	Days to complete 1 plan		- turnover - grievances - rewriting costs	% turnover # grievances cost/person	
C. Personnel Data Entries	1 transaction	Accurate, no "fail"	Minutes to complete 1 transaction		- no complaints - no errors	# complaints # "fails" to be corrected	
Your products or services 1.							
2.							
3.							

a. Identify your *product or service*, for example, career counseling, wage and compensation planning, legal services.

b. Identify *one unit output* of what you do. A question you can ask yourself is: If you were buying your product or service from an external professional service firm, what would a unit of your product or service be? For example:

Career counselor.   One career counseling session, or one employee with a good career plan.

Wage and compensation planner.   One plan.

Trainer.   One course delivered or one student trained.

Market researcher or strategic planner.   One completed report.

Consultant.   One completed project.

c. Identify *quality control standards* for the product or service. For example: What is a "good" career plan? A quality control standard might be "a written plan using a standard form, signed by both the employee and his or her supervisor."

d. Identify *unit inputs* required to produce the output. For human resource and knowledge workers, these inputs are mostly people's time (e.g., the *hours* of counselor time to deliver one hour of counseling, or *days* of strategic planner time to produce one strategic planning report).

Other input costs might be materials, for example, a career planning guide given counseled employees, travel, per diem, purchased services (e.g., consultant fees), equipment, and facilities (e.g., rooms rented).

e. Calculate the *total dollar cost* of the inputs needed to produce one unit output. Chapter 3, "Calculating Costs," will show you how to do this calculation.

2. Identify effectiveness measures. Identifying effectiveness measures, the ultimate value to the organization of your product or service, is more challenging. You must identify the real mission or purpose of the service you provide and relate it to financial consequences for your firm.

a. Identify *the value* of your product or service *to your clients.*

The following questions may help:

Who are your clients: individuals and/or organizations?

What is the consequence or benefit to your client of your product or service?   For a career counselor, for example, the benefit for employees might be greater satisfaction or a higher likelihood of getting promoted. For the organization it might be lower turnover by unsatisfied employees, higher productivity, and fewer grievances or equal employment opportunity complaints and suits filed by people who did not feel they had fair advancement opportunities.

What is the consequence of not providing your service? Very often benefits result from "costs avoided," for example, a person not leaving, a medical case or claim avoided, a grievance or affirmative action suit not filed. For career counseling, loss of the service for individuals might result in greater dissatisfaction, leading to lower productivity and higher turnover, and for the organization it might result in fewer people available for promotion (hence higher outside recruiting costs) and more grievances, complaints, and suits.

It may help you to identify effectiveness measures to trace the impact of your product or service through to the organization's revenues or costs. An example is given in Figure 2.7 for two types of communications skills training in public utilities: public speaking for executives and communication skills for customer service representatives.

How might one show the ultimate dollar value of teaching executives to be public speakers? A key part of the senior utility executive's job is maintaining good community relations and persuading the public that the utility is providing good services at a fair price.

The *learning* outcome of the public-speaking course was presumably more knowledge of effective speaking techniques.

The *behavior* outcome was the increased number of "good" speeches actually given by executives trained. In this case,

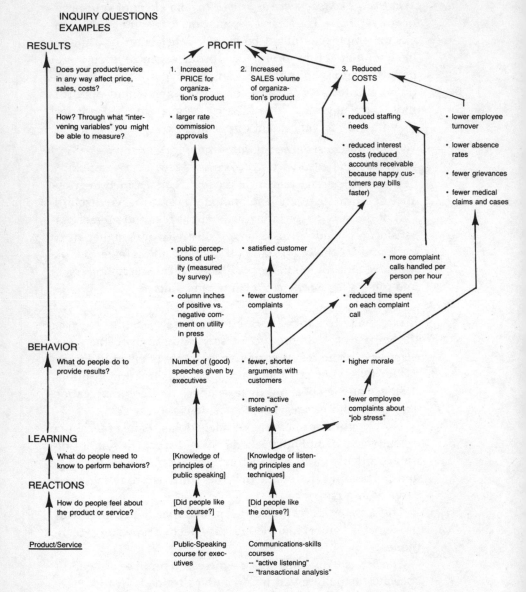

FIGURE 2.7
Identifying Results Benefit Measures

INQUIRY QUESTIONS
EXAMPLES

RESULTS

Does your product/service in any way affect price, sales, costs?

How? Through what "intervening variables" you might be able to measure?

PROFIT

1. Increased PRICE for organization's product
   - larger rate commission approvals
   - public perceptions of utility (measured by survey)
   - column inches of positive vs. negative comment on utility in press

2. Increased SALES volume of organization's product
   - satisfied customer
   - fewer customer complaints

3. Reduced COSTS
   - reduced staffing needs
   - reduced interest costs (reduced accounts receivable because happy customers pay bills faster)
   - more complaint calls handled per person per hour
   - reduced time spent on each complaint call
   - lower employee turnover
   - lower absence rates
   - fewer grievances
   - fewer medical claims and cases

BEHAVIOR

What do people do to provide results?

Number of (good) speeches given by executives

- fewer, shorter arguments with customers
- more "active listening"

- higher morale
- fewer employee complaints about "job stress"

LEARNING

What do people need to know to perform behaviors?

[Knowledge of principles of public speaking]

[Knowledge of listening principles and techniques]

REACTIONS

How do people feel about the product or service?

[Did people like the course?]

[Did people like the course?]

Product/Service

Public-Speaking course for executives

Communications-skills courses
-- "active listening"
-- "transactional analysis"

24

the "goodness" of the speech was measured by a reaction survey given to members of the audience. The survey asked whether or not the people listening liked the speech, understood the utility's position, and believed it was fair. The link from good public speaking to the *results* outcome was measured "unobtrusively" by using an intermediate reaction measure. The number of column inches of positive versus negative comment on the utility in the press was shown to predict public perceptions of the utility as measured by customer attitude surveys. Studies further showed that utilities with higher public satisfaction ratings are granted larger rate increases by state rate commissions. Approval of higher prices for the utility's product directly increased the firm's revenues. The benefits of public-speaking training could be traced through effects on community and public relations measures to the utility's bottom line.

How might one show the dollar value of communications skills courses for customer service representatives? Customer service representatives are people who answer telephones and respond to customers' questions and complaints about utility bills. Turnover among these people is very high, as much as 300%. People who leave say they could not stand being beaten up on the telephone all day.

The communications skills course taught service representatives principles of "active listening" (how to repeat what customers said, leading the customer to feel understood), and transactional analysis (how to maintain one's "adult" emotional self-control and respond objectively to angry customers).

The *behavior* outcome of these workshops was more active listening and fewer and shorter arguments with customers, as measured unobtrusively by listening in on service representatives' conversations with customers.

Intermediate *results* included fewer customer complaints ("I demand to speak to your boss!"), which meant reduced time spent on each complaint call by service representatives and their superiors. This in turn meant more complaint calls could be handled per person per hour, which led to reduced staffing needs. Service representatives reported higher morale and job satisfaction and fewer complaints about job stress. This led to lower employee turnover, lower absence rates, fewer grievances, and fewer medical cases and claims—all of which resulted in reduced personnel costs.

Customers who were satisfied that their bill was fair paid faster. This led to reduced accounts receivable, collection efforts, and interest costs. It is questionable whether satisfied customers bought more electricity, but increased customer satisfaction usually predicts increased sales volume, directly increasing firms' revenues.

b. *Identify measures of your effectiveness results.* Identify the "perfect score" for your effectiveness outcomes, for example, zero turnover, zero absenteeism, 100% of bills paid within 30 days. A perfect score is useful because it defines one end of a scale. As soon as you have identified the perfect score, you can measure how an individual or organization is doing in terms of it.

c. *Calculate the dollar value* of one effectiveness result. Chapter 4, "Calculating Benefits: Basic Strategies" will show you how to do this calculation.

Method Guidelines

Identify Output Results Versus Input or Process Measures. For example, people trained per year, telephone calls made, or meetings attended are not good measures, because the *results* of training, meetings, or telephone calls are not specified. A better measure for training is cost per person trained (an efficiency measure), or even better, increase in sales per person trained (an effectiveness measure).

Be Sure Your Output Measure Is the Result the Organization Really Wants. For example, lawsuits litigated per lawyer is probably not a good measure of legal services. Good lawyers keep their clients out of trouble and hence have fewer lawsuits to litigate. Better measures would be legal problems resolved per lawyer or cost per legal problem resolved. Cost per patient bed day is a poor measure of hospital performance because it rewards "bed stuffing"—keeping patients in a hospital longer than they need to be to spread fixed costs over more patient bed days. This may increase hospital revenue, but it also increases the cost of patient care. A better measure would be "cost per patient with a given illness returned to normal state of health." In fact, this is the approach governments and insurers are taking to cost containment in health care services.

Be Sure Your Output Measures Are Within Your Control, Within the "Boundary" of Your Department. For example, tons of steel per secretary or typhoons tracked per meteorologist are not good measures, because secretaries have very little to do with producing a ton of steel and meteorologists cannot control whether typhoons develop. (Mundel [1983] reports in all seriousness that the U.S. weather bureau was criticized for low productivity because it tracked 26 typhoons in a base year, and then 17 the next year, leading some bureaucrat to conclude that meteorologists' productivity had fallen 9/26 typhoons = 35%!)

For example, a college relations department decided that cost per new college hire was not a good output measure, because many other factors—such as salary, or skill of employment interviewers—influence whether or not a college graduate actually comes to work for the firm. An output over which college relations specialists *did* have control was cost per good lead, where the quality control definition of "a good lead" was a candidate in the top 10% of his or her class, from one of the top ten schools in computer science. This figure turned out to be $485 for a majority candidate and $670 for a minority candidate.

Output measures should be appropriate to the size of the organizational unit responsible for them. Mundel (1983) suggests that work unit output measures can be divided into eight levels (shown in Table 2.1), from the smallest part of the task to the ultimate result of a number of programs for an organization.

My experience is that the most useful level for human resources and knowledge workers is Level 5: the end product or one unit of a program, for example, one performance appraisal or one career plan. Level 3 tasks (e.g., one career counseling session), and Level 2 elements of tasks (e.g., scheduling one session) are useful in calculating the dollar cost of a specific end product, as will be seen in Chapter 3, "Calculating Costs." Higher level measures of the results of a program, groups of programs, or the overall result for the organization can always be calculated by adding up or extrapolating from Level 5 work unit costs and benefits.

Consider Efficiency Versus Effectiveness Trade-Offs. Efficiency measures particularly must be quality controlled to ensure that efforts to increase efficiency do not harm the organization by decreasing overall effectiveness. For example, management could lean on career counselors seeing clients for one-hour sessions to triple productivity by seeing three clients an hour, each for 20 minutes. The effectiveness question is, ''Are people going to get any meaningful career counseling in one third of an hour?'' To answer this, one must consider the real purpose of career counseling, for example, to prepare people for promotion or reduce turnover. Increased efficiency in this case is valuable only if employees produce equally good career plans as a result of their shorter counseling sessions—and there is no decrease in promotion and turnover effectiveness measures.

Similar examples are: faster sales calls may save money but result in lower sales. Shorter repair calls may lead to more callbacks because equipment was not repaired properly. Fewer clerks can cause customers to perceive lower level service and lead to a decline in sales. Fewer lab technicians could lead to longer hospital stays or patient complications (and malpractice suits) if late diagnoses prevent care from being given in time.

In each case you must define quality control standards or an effectiveness measure for the service and ensure that the quality is maintained and/or that effectiveness is not reduced.

Effectiveness measures must also be quality controlled to be sure short-term savings do not result in long-term losses to the organization. Examples are grievances in industry and disciplinary actions in the military. Both cost money, approximately $1000 a grievance or disciplinary action. Zero grievances and zero disciplinary actions are clearly cost beneficial and might be considered an indicator of a high performing organization. Zero grievances may, however, mean management is so soft and quick to give into the union that it is ''giving away the store,'' establishing damaging precedents in work concessions that result in higher labor costs. Similarly, few disciplinary actions in a military unit may be an indicator of lax discipline, which will show up in poor performance in an emergency situation. In dealing with grievances, managers must

TABLE 2.1

Levels of Work Unit Output Measures

Level	Name	Definition	Example	Measure
8.	Result	What achieved because of output of activity	Personnel (Succession) planning	2 backup candidates for all (100) key positions
7.	Gross Output (of several programs)	End Products, completed services of several related programs (e.g., performance appraisal, career path analysis, career counseling, etc.	Career plans	Completed career plans for top 3 levels of management (500 people)
6.	Program	Output of 1 program	Performance Appraisal	Completed performance appraisals for top 5 levels of management (7,500 people)
5.	End Product	1 unit of final output, measure	1 performance appraisal	Completed performance appraisal forms signed by boss and subordinate a. Boss-Subordinate Agreement Form b. Boss Rating Form c. Subordinate Rating Form
4.	Intermediate product	Part of 5 unit output, or required for it	1 Boss-Subordinate Agreement Form	1 completed form
3.	Task	Activity in performance of unit	1 boss-subordinate meeting	1 meeting
2.	Element	Part of task	schedule 1 meeting	1 meeting entered on boss and subordinate's calendar
1.	Motion	Smallest part of task	reach for phone	1 motion

29

trade off the immediate saving of not contesting an issue with the worker against possible higher labor costs in the future. Military officers must trade off savings and reduced disciplinary actions against possible reduction in combat-readiness quality standards if discipline is relaxed.

Unfortunately, there is no right or final answer to developing efficiency and effectiveness measures. Human resource and knowledge workers must continually work to define meaningful work units for their services and experiment with different levels of service to deliver optimum quality and effectiveness benefits for the least cost. As you will see, cost benefit analysis methods are of great help in trading off the savings from short-term efficiency increases against the possible reduced benefits in longer-range effectiveness measures.

CHAPTER 3

Calculating Costs

This chapter shows you how to calculate the costs of delivering *any* human resource or staff service.

We will start with *costs* for two reasons:

1. The *outcomes* of human resources development programs are meaningful only in the context of what it cost the organization to achieve them

2. The secret of calculating *benefits* is the ability to *cost* peoples' behavior and problem situations. Most benefits come from reducing costs (''cost avoidance''). You must be able to calculate these costs avoided to show benefits

Key concepts:

Costs are easy—just like preparing a budget. The key is using simple cost worksheets.

Manage *internal* knowledge worker groups with the methods used by their external ''professional service firm'' counterparts.

The costs involved in delivering any service are:

Outlay (Out-of-Pocket) Direct Costs.   Expenses you actually pay out money for in delivering a service, such as travel, per diem, learning materials, purchased services (e.g., consultants' fees), equipment, and facilities (e.g., room rentals)

Labor Costs.   The dollar value of the time of all people directly involved in delivering a service: service providers *and* clients (e.g., trainees)

Overhead Costs.   The indirect costs of doing business (e.g., fringe benefits, offices, and the like) associated with labor

Opportunity Costs.   Money the firm loses by using people and resources one way rather than another (e.g., sales or production lost when people attend a training program instead of selling or making widgets)

OUTLAY DIRECT COSTS

Direct outlay costs.   These can be either *expense* costs or *capital* costs.

Expense Costs.   These are materials or services that are "used up" in less than a year. Examples are airfares, per diem meal and hotel bills, consultants' fees or a course book that a trainee uses in a course.
Expense costs are calculated in the following format. You simply:

1. *Identify the expense:*
   a. "Round trip airfare to Chicago"
   b. "Participant workbooks"
   c. "Training room with coffee and donuts"
2. *Identify what one unit of the expense costs (cost/unit):*
   a. *One* round trip airfare to Chicago (cost/trip)
   b. *One* participant workbook (cost/workbook)
   c. *One day* room rental and *one day's* coffee and donuts (cost/room-day)
3. *Identify how many units of the expense are used (# units)*
   a. *Two* trainees RT to Chicago (2 units)
   b. *20* participants (20 units)
   c. *Three* days room rental and service (3 units)
4. *Multiply* (2) cost/unit × (3) # units to get (4) expense cost

Examples:

(A) Expense	(B) Cost/Unit	×	(C) # Units	=	(D) Cost (B) × (C)
RT Airfare to Chicago	$600/trip	×	2 trainers	=	$1200
Participant Course Books	$75/trainee	×	20 trainees	=	$1500
Room Service	$150/day	×	3 days	=	$450

Capital Expense Costs. Accounting for *capital* expense costs is slightly more complex. A *capital cost* is a thing or service that has a useful life or more than one year. Capital items are "expensed" (amortized or charged off) as outlay costs over the period they are used up. For example, a $3000 personal computer with a useful life of three years is "expensed" at $3000 ÷ 3 years = $1000 per year.

Capital items can also be expensed by charging a portion of their costs to courses or events in which they are used. For example, a $500,000 nuclear reactor control panel simulator used to train 100 operators in 20 courses could be expensed:

By course: $5,000,000/20 courses = $25,000/course or

By trainee: $500,000/100 trainees = $5000/trainee

Table 3.1 shows typical outlay and capital expense units and cost/unit.

Expected Values. The expense cost format can also be used to value events that occur only a certain percentage of the time or with some known probability. This method is called "expected value" analysis. The expected value, E(v) of an event is its dollar value (V) times the probability or percentage of the time it occurs (P):

$$E(v) = V \times P$$

For example, the expected value of a strike that will cost a firm $1 million if it occurs, and has a 50% chance of occurring, is $1 million (V) × .5 (P) = $500,000.

The total expected value of an event is the sum of expected values of all of its possible outcomes. The other possible outcome of the strike situation is no strike, which has an expected value of: E(v) = $1 million × 0 = 0; the total expected value is $500,000 + 0 = $500,000. (You can be sure you have included all alternatives if your "P" percentage or probability values add up to 1.00.)

For example, assume you are a student registrar and want to calculate a registration cost per student which includes the cost of last minute

TABLE 3.1
Units of Direct Cost

Expense	Cost/Unit	X	# Units	= Total Cost
1. Travel				
Air Fare	Cost/Trip	X	# trips	= _____
Ground	Cost/Mile	X	# miles	= _____
Transportation	Cost/Day	X	or # days	= _____
2. Per diem (room, food, other living expenses)	Cost/Day	X	# days	= _____
3. Materials* (e.g., participant workbooks, if these must be purchased)	Cost/participant	X	# participants	= _____
	Cost/Student Day	X	#student/days	= _____
	Cost/Course	X	# courses	= _____
(Materials are usually defined as things consumed in delivering a service)				

(continued)

---

* A good way to recover material development costs is to "amortize" total development costs over the number of people trained. The development amortization cost added to the out-of-pocket costs of printing a seminar workbook =

$$\frac{\text{Total development costs}}{\text{\# people trained}}$$

For example, if you spent $10,000 developing workbooks used to train 100 people, you would add:

$$\frac{\$10,000 \text{ development cost}}{100 \text{ workbooks}} = \$100/\text{workbook}$$

to the cost of each workbook to recover your development costs. If the workbooks actually cost $25 to print, your total workbook cost to participants should be $100 (development cost) + $25 (printing cost) = $125 per workbook.

Table 3.1 continued

Expense	Cost/Unit	X	# Units	= Total Cost
4. Purchased Services, (e.g., consultants hired by the day or paid a fixed fee to conduct a training program.)	Cost/Day	X	# days	= _____
	Fixed Fee/Course	X	# courses	= _____
5. Equipment* (e.g., renting a projector or amortizing the cost of a simulator)	Rental (or Amortization) Cost/Unit	X	# pieces of equipment	= _____
	Rental (or Amortization) Cost/Day	X	# equipment-days	= _____
(Equipment, unlike materials, is usually defined as things which will be used in delivering more than one unit of service.)	Rental (or Amortization) Cost/Course	X	# courses	= _____

(continued)

* Expensive equipment built or purchased for a specific course should be amortized in the same way as materials development cost. For example, a mock-up of a nuclear reactor control panel costing $500,000 and used to train 100 operators in 10 training courses can be charged off at:

$$\frac{\$500,000 \text{ cost}}{100 \text{ trainees}} = \$5000/\text{trainee}$$

or $500,000 cost/10 courses = $50,000 per course A "Resuscitation Annie" – a life size human dummy costing $2000 used to teach CPR (cardio-pulmonary resuscitation) – is demolished after being pounded on by 20 classes of 15 students, 300 total trainees. The "Annie's" amortization cost would be $2000 cost/20 classes = $100 per course or $2000 cost/300 students = $6.67 per student.

TABLE 3.1 continued

Expense	Cost/Unit	X	# Units	= Total Cost
6. Facilities,* (e.g., room rentals includ- ing coffee, do- nuts and other service charges).	Cost/Day	X	# days	= _____
	Cost/Person Days, Week, etc.	X	# person/ days, weeks, etc.	= _____
(Facilities costs may include the facilities' total budget (administra- tion maintenance, depreciation, etc.) and be charged to projects by the number of days used per year.)	Cost/Course	X	# courses	= _____

---

* Facilities costs can be amortized in the same way as materials development and equipment costs. For example, for a school having a total budget of $1,200,000 and delivering 4000 student-weeks of training costs:

$$\frac{\$1,200,000 \text{ total school budget}}{4000 \text{ student weeks}} = \$300/\text{student week}$$

cancellations. Regular registration paperwork costs $25/student. One time in 10 last-minute cancellations cost an additional $70 in guaranteed hotel reservation and additional paperwork expenses, a total of $95 per cancellation. The "expected value" of the 1-time-in-10 cancellation is the $95 it costs times 10% (.1), the percentage of the time or probability it occurs: E(v) = $95 × .1 = $9.50. The other 90% of the time, registration costs $25, and the E(v) of this outcome is $25 × .9 = $22.50. The total you need to charge for registration to pay for the 10% of registrations which cost the additonal $70 is $9.50 + $22.50 = $32.00:

(A)	(B)		(C)		(D)
Expense	Cost/Unit	×	# Units	=	Cost
					(B) × (C)
Expected Value	Value	×	Probability	=	E(v)
Last Minute Cancellation	$95.00	×	.1 (10%, 1 time in 10)	=	$ 9.50
Registration	$25.00	×	.9 (90%, 9 times in 10)	=	$22.50

Total Registration Costs/Student $32.00

Out-of-pocket expenses are the most visible, easily understood, and accounted for costs of programs. These costs are, however, rarely more than 10% of total program costs. *The real costs of staff efforts are the labor costs of people's time.*

LABOR COSTS

Labor cost is the dollar value of the time people spend working on or participating in a specific task or project. There are several ways of calculating labor costs. The most common methods are described here, with some of their pros and cons. Before you choose a method, ask your comptroller which method your organization uses. This will ensure that your figures are consistent with and credible to others in your firm—and its auditors, clients, and government regulators.

Labor cost based on days paid in a standard year.   This is a person's salary divided by the number of days (hours or minutes) he or she is *paid* in a year. A standard U.S. industry pay year is 260 days (2080 hours or 124,800 minutes). For example, a trainer earning the current average personnel salary of $25,000 a year and paid 260 days has a labor cost of $25,000 ÷ 260 days = $96.15 per day.

TABLE 3.2
Labor Cost Calculation

Salary/Year   ————————— A1

Time Paid/Year   ————————— A2
(Standard: 260 days,
          2080 hours,
      124,800 minutes)

Labor Cost/Time Unit ————————— A3 = A1/A2

Example	Formula	Your Data
For a person making $25,000 a year:		
Salary/year $25,000	_____ A1	Your Salary [ ]
divided by		divided by
Time paid/ ÷ 260 Days	_____ A2	Time ÷ [ ]
year		Days (hours, minutes) you
equals		are paid/year
		equals
Labor cost/ = $96.15/Day	_____ A3 = A1/A2	Your labor = [ ]
time unit		cost/day
		(hour, minute)

If this trainer spends two days preparing for and then three days conducting a communications workshop, his or her salary cost for this workshop is 5 days × $96.15/day = $480.75.

This method of calculating labor costs understates true labor cost by as much as two thirds. The biggest cost of staff people is not their direct salaries but their indirect fringe and overhead expenses. (See Table 3.5.)

Full Labor Costs. These include indirect expenses—fringe benefit and overhead costs that may not appear to be directly chargeable to specific activities or projects but that *are* a major cost of providing services.

Fringe Benefits. These are the (1) costs of time paid but not worked, such as, vacations, sick leave, and holidays, (2) legally required taxes and insurance: FICA (social security), unemployment, and workers compensation, plus (3) other indirect employee compensation; such as health insurance, pension payments, education, parking, child care, and so forth. Fringe benefits in American industry currently average 35%[1] of salary costs per year.

There are two ways of "loading" or adding fringe expenses to calculate direct labor costs.

Direct Labor Cost Based on Days Worked in a Standard Year

One way is to divide yearly salary by days actually *worked* (current U.S. average = 230 days[2]) instead of the 260 days actually paid. For example, the "loaded" cost of a person making $25,000 a year is $25,000 ÷ 230 days = $108.70 a day.

---

[1]Fringe benefit rates vary substantially by size and type of firm. *Employee Benefits* (US Chamber of Commerce, 1983) cites a fringe benefit rate of 36.6% based on a survey of 1454 companies. *Operating Statistics of Professional Firms* (Harper, 1984) cites a fringe benefit rate of 20.6% based on a sample of 46 consulting and engineering firms.

[2]Average *days worked* in American industry, calculated as follows: 365 days in a year, less 104 weekend days (52 weekends × 2 days/weekend), 15 days (3 weeks) vacation, 11 holidays, and 5 sick or personal leave days.

Salary/Year   ——————— A1

Time Worked/Year   ——————— A2
(Standard: 230 days,
    1840 hours,
  110,400 minutes)

Labor Cost/Time Unit   ——————— A3 = A1/A2

Example	Formula	Your Data
For a person making $25,000 a year		
Salary/year $25,000	——————— A1	Your Salary ☐
divided by		divided by
Time worked/ ÷ 230 Days year	——————— A2	Time Days (hours, minutes) you work/year ÷ ☐
equals		equals
Labor Cost/Day = 108.70/Day "loaded" for time paid but not worked	——————— A3 = A1/A2	Your Labor Cost/ = ☐ Day (Hour, Minute)

41

This method accounts for fringe benefits taken as "days paid but not worked"—vacation, holiday, and leave time—but not other benefits like taxes, health insurance and pensions. If 30 of 260 days are paid fringe days, fringe benefits are accounted for as salary X 30/260 days = 11.5% of salary. If total fringe rate is 35% of salary, 35% − 11.5% = 23.5% of *"out of pocket"* fringe costs are missed. (See Table 3.4.)

Direct Labor Cost "Loaded" with Total Fringe Benefits

A better way to account for fringe benefits is to add to direct labor cost (salary/days paid × days worked) the dollar value of all fringe benefits (salary/year × total fringe rate) and divide this total direct labor + fringe cost/year by days worked/year. (See Table 3.4 for an example of our $25,000 a year employee with a daily direct labor cost "loaded" with fringe benefits of 35% salary.)

This figure is still not the real cost of a person's time. We must add in overhead costs.

OVERHEAD COSTS

Overhead costs are all the indirect costs of doing business:

1. Professionals' "downtime" when they are not working on specific projects (what we will call "unapplied," "indirect," or "nonbillable" time)
2. Managers' and support staff (e.g., secretaries) salaries
3. Occupancy costs: office rentals, light and heat, copying machines and other equipment, and general office supplies
4. Legal and accounting expenses, insurance, and interest on the firm's debt

Overhead costs in U.S. professional firms currently average about 115% of direct labor plus total fringe costs/year, assuming no professional

TABLE 3.4
Direct Labor Cost Loaded With Full Fringe

Salary/Year	_____ A1
Fringe Rate	_____ A2
Fringe Cost	_____ A3 = A1 × A2
Labor Cost/Year: Salary (A1) + Fringe (A3) Cost	_____ A4 = A1 + A3

Example	Formula	Your Data
For a person making $25,000 a year:		
(1) Salary/year　$25,000 　　multiplied by	$\dfrac{S}{\quad}$ A1	(1) Your salary/year ☐ 　　multiplied by
(2) Fringe Rate　× 35% 　　equals	$\dfrac{.35}{\quad}$ A2	(2) Your Fringe Rate × ☐ 　　equals
(3) Fringe Cost　= $8750 　　added to salary (1) + 　　equals	$\dfrac{.35S}{\quad}$ A3 = A1 × A2	(3) Your Fringe Cost = ☐ 　　added to salary (1) + 　　equals
(4) Labor cost/year = $33,750 　　(Salary + 　　Fringe Cost) 　　divided by	$\dfrac{1.35S}{\quad}$ A4 = A1 + A3	(4) Your Labor Cost/ = ☐ 　　year 　　divided by
(5) Time worked/　÷ 230 Days 　　year 　　equals	$\dfrac{230}{\quad}$ A5	(5) time worked/ ÷ ☐ 　　year 　　equals
(6) Labor Cost/ = $146.74/Day 　　Day 　　(hour, minute)	$\dfrac{\dfrac{1.35S}{230}}{\quad}$ A6 = A4/A5	(6) Your Labor = ☐ 　　Cost/Day 　　(hour, minute)

"downtime" is included in overhead.[3] (The cost of downtime will be accounted for by adjusting costs for professionals' "applied" or "billable" rates below). If you are in a cost center or know your department's budget, you can get a quick estimate of your overhead rate by subtracting total delivery professionals' salaries plus fringe from total costs and dividing by total delivery professionals' salaries plus fringe:

$$\text{Overhead rate} = \frac{\begin{array}{c}\text{total cost center budget} - \\ \text{total delivery professionals salaries} \\ + (\text{salaries} \times \text{fringe \%})\end{array}}{\begin{array}{c}\text{total delivery professionals' salaries} \\ + (\text{salaries} \times \text{fringe\%})\end{array}}$$

Your total cost center budget should include all payroll and fringe costs, plus occupancy, supplies, purchased services, equipment depreciation and administrative costs (e.g., legal, accounting, and interest costs) allocated to it. A "delivery professional" is a person who directly provides a service, for example, training, course design, planning, or counseling. People who "deliver" and also manage should include in "delivery professionals salary + (salaries × fringe%)" their total salary plus fringe multiplied by the percentage of time they deliver services: manager/deliverer salary + fringe × % delivery time/total time worked.

For example, the overhead rate for a wage and compensation planning group of four delivery professionals making a average of $30,000 each, with a 35% fringe benefit rate (a benefit cost of .35 × $30,000 = $10,500 per person) and a total cost center budget of $350,000 is:

$$\text{Overhead rate} = \frac{\$350,000 \text{ budget} - 4\,(\$30,000 + 10,500)}{4\,(\$30,000 + 10,500)}$$

$$= \frac{\$350,000 - 162,000}{\$162,000} = 116\%$$

---

[3] See "Overhead" under "Applications" at the end of this chapter for a breakdown of overhead costs. Accounting for overhead can be complex and good industry average data on overhead rates are hard to find. Fultz (1980) provides worksheets for eight different ways of calculating overhead, which give a range of overhead rates from 46.54 to 102.86% using the same data for a typical firm. Harper (1984) found an average overhead figure of 170% for a sample of 46 professional service firms, but this figure includes in overhead substantial professional "downtime": 37.5% of days paid (97.5 days in a 260-

Full Labor Cost

Full labor cost is a person's salary *plus* total fringe benefits, *plus* overhead, divided by days worked. Table 3.5 shows the calculation of the full cost of a person's time.

Overhead costs are calculated as a percentage of direct labor plus total fringe costs per year, and this cost is added to the direct labor plus fringe "base" to get the "full" labor plus fringe plus overhead cost of a professional's time. If the person is in a profit center or firm, profit calculated as percentage of full cost is added to full cost to find the total revenue a professional has to bring in to cover all of his or her costs and make the desired profit. (In Table 3.5, profit rate and profit are assumed to be 0, as in a typical internal professional cost center in a firm.)

Note that a good estimate of the full cost of a person's time is 2.7 times the cost per day worked (salary/230 days) or *three times* his or her salary cost per day paid (salary/260 days). This figure, called a "full cost multiplier," provides a useful rule of thumb for estimating human resource costs. (See the *Business Week* article quoted on page 209 of Chapter 6.).

Because most people think in terms of standard years of 260 days (2080 hours or 124,800 minutes), a full cost multiplier of 3 and standard times are used in most examples in this book. This figure is easy to use and is precise enough for most decisions you will evaluate using cost benefit analysis. The worksheets shown in Tables 3.5 and 3.7 and computer programs in Appendix A provide exact full labor costs for use when you need greater precision.

You might ask whether it really makes sense to add overhead expenses to the cost of people's time.

Direct labor costs are clearly "variable costs," expenses that change when the volume of work increases or decreases. If people work on a project, project costs go up; if people spend less time on the project, project costs go down.

Overhead costs appear to be "fixed costs," expenses that don't change when the volume of work changes, that "have to be paid any-

---

day standard year). This equates to a base overhead rate of 120% if professional downtime is not included. Again, readers are best advised to get help from their firm's comptroller in choosing an overhead figure.

TABLE 3.5
Calculating the Full Cost of a Person's Time

```
BASE                                          EXAMPLE
                                   For person making $25,000/year
 1) Salary/Year                                      $25,000.00
    divided by
 2) Days paid/standard year          260
    equals
 3) Labor cost/day paid                                  $96.15
    (2) Days paid minus
 4) Paid Days off                     30
    equals
 5) Direct Labor Days Worked/Year    230
    x (3) labor cost/day equals
 6) Direct Labor Cost/Year                           $22,115.38

FRINGE
    (4) Days off/(2) Days paid equals
 7) Paid days off fringe %          0.115
    x (1) Salary/year equals
 8) Paid days off fringe cost              $2,884.62
 9) Out of pocket fringe %          0.235
    x (1) Salary/year equals
10) Out-of-pocket fringe cost              $5,865.38
11) Total fringe %                  0.350
    x (1) Salary/year equals
12) Total Fringe cost                                 $8,750.00
    (6) Direct labor + (12) Total fringe =
13) SUBTOTAL: Direct Labor + Fringe Cost             $30,865.38

OVERHEAD
14) Overhead %                      1.15
    x (13) Direct Labor + Fringe equals
15) Overhead Cost                                    $35,495.19
    plus (13) Direct Labor + Fringe equals
16) TOTAL FULL COST: Drct Lbr+Frng+Ohd               $66,360.58

FULL LABOR COSTS
    (16) Full cost divided by Time Unit worked/year
17) Full Labor cost/day         230  days/year=         $288.52
18) Hours paid/day                8
19) Full labor cost/hour       1840  hours/year=         $36.07
20) Full labor cost/minute   110400  min./year=           $0.60

FULL COST MULTIPLIER
    (16) Full cost/(3) Sal. cost/day paid equals
21) Full cost multiplier                                   3.00
```

46

TABLE 3.5 continued

FORMULA S=Salary	YOUR DATA	
<u>S</u> A1	1) Salary/Year divided by	
<u>260</u> A2	2) Days paid/standard year equals	260
<u>S/260</u> A3=A1/A2	3) Labor cost/day paid (2) Days paid minus	
<u>30</u> A4	4) Paid Days off equals	
<u>230</u> A5=A2-A4	5) Direct Labor Days Worked/Year x (3) labor cost/day equals	260
<u>.885S</u> A6=A5*A3	6) Direct Labor Cost/Year	
	FRINGE	
	(4) Days off/(2) Days paid equals	
<u>.115</u> A7=A4/A2	7) Paid days off fringe % x (1) Salary/year equals	
<u>.115S</u> A8=A7*A1=A3*A4	8) Paid days off fringe cost	
<u>.235</u> A9	9) Out of pocket fringe % x (1) Salary/year equals	
<u>.235S</u> A10=A9*A1	10) Out-of-pocket fringe cost	
<u>.350</u> A11=A7+A9	11) Total fringe % x (1) Salary/year equals	
<u>.350S</u> A12=A8+A10=A11*A1	12) Total Fringe cost	
	(6) Direct labor + (12) Total fringe =	
<u>1.235S</u> A13=A6+A12	13) SUBTOTAL: Direct Labor + Fringe Cost	
	OVERHEAD	
<u>1.15</u> A14	14) Overhead %	
	x (13) Direct Labor + Fringe equals	
<u>1.420S</u> A15=A13*A14	15) Overhead Cost	
	plus (13) Direct Labor + Fringe equals	
<u>2.655S</u> A16=A13+A15	16) TOTAL FULL COST: Drct Lbr+Frng+Ohd	
	FULL LABOR COSTS	
	(16) Full cost divided by Time Unit worked/year	
<u>2.655S/230</u> A17=A16/A5	17) Full Labor cost/day	260 days/year=
A18	18) Hours paid/day	8
<u>2.655S/1840</u> A19=A16/(A18*A5)	19) Full labor cost/hour	2080 hours/year=
<u>2.66S/110400</u> A20=A16/(A5*A19*60)	20) Full labor cost/minute	124800 min./year=
	FULL COST MULTIPLIER	
	(16) Full cost/(3) Sal. cost/day paid equals	
<u>3.00S</u> A21=A17/A3	21) Full cost multiplier	

way," whether people have work to do or not. Some examples *might be* managers' salaries, or occupancy, or legal costs: "might be" because *there is no such thing—and should be no such thing—as a truly fixed cost.* When work goes away, firms can and do reduce management staff, sublease office space, and find cheaper lawyers.

There are three reasons to use full costs:

1. Full costs provide a constant reminder of how much overhead is costing—and a constant incentive to reduce it, to make it as "variable" as possible. Costs left "buried" in overhead are costs over which you have abdicated control! Indirect costs are *twice* payroll, *two thirds* of the cost of delivering services—*a lot* over which to abdicate control!

2. In a cost or profit center—and more and more internal staff groups are managed this way—the full cost of people's time is what you actually have to charge to cover all your costs of doing business.

3. To calculate benefits offered by "make versus buy" alternatives, or return on investment in labor saving equipment, you must know the full cost of your present way of delivering a service.

If you are not in a cost or profit center, full costs are still the best measure of how much it actually costs your firm to deliver service. As you will see, *the full costing of people's time is the key to calculating the costs and benefits of human resource efforts.*

CALCULATING THE COSTS OF PEOPLE, PROJECTS, AND OFFICES

To calculate—and cut—the full costs of delivering services, you must account for and value people's time. The best way to do this is to manage all knowledge workers, projects, and offices as they would be in a well-managed professional service firm (PSF). Examples of professional service firms are law, accounting, consulting, architectural, and engineering firms. Essentially any internal or external staff group or department *is* a professional service firm. Established cost-accounting methods and standards exist for managing such firms (Fultz, 1980; Jones and Trentin, 1968). These methods include the following steps.

Keep Time Sheets

All staff people should keep time sheets and "bill" their time on an hourly basis to all projects, clients, or other activities on which they spend time. You or your subordinates may resist keeping time sheets because you feel they mean "management doesn't trust us or is checking up on us . . . it takes too much time . . . we are professionals and shouldn't be treated this way." Appeals that managers of knowledge workers can use to introduce time sheets include:

Planning. "We need time data on how long it takes us to deliver various services for our own internal planning and budgeting. How else can we know how to reschedule staff or how many new people to hire if we suddenly get three new jobs . . . ?"

It's Easy. "In fact, time sheets rarely take more than five minutes a day to fill out."

Personal Time Management. "Time sheets will help you make the best, most efficient use of your time."

Professional Practice. "In fact, all well-managed professionals the world over—members of top law, accounting, consulting, or engineering firms—*do* keep time sheets."

If these appeals fail, you as boss can always mandate time sheets by fiat: "This is the way we are going to do business from now on" or (the practice in most professional firms and most effective!) "Payroll won't issue salary checks until they receive your time sheet for the pay period." People may grouse for a week but quickly adapt: keeping time sheets soon becomes routine.

Figure 3.1 provides a sample time sheet for a staff person or office. This form collects the following data:

Time Period

Time sheet data in this example are collected every two weeks. You can, of course, tailor this period to your accounting needs.

FIGURE 3.1
Time Sheet

Consultant Name _____ Date _____ Period Ending _____

	Project	Date										
Applied	1.											
	2.											
	3.											
	4.											
Unapplied	Admin											
	Mktg											
	R&D											
	Prof Dev											
	Staff 1.											
	Staff 2.											
	Holiday											
	Sick											
	Vacation											
	Hour Totals											

Employee Signature _____ Approval _____

Applied Hours/Period: _____ A1

Hours Paid/Period: _____ A2

"Gross applied rate" _____ A3 = A1/A2

Hours worked/period _____ A4

"Net applied rate" _____ A5 = A1/A4

Applied and Unapplied Billing Entries

Applied. Known also as "billable" entries are time spent on specific projects, activities, or clients. In private law or consulting firms, applied time is hours or days for which a client can be billed. Projects or clients are usually given numbers that are entered under the "applied" heading. Time spent (in hours) on each applied project is entered for each day of the time period.

Unapplied (indirect or non/billable). These entries include "overhead" time spent on all other things a staff person does that cannot be associated directly with a specific project or client. In private professional service firms, or internal groups that cross-charge for their time, this is time a client *cannot* be billed for. Some examples of typical unapplied entries are:

1. *Administration.* Time spent on routine "maintenance" activities and paperwork, for example, attending staff meetings, filling out one's time sheet and expense account, answering correspondence, and travel that cannot be charged to a client.

2. *Marketing.* Time spent writing proposals, making presentations to potential clients, preparing brochures and mailings, and making phone calls to sell services. Efficient internal as well as external service people must market their services to prospective clients. Professionals who begin keeping time-sheet data on marketing activities are often surprised at how much time they spend explaining and promoting what they do.

3. *Professional Development.* Time spent attending courses and conferences, and reading professional books and journal articles.

4. *Research and Development.* Time spent developing new services, products, or information. Technically, both professional development and research and development (R&D) time are "investments." Although usually not formally capitalized, this is important time. Knowledge workers are essentially in the business of selling information. They must spend more time renewing or investing in their intellectual capital and inventory in order to have something valuable to offer.

5. *Staff Work.* Time spent doing research, preparing reports or writing memoranda on projects not directly related to your job. Professional people are continually asked to do collateral work— for example, the request from some higher-up to prepare an affirmative action report, or "look at what an increased Hispanic population may mean for us in the 1990s." Time spent on staff work should be tracked. Whenever possible, you should get staff work identified as *applied* work for a specific project or client. Otherwise, you are likely to get stuck with and lose credit for time spent on staff work.

6. *"Other."* Overhead or administrative "down-time" includes preparatory, travel and compensatory "staring into space" time needed to recover from the five straight weeks on the road (e.g., personal time doing laundry, paying bills). Where possible, preparatory, travel, and compensatory time should be billed to applied projects or clients.

7. *Holiday, sick,* and *vacation time.*

Time sheets can and should be tailored to your job and to your firm's accounting procedures. You may want to subdivide applied projects into steps, for example, Project 100.000, New Supervisor Course, into 100.01 Needs Assessment, 100.02 Course Design.

Managers of staff groups often spend some time managing and some time delivering services. Management time "overhead" paid for by the overhead multiplier can be accounted for separately. Managers may find it useful to expand the "admin" category to track time spent on specific management activities.

Numerous software programs for managing time billings are available for mainframe, mini, and micro "personal" computers. In fact, the "electronic time sheet"—direct data entry on computer terminals—is rapidly replacing the paper time sheet. Direct data entry is a great boon to PSF management. It permits instantaneous project (and personnel) planning, monitoring and invoicing.

Once you have completed your time sheet for a time period, total the hours spent each day (daily column totals) and on each applied and unapplied activity (account row totals). Applied and unapplied hour totals are summarized in the lower left-hand corner of the time sheet to calculate an extremely important figure: your *applied rate*.

Calculate Applied Rates

Your applied rate is the number of hours you billed to applied projects or clients, divided by the total number of hours that you were *paid* ("gross" applied rate) or *worked* ("net" applied rate) in a given time period. In the Figure 3.1 example, this person's "gross" applied rate is 51 hours divided by 80 hours, or 64%. *A staff person's applied rate is the single most important indicator of his or her productivity.*

A well-established standard for professional service firms is that people should maintain a "gross" applied rate of 75%, for example, 15 days out of 20 days worked in a month. On a yearly basis, a 75% applied rate means a person is billable .75 × 260 days = 195 days. Thirty of these days are vacation, holiday, and leave time. This leaves 260 − 30 = 230 days actually worked. If 195 days are applied, this leaves 230 − 195 = 35 days, about 35 days/12 months = 3 days a month for administrative, marketing, professional development, R&D staff, and "other" time. A 75% "gross" applied rate means a billable rate of 195 days/230 days worked = a "net" applied rate of 85%, 85% of days on the job. Applied rates much above this level cannot be sustained; applied rates much below this level indicate that people are not being used efficiently.

$$\text{"Gross" applied rate} = \frac{\text{time applied or billable/period}}{\text{time } \textit{paid}/\text{period}}$$

For example, the gross applied rate for a person billable 195 days/year and paid 260 days/year is:

$$\text{Gross applied rate} = \frac{195 \text{ "billable" days/year}}{260 \text{ days paid/year}} = 75\%$$

$$\text{"Net" applied rate} = \frac{\text{time applied or billable/period}}{230 \text{ days } \textit{worked}/\text{year}}$$

For example, the net applied rate for a person billable 195 days/year who works a 230 day year is:

$$\text{Net applied rate} \ = \ \frac{195 \text{ ''billable'' days/year}}{230 \text{ days worked/year}} \ = \ 85\%$$

Private professional service firms with gross applied rates below 75% risk going bankrupt or pricing themselves out of the market. As will be seen, the lower a person's applied rate, the more he or she costs. Internal staff groups with low applied rates sooner or later have their budgets and staff levels reduced, when senior managers see them sitting around without enough work.

Conversely, sustained gross applied rates above 75% can cause people to burn out. Many professionals get into the habit of working nights and weekends to get their "unapplied" work done, for example, answering correspondence or preparing budgets. People who consistently work and travel 85% to 90% of the time sooner or later fail to renew their "intellectual capital." Often they develop medical or emotional problems: get depressed, start drinking a lot, begin having marital or family problems, become ineffective with clients, and resign or are fired. The art of managing professional service groups is scheduling people and work so everyone has a high but realistic and sustainable applied rate.

Applied rate objectives can vary with the type of job. For example, the manager of a staff group may have a 50% applied rate objective, with the other 50% of his or her time reserved for management activities. A technical person in a job that does not require travel (e.g., a graphic artist who can be billed to projects almost continually) may have a gross applied rate objective of 85%, 221 billable days out of 230 days worked (a net applied rate of 96% of available time).

Knowing staff persons' full cost per day and their applied rates enables you to calculate a second key direct labor cost: *"billing rate"* or *cost per applied person-day.*

Calculate Billing Cost per Applied Person-Day

This is the dollar amount the person has to charge for each day applied or "billable" to a client to cover all direct (salary) and indirect (fringe and overhead) costs if he or she is in a cost center or external service firm. A person's billing cost per applied person-day (*"billing rate"*) is his or her full cost per day divided by his or her net applied rate.[5]

$$\frac{\text{Cost per applied}}{\text{person day}} = \frac{\text{Full cost/day}}{\text{net applied rate}}$$

For example, a $25,000-a-year person with a full cost/day of $292 and a 85% net applied rate must bill

$$\frac{\$292 \text{ full cost/day}}{.85 \text{ net applied rate}} = \$344/\text{day}$$

Another way to calculate your billing rate is to divide your total cost center budget by the number of days (or hours) delivery professionals in the group have available to work per year. For example, at a 75% gross applied rate, available days = 260 days × 75% = 195 days (or available hours = 2080 hours × 75% = 1560 hours) × the number of people in the cost center, billing rates for the 4 person wage and compensation cost center with a total budget of $350,000 are:

$$\text{Billing rate/day} = \frac{\$350,000}{4 \text{ people} \times 260 \text{ days} \times 75\% \text{ applied rate}}$$

$$= \frac{\$350,000}{780 \text{ days available}} = \$448.72/\text{day}$$

or,

$$\text{Billing rate/hour} = \frac{\$350,000 \text{ cost center budget}}{4 \text{ people} \times 2080 \text{ hours} \times 75\% \text{ applied rate}}$$

$$= \frac{\$350,000}{6240 \text{ hours available}} = \$56.09/\text{hour}$$

[5]Assuming that no "unapplied time" is included in the organization's overhead rate. If unapplied time *is* included in the overhead multiplier, "applied rate" (in the cost per applied person-day equation) = "actual applied rate ÷ budgeted applied rate." For example, a person applied 64% with a budgeted applied rate of 75% would divide his or her full cost per day by .64 ÷ .75 = .85. Professional service groups normally use the average applied rates for all professionals in the group to calculate billing rates.

Note that the rule of thumb for professionals applied at the standard 75% gross applied rate is that their *cost* per applied person-day equals *3.5 times* their *salary cost per day paid* (salary/260 days). This is because full cost per day equals salary cost per day × 2.6, and 2.6× ÷ .75 gross applied rate = 3.5×.

Full cost per day must be divided by the applied rate because people cannot apply or charge 100% of the time they work: some days are spent in unapplied activities such as administration or vacation time. Staff people cost or must charge enough for their smaller number of applied or billable days to pay for *all* of their time.

This can be seen in Figure 3.2, which shows all the costs of a PSF. Only the shaded part of the pie, directly applied and billable labor and expenses, brings money into the firm or cost center. Variable out-of-pocket costs, called "in-outs," don't help because, although you can bill a client for your travel ("in"), the money you get goes right back "out" to airlines, hotels, and other suppliers. Direct billable labor must bring in enough money to pay the salaries of the people doing the work *and* their unapplied time *and* all indirect overhead costs. The smaller the direct billable share of the pie, the more must be charged to pay for the rest. Dividing your full cost by your applied rate tells you how much you have to charge to cover your share of the total overhead pie.

Cost per applied person-day calculations can also include amortization of training costs incurred in preparing for a job (e.g., trainer training to teach a specific course a certain number of times). This amortization figure is calculated by dividing the total training costs by the number of days the person is expected to perform the function.

$$\frac{\text{Cost per}}{\substack{\text{applied} \\ \text{person-day}}} = \frac{\text{full cost/day}}{\text{net applied rate}} + \frac{\substack{\text{Amortization cost:} \\ \text{cost of training}}}{\text{\# days in job}}$$

For example, if it costs $1600 to train a staff person to score assessment center exercises and the person will observe eight two-day sessions, the amortization cost of the training is $1600 ÷ 16 days = $100/day. If this person's cost per applied person day is $300/day, the total that should be charged for his or her time is $400/day.

The quick rule of thumb for *client* or *participant* full cost per day remains simply *three times* the *salary per day* (salary/260 days). This is be-

FIGURE 3.2
Direct Applied and Indirect Overhead Costs
as a Percentage of Total Professional Service Firm Costs

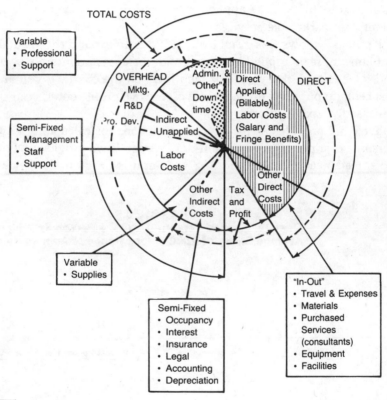

Applied billable time and "in-outs" which bring money into the PSF

costs and profits

Additional billable time from increasing applied rates and decreasing unapplied overhead time and costs

costs and profits with higher applied rates and lower overhead

57

cause employees in a firm must be assumed to be 100% applied (i.e., worth what they are paid per day).

Calculating one's cost per applied person-day makes it easy to see why applied rates are so important in determining the costs of services. The fewer days you are applied or billable, the more you must charge for each day to cover your full cost.

Table 3.6 shows the cost per applied person-day for a human resource person earning the average salary of $25,000, for a range of applied rates from 10% to 100%. Low applied rates lead to very expensive and frequently unmarketable services.

Figure 3.2 shows this graphically: if you can expand the shaded area by billing more unapplied time, revenues increase and indirect overhead and total costs decrease (the dashed lines on the chart). If you are in a cost center, your costs go down. If you are in a profit center, your profits (and, sadly, taxes) go up.

Table 3.7 provides step-by-step instructions for calculating any staff person's cost per applied person-day. Appendix A provides a Lotus 1-2-3 spreadsheet template and BASIC computer program that walks you

TABLE 3.6
Cost Per Applied Person—Day for a Person Earning an
Average Salary of $25,000 for a Range of Applied Rates

Cost Per Applied Person-Day = $\dfrac{\text{full cost per day: (\$292)}}{\text{Net applied rate}}$

Applied Rate	Cost Per Applied Person-Day
10%	$2,921/day
20%	1,460/day
30%	974/day
40%	730/day
50%	584/day
60%	487/day
70%	417/day
80%	365/day
90%	325/day
100%	$ 292/day

through calculation of direct and full costs for staff people, given a person's or firm's fringe, overhead, profit and applied rates.

OPPORTUNITY COSTS

Opportunity costs are any costs or benefits that the firm loses in addition to labor, overhead, and outlay costs. In most cases, the full labor costs of people's time *is* the opportunity cost of their participation in a project. Occasionally there may be opportunity costs in addition to the cost of participants' time. An example would be the value of production lost if an assembly line is shut down to permit workers to attend a safety training course, the additional costs of temporary workers hired to keep the line running, or overtime paid if production is made up after hours.

Opportunity costs are calculated using the same format as outlay costs. For example, assume you took 10 workers off an assembly line for a day of safety training. Plant management makes up production by hiring five temporary workers at $10/hour, $100/day, and paying five of your trainees four hours of overtime at $18/hour that evening. (Total: 20 hours of overtime.)

The additional "opportunity cost" of the safety training is $860:

(A) Expense	(B) Cost/Unit	×	(C) # Units	=	(D) Cost (B) × (C)
"Opportunity Costs"					
Temporary Workers	$100/day	×	5 temps	=	$500
Overtime	$18/hour	×	20 hours	=	$360
Total Opportunity Costs					$860

CALCULATING THE COST OF DELIVERING A SERVICE

Once you know

the cost per applied person-day *labor costs* of everyone involved in

TABLE 3.7
Calculating the Full Cost of a Person's Time

BASE

		EXAMPLE
		For person making $25,000/year
1) Salary/Year		$25,000.00
divided by		
2) Days paid/standard year	260	
equals		
3) Labor cost/day paid		$96.15
(2) Days paid minus		
4) Paid Days off	30	
equals		
5) Direct Labor Days Worked/Year	230	
x (3) labor cost/day equals		
6) Direct Labor Cost/Year		$22,115.38

FRINGE

(4) Days off/(2) Days paid equals		
7) Paid days off fringe %	0.115	
x (1) Salary/year equals		
8) Paid days off fringe cost		$2,884.62
9) Out of pocket fringe %	0.235	
x (1) Salary/year equals		
10) Out-of-pocket fringe cost		$5,865.38
11) Total fringe %	0.350	
x (1) Salary/year equals		
12) Total Fringe cost		$8,750.00
(6) Direct labor + (12) Total fringe =		
13) SUBTOTAL: Direct Labor + Fringe Cost		$30,865.38

OVERHEAD

14) Overhead %	1.15	
x (13) Direct Labor + Fringe equals		
15) Overhead Cost		$35,495.19
plus (13) Direct Labor + Fringe equals		
16) SUBTOTAL: Drct Lbr+Frng+Ohd		$66,360.58

PROFIT

17) Profit %	0	
x (16) Lbr+Frng+Ohd equals		
18) Profit		$0.00
plus (16) Lbr+Frng+Ohd equals		
19) TOTAL: Full labor cost/year+Profit		$66,360.58

FULL LABOR COSTS

(19) Full cost divided by Time Unit worked/year		
20) Full Labor cost/day	230 days/year=	$288.52
21) Hours paid/day	8	
22) Full labor cost/hour	1840 hours/year=	$36.07
23) Full labor cost/minute	110400 min./year=	$0.60

FULL COST MULTIPLIER

(20) Full cost/(3) Sal. cost/day paid equals		
24) Full cost multiplier		3.00

APPLIED (DIRECT "BILLABLE") COSTS

25) "Gross" applied rate %	0.75 x days paid/year	
x (2) Days paid/(5) Days worked=		
26) "Net" applied rate %	0.85 x days worked/year	
x (5) Days worked=		
27) Applied/billable days	195 /year	
(19) Full cost/(27) Applied days=		
28) Full cost/applied day		$340.31
(19) Full cost divided by		
29) Applied/billable hours	1560 /year	
equals		
30) Full cost/applied hour		$42.54
(19) Full cost divided by		
31) Applied/billable min.s	93600 /year	
equals		
32) Full cost/applied min.		$0.71

BILLING RATE MULTIPLIER

(28) Full cost/applied day/(3) Sal.cost/day=		
33) Billing rate multiplier		3.54

FORMULA S=Salary		YOUR DATA	
$\underline{S}$ A1	1) Salary/Year divided by		[ ]
$\underline{260}$ A2	2) Days paid/standard year equals	260	
S/260 A3=A1/A2	3) Labor cost/day paid (2) Days paid minus		[ ]
$\underline{30}$ A4	4) Paid Days off equals	[ ]	
$\underline{230}$ A5=A2-A4	5) Direct Labor Days Worked/Year x (3) labor cost/day equals	260	
.885S A6=A5*A3	6) Direct Labor Cost/Year		[ ]

FRINGE

	(4) Days off/(2) Days paid equals		
.115 A7=A4/A2	7) Paid days off fringe % x (1) Salary/year equals	0.000	
.115S A8=A7*A1=A3*A4	8) Paid days off fringe cost		$0.00
.235 A9	9) Out of pocket fringe % x (1) Salary/year equals	[ ]	
.235S A10=A9*A1	10) Out-of-pocket fringe cost		$0.00
.350 A11=A7+A9	11) Total fringe % x (1) Salary/year equals	[ ]	
.350S A12=A8+A10=A11*A1	12) Total Fringe cost (6) Direct labor + (12) Total fringe =		[ ]
1.235S A13=A6+A12	13) SUBTOTAL: Direct Labor + Fringe Cost		[ ]

OVERHEAD

1.15 A14	14) Overhead % x (13) Direct Labor + Fringe equals	[ ]	
1.420S A15=A13*A14	15) Overhead Cost plus (13) Direct Labor + Fringe equals		[ ]
2.655S A16=A13+A15	16) SUBTOTAL: Drct Lbr+Frng+Ohd		[ ]

PROFIT

0 A17	17) Profit % x (16) Lbr+Frng+Ohd equals	[ ]	
0 A18=A16*A17	18) Profit plus (16) Lbr+Frng+Ohd equals		[ ]
2.655S A19=A16+A18	19) TOTAL: Full labor cost/year		[ ]

FULL LABOR COSTS

	(19) Full cost divided by Time Unit worked/year		
2.655S/230 A20=A19/A5	20) Full Labor cost/day 260 days/year=		[ ]
A21	21) Hours paid/day 8		
2.655S/1840 A22=A21*A5	22) Full labor cost/hour 2080 hours/year=		[ ]
2.66S/110400 A23=A19/(A5*A21*60)	23) Full labor cost/minute 124800 min./year=		[ ]

FULL COST MULTIPLIER

	(20) Full cost/(3) Sal. cost/day paid equals		
3.00S A24=A20/A3	24) Full cost multiplier		[ ]

APPLIED (DIRECT "BILLABLE") COSTS

A25	25) "Gross" applied rate % [ ] x days paid/year x (2) Days paid/(5) Days worked=	
A26=A25*A2/A5	26) "Net" applied rate % [ ] x days worked/year x (5) Days worked=	
A27=A25*A2	27) Applied/billable days [ ] /year (19) Full cost/(27) Applied days=	
2.655S/195 A28=A19/A27	28) Full cost/applied day (19) Full cost divided by	[ ]
A29=A27*A21	29) Applied/billable hours [ ] /year equals	
2.655S/1560 A30=A19/A29	30) Full cost/applied hour (19) Full cost divided by	[ ]
A31=A29*60	31) Applied/billable min.s [ ] /year equals	
2.655S/93600 A32=A19/A31	32) Full cost/applied min.	[ ]

BILLING RATE MULTIPLIER

	(28) Full cost/applied day/(3) Sal.cost/day=	
3.54S A33=A28/A3	33) Billing rate multiplier	[ ]

delivering a service—trainers or consultants *and* client participants and

the *outlay costs* involved,

it is very easy to calculate the total cost of a project or service. Table 3.8 provides a worksheet for calculating the cost of any service or project. Appendix A provides a Lotus 1-2-3 spreadsheet template and BASIC program for this worksheet that prompts you for data needed and does all calculations.

1. First, *identify* all the *steps* of your project; for example, for a train-ing program: (1) training needs assessment, (2) curriculum de-velopment, (3) training, (4) delivery, and (5) evaluation. Write the step name in the space provided in Column A of the work-sheet.

    Labor costs. For each step calculate the *labor costs* of the service or project as follows:

2. Identify *who is involved in each step.* Include both staff or human resource people *and* participants from your client organization. Write the name or title of the person(s) in column B.

3. If more than one person in the same job or salary grade (e.g., "first-level supervisors" or "nonexempts who responded to the survey") was involved, ask *how many* people spent time on the step. Put the number of people in column C.

4. *Calculate the full cost of each person's time per day/hour/minute.* Col-umn D provides the equation for finding a person's approxi-mate full cost:

$$\frac{S \quad \times M}{T} = \underline{\hspace{2cm}}$$

where   S = salary per year

   M = Full cost (or overhead) multiplier—usually about 3

   T = time unit: 260 days, 2080 hours, 124,800 minutes in a standard working year

TABLE 3.8
Costing Worksheet

A Analysis Step*	B Labor ("Who?")	C #	LABOR COSTS	D Time	E Time	F Cost C x D x E	OUTLAY OR OPPORTUNITY COSTS	G Expense	H Cost/Unit	I # Units	J Cost H x I	OPTION TOTALS	K1: TOTALS* F + J	K2: TOTALS* F + J
			Full Cost/Time											
			$ ___ x M = ___ / T		x ___ =					x	=			
			$ ___ x M = ___ / T		x ___ =					x	=			
			$ ___ x M = ___ / T		x ___ =					x	=			
			$ ___ x M = ___ / T		x ___ =					x	=			

Total Labor Cost/Step ═══   Total Direct Costs ═══   Total Cost ═══   Total Cost

$ = Salary/year   M = full cost multiplier (e.g.3)   T = time: 260 days, 2080 hours, 124800 minutes per year

*Fill in number and name of step; draw heavy horizontal line to show where one step ends and next begins; put step, labor, and direct cost subtotals on this line. Continue this procedure, using as many of the costing worksheets as you need.

63

You can use either hours or minutes as your unit of time as appropriate, but whatever unit of time is used must be consistent.

If several people making about the same amount were involved in the step, you can use their average salary per year. Put the person's full cost in the space to the left of the "equal" sign in Column D.

5. Identify *how much time* in days (hours or minutes) each person spends on the task.

6. *Calculate the total labor cost* by multiplying (C) the number of people involved × (D) their cost per day × (E) the number of days (hours or minutes) they spent on the step. Put this number in column F.

   Outlay costs. Next calculate the out-of-pocket *direct costs* for the step, as follows:

7. Identify *what expenses were involved* (e.g., materials, travel, per diem, computer time). Write the expense name in column G.

8. Identify the *cost per unit of the expense* (e.g., the cost of one workbook, one trip, one day's per diem). Put this figure in column H.

9. Identify the *total number of units* involved in the step (e.g., the number of workbooks or trips). Put this figure in column I.

10. *Calculate the total outlay expense cost* by multiplying (H) the cost per unit × (I) the number of units.

    Step totals: Sum full labor costs (figures in column F) to find the total full labor cost for the step. Sum outlay expense costs (figures in column I) to find total direct costs.

11. Add total *full labor costs (column F sum) to total outlay costs (column I sum)* to find the *total cost* for the step. Put this figure in column K.

Draw a line under the labor, outlay and total step costs to separate Step 1 from Step 2.

Repeat the process for Steps 2, 3, and so on, until you have accounted for costs of all steps in the program.

Sum the total costs for each step to find the total cost of the program.

This procedure is illustrated in Table 3.9, calculation of the cost of a management training program for foremen, conducted by the training department of a large manufacturing concern.

STEP 1:   DEVELOPMENT OF THE COURSE

Mr. Smith spent 10 days developing a 16-hour course on basic supervisory principles for plant foremen. The course was to be delivered in eight two-hour segments.

Full labor costs.   Smith's salary was $30,000 a year. His full cost per day was $30,000 × 3/260 days = $346/day. The full cost of his time for Step 1 was $346/day × 10 days = $3460.

Outlay costs.   Expenses for this step were $260 for off-the-shelf training materials purchased from vendors.

The *total cost* of Step 1 is $3460 (labor) + $260 (expenses) = $3720. Note that at five development days for each day of training delivered, this was particularly efficient course development. Industry norms range from between 10 to 75 development days for each day of training. Most course development efforts involve additional steps (e.g., "discussion with clients," "needs assessment," "course design") before the development step. See Table 3.11 for a list of typical steps in a training program.

STEP 2: TRAINER TRAINING

Next, Smith conducted a five-day trainer training session to teach plant supervisors from eight locations to deliver the program developed in Step 1 at their plants.

Full labor costs   for this step were the five days of Smith's time at $346/day ($346/day × 5 days = $1730), plus five days each of the eight plant supervisors' time at $288/day (5 days × $288/day × 8 people = $11,520), for a total of $1730 + $11,520 = $13,250.

TABLE 3.9
Plant Supervisor Management – Training Program
COSTING WORKSHEET

A Analysis Step*	B Labor ("Who?")	LABOR COSTS C #	D Full Cost/Time	E Time	F Cost C×D×E	OUTLAY OR OPPORTUNITY COSTS G Expense	H Cost/Unit	I # Units	J Cost H×I	TOTALS* K = F+J
1. Development of course	Smith (HR person)	1	$\frac{S\ \$30K \times M\ 3}{T\ 260}$ = $346/day	× 10 days	= $3,460	Materials	$260	× 1	= $260	$3,720
Step 1 Total										$3,720
2. Trainer training	Smith (Trainer)	1	$\frac{S\ \$30K \times M3}{T\ 260}$ = $346/day	× 5 days	= $1,730	Per diem	$20	× 5 days	= $100	$1,830
	Plant Supervisors		$\frac{S\ \$25K \times M\ 3}{T\ 260}$ = $288/day	× 5 days	= $11,520	Materials	$50/person	× 8 people	= $400	$11,920
			$\frac{S \times M}{T}$			Travel to training site	$350/person	× 8 people	= $2,800	$2,800
			$\frac{S \times M}{T}$			Per diem	$75/person/day	× 5 days x 8 people = 40	= $3,000	$3,000
			$\frac{S \times M}{T}$			Training room	$150/day	× 5	= $750	$750
Step 2 Total										$20,300

TABLE 3.9
Plant Supervisor Managment – Training Program
Costing Worksheet

A Analysis Step*	B Labor ("Who?")	LABOR COSTS C #	D Full Cost/Time	E Time	F Cost C×D×E	OUTLAY OR OPPORTUNITY COSTS G Expense	H Cost/Unit	I × # Units =	J Cost H×I	TOTALS* K = F+J
3. Delivery of training	Plant Supervisors (Trainers)	8	S $25K x M 3 / T 260 = $288/day	× 3 days = (16 hrs delivery, 8 hrs prep)	$6,912					$6,912
	Head Foreman	80	S $20K x M3 / T 260 = $231/day	× 2 days =	$36,960	Materials	$50/person	× 80 people =	$4,000	$40,960
Step 3 Total										$47,872
4. Evaluation	Smith (HR Person)	1	S $30K x M 3 / T 260 = $346/day	× 3 days =	$1,038	Telephone & computer time	$100	× 1	$100	$1,138
Step 4 Total										$1,138

Total Labor Cost/Step $61,620   Total Direct Costs $11,410

$73,030
Total Cost

*Fill in number and name of step; draw heavy horizontal line to show where one step ends and next begins; put step, labor, and direct cost subtotals on this line. Continue this procedure, using as many of the costing worksheets as you need.

67

Outlay costs for this step were Smith's per diem ($20/day for meals at a local restaurant × 5 days = $100); materials for the eight trainees at $50 per course book; travel to the training site for each of the trainees at $350 average per person; $75 per person/day per diem for eight people for five days ($75/day × 8 people × 5 days = $3000); and $150/day for the room in which the training was conducted ($150/day × 5 days = $750).

Total costs of Step 2 were $13,250 (labor) + $7050 (expenses) = $20,300.

STEP 3: DELIVERY OF TRAINING

The plant supervisors trained 10 forepeople in each of their factories.

Full labor costs for the eight trainers were their full costs of $288/day for three days (16 hours of training, plus one hour of preparation for each of the eight sessions): 8 people × $288/day × 3 days = $6912. Full labor costs for the 80 trainees were their full costs of $231/day for two days: 80 people × $231/day × 2 days: $36,960.

Direct costs for this step were $50 per person for course-book manuals for 80 participants: $50/person × 80 people = $4000.

Total costs for Step 3 were $43,872 (labor) + $4000 (expenses) = $47,872.

STEP 4: EVALUATION

Smith subsequently spent three days contacting the eight supervisory trainers and analyzing a reactions questionnaire given to each of the head foreperson.

Full labor costs for this step were Smith's three days × $346/day = $1038.

Outlay costs for this step were $100 for telephone charges and computer time.

Total costs of Step 4 were $1138.

This plant-management training program cost a total of $73,030. Typically, 85% of the cost of the program was in people's time—both trainers' and participants' time. Note that in Steps 2 and 3 the cost of *participants'* time was much greater than the cost of the trainers' time. This is true in most human resource interventions: *the real cost of the program is the clients' time.*

This simple costing procedure (similar to preparing a budget) can be used to cost virtually any human resource project or program. The figures involved are not complex, but, in practice, you will find few people know (or think they know) the data required to calculate the costs of services using the format shown in Tables 3.8 and 3.9. Most will not know their applied rates or cost per applied person-day—or even know what these terms mean. Few will have kept accurate track of their time using time sheets. *People do, however, have data they do not know they have. These data are easy to get if you ask them the right questions.* I call this an "inquiry strategy." Figure 3.3 shows the questions to ask to fill out the costing worksheet:

Q1:   What are the *steps* involved in delivering the service?

Then for *each step*:

Q2:   *Who* is involved at each step?

Q3:   *How many* people of the same title or salary level are involved?

Q4:   *How much do each* of these people *make* (*salary* per year)?

Q5:   How much *time* does each person involved spend during the step?

Q6:   Are there any *direct outlay* involved in the step? If yes,

Q7:   *How much* does each unit of the outlay expense cost?

Q8:   *How many* units are involved in the step?

EXAMPLE. *Centralizing versus decentralizing the hiring of minority engineers:*

I was asked to referee a dispute between corporate headquarters and division recruiters about who should take what steps in hiring minority

FIGURE 3.3
"Inquiry Strategy" Questions
To Find the Cost of An HR Program

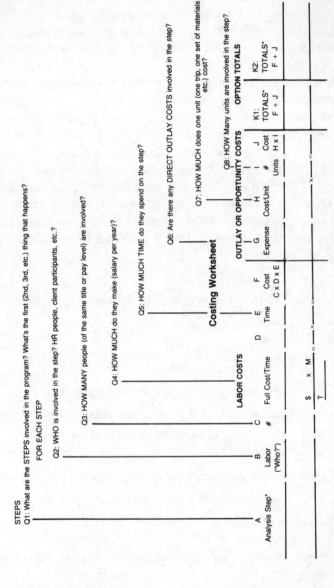

STEPS
Q1: What are the STEPS involved in the program? What's the first (2nd, 3rd, etc.) thing that happens?

FOR EACH STEP

Q2: WHO is involved in the step? HR people, client participants, etc.?

Q3: HOW MANY people (of the same title or pay level) are involved?

Q4: HOW MUCH do they make (salary per year)?

Q5: HOW MUCH TIME do they spend on the step?

Q6: Are there any DIRECT OUTLAY COSTS involved in the step?

Q7: HOW MUCH does one unit (one trip, one set of materials etc.) cost?

Q8: HOW Many units are involved in the step?

Costing Worksheet

	LABOR COSTS					OUTLAY OR OPPORTUNITY COSTS				OPTION TOTALS	
A Analysis Step*	B Labor ("Who?")	C #	D Full Cost/Time	E Time	F Cost C × D × E	G Expense	H Cost/Unit	I # Units	J Cost H × I	K1: TOTALS* F + J	K2: TOTALS* F + J
		$ × M =						×	=		
		T									

$ = Salary/year   M = overhead multiplier (e.g.3)   T = time: 260 days, 2080 hours, 124800 minutes| per year

*Fill in number and name of step; draw heavy horizontal line to show where one step ends and next begins; put step, labor, and direct cost subtotals on this line. Continue this procedure, using as many of the costing worksheets as you need.

70

engineers. This case shows how a simple costing inquiry strategy can be used to "cost-benefit analyze" a problem involving three personnel issues: centralization versus decentralization, hiring, and affirmative action.

The corporate recruiters argued for keeping this function centralized to avoid "duplicating functions and reinventing the wheel: if recruiters from four divisions do what we are doing, it will cost four times as much!"

Division recruiters argued for decentralizing this function on the basis of reducing turnover. They claimed that line managers would make better job-person match decisions. Fewer recruits would feel the job or location had been misrepresented—and be less likely to quit.

I asked the logical questions: "Well, what does it cost to do it each way (centralized versus decentralized)?" "How many more engineers would you have to keep each year to make decentralization worthwhile?" Both corporate and divisional people threw up their hands and said, "How do we know, no one keeps track of costs of this kind." I proceeded with the inquiry strategy shown in Table 3.10 and was able in about 20 minutes (literally on the back of a napkin in the company cafeteria) to get a fairly complete cost for both the centralized and decentralized options. The conversation went somewhat as follows:

Analyst: OK, let's walk through the steps it takes to hire a minority engineer. We'll keep a running total of how much it costs you to do it now, centralized, versus how much it would cost you to do it decentralized. I'll start with the way you're doing it now at headquarters. How many people do you have?

Answer: Three.

Analyst: How much do they make?

Answer: One makes $25,000, one makes $30,000, and one makes $35,000.

Analyst: How many days per year do you work?

Answer: Well, let's see. We have a standard 260-day year, we get three weeks of vacation (15 days), 11 holidays, and four sick and personal leave days. That leaves 230 work days.

TABLE 3.10 INQUIRY STRATEGY: PROBING COSTS OF CENTRALIZED VERSUS DECENTRALIZED FUNCTION

Probe	Answer	Calculation
		Labor
		Salary/days = cost × OHD factor* = Full labor cost
1. How many people at headquarters would work on this project?	3	
2. How much does each make?	1@$25K 1@$30K 1@$35K	$25K/260 = 96 × 3 = $288/day $30K/260 = 115 × 3 = $346/day $35K/260 = 135 × 3 = $404/day
3. How many days/year do they work?	230 − 11 days holidays, 4 sick days average, 3 weeks' vacation (15)	260 − 30 = 230 Direct labor = 230/260 = 89% salary
4. What's your (a) Fringe rate? (b) OHD rate?	43% of annual salary (.43S) 120% of salary + fringes (.89S + .43S) = 1.6S	Direct labor + Cost of fringes + Cost of OHD = full cost multiplier .89S + .43S + 1.2(.89S + .43S) = 2.9S ~ 3S

	Cost of Full Labor	Direct Cost of Travel and Expenses	Cost Centralized	Cost Decentralized
5. What are the steps in recruiting a minority employee?				
I. College Relations Visits				
6. How much time does each person spend on this a year? 50% of $35K/yr person 50% of $25K/yr person 10% of $30K/yr person	115 days × $404/day = $46.5K 115 days × $288/day = 33.1K 23 days × $345/day = 7.9K Total = $87.5K			
7. How many trips are made in all? 2 trips to each of 35 schools = 70 trips		70 trips × $300/trip = $21K	21.0K +87.5K $108.5K	$108.5K

8. How much do travel and per diem costs average per trip?

   $300

II. Conducting Exploratory Interviews

9. How many people visit how many schools?

If we stay *centralized*: One of the 3 of us (average salary = $30K) makes 2 2-day trips to the 35 schools

   2 trips × 2 days × 35 schools = 140 days

   140 days × $346/day = $48.5K

   70 trips × $300/trip = $21K $69.5K

If we *decentralize*: Each of the 4 divisions sends a fairly high-level person ($35K) on 2 1-day trips to the 35 schools

   280 days × $404/day = $113.1K (2 trips × 4 div.) × 1 day × 35 schools

   280 trips × $300/trip = $84K $197.1K

III. Collecting interview reports

10. Separately costed?

   No, accounted for in overhead

IV. Reviewing files at weekly staff meetings.

11. How many meetings take place?

   50/year

12. How long does each meeting last?

   2 hours

13. How many people attend?

   2 reps

14. How much does each rep. make?

   $25K/yr

15. What is the annual cost?

   12 reps × $288/day × 2 hrs ÷ 8 hrs/day × 50 meetings = $43.2 $43.2K $43.2K

(cont.)

TABLE 3.10 continued

	Cost of Full Labor	Direct Cost of Travel and Expenses	Cost Centralized	Cost Decentralized
V. Contacting applicants for second interview				
16. Separately costed? No, accounted for in overhead				
VI. Interviewing applicants at headquarters				
17. How many applicants are invited? 400				
18. Are interviewees paid? No				
19. What is average cost of travel and expenses for an applicant to come for an interview? $300/applicant		400 applicants × $300 each = $120K		
20. How long is the inverview? 1 hour				
21. How many interviews does each applicant have? 5				
22. How much do interviewers make? $35K				
23. What is the cost of conducting interviews? *If we stay centralized:*	400 applicants × 5 interviews × $\frac{1}{8}$ day = 250 interviewer-days × $404/day = $101.0K			
If we decentralize: 4 people make 2 trips to HQ (@ $400/ trip each) and spend 20 days @ $75 per diem/day		$4 \times 2 \times \$400 = \$3.2K$ $4 \times 20 \times \$75 = \underline{\$6.0K}$ $9.2K$	$221.0K	$230.2K

VII. Making job offers

24.	Separately costed?	No, accounted for in overhead		
25.	How many of 400 people do you hire?	100		
26.	Are there any other hiring costs?	Yes: moving allowances of $3,000 per person hired	100 hires × $3,000/hire = $300,000	$300K	$300K

Total recruitment cost to hire 100 people

		$742.3K	$879.1K
Cost/hire		$7423	$8791

Analyst: OK, so your direct labor time is 230 days worked divided
            by 260 days paid equals .89% of salary. What is your fringe
            rate?

Answer: Forty-three percent.

Analyst: How about your overhead rate? [Blank stares. One person
            in the group looks up and sees the company's comptroller
            entering the cafeteria and yells, "Hey Joe, what's our over-
            head rate?"]

Answer: One hundred and twenty percent.

Analyst: With these data it's easy to calculate your headquarters re-
            cruiters' full labor costs. Your full cost multiplier is each per-
            son's direct labor, 89% of salary (.89 salary) plus 43% fringe
            (.43 salary) plus 120% (.89 salary + .43 salary) overhead =
            1.3 salary + 1.6 salary = 2.9 × salary. To make things easy,
            I'll just use 3, the U.S. industry average. This means your
            $25,000/year recruiter has a direct cost of $25,000 ÷ 260 days
            = $96 × 3 = $288/day. Your $30,000/year person costs
            $30,000 ÷ 260 days = $115/day × 3 = $346/day. Your
            $35,000/year person costs $35,000 ÷ 260 days = $135/day
            × 3 = $404/day. Now I have all the information I need to
            calculate your recruitment costs. What are the steps in re-
            cruiting a minority engineer? What is the first thing what
            you do?

Answer: Our first step is college relations visits. We don't advertise,
            but we spend a lot of time wining and dining college deans
            at small southern schools.

Analyst: How much time does each person spend on this per year?

Answer: Well, I'd say 50% of the $35,000/year person's time, 50% of
            the $25,000/year person's time, and 10% of the $30,000/year
            person's time.

Analyst: [Scribbling on napkin.] OK, it you work 230 days, 50% of
            the $35,000/year person's time is 115 days × $404/day =
            $46,460; 50% of the $25,000/year person's time is 115 days
            × $288/day is $33,120; and 10% of the $30,000/year per-
            son's time is 23 days × $346/day = $7958. That adds up to

$87,538 worth of time spent wining and dining college deans. How many trips do you take to the schools?

Answer: We make two trips to 35 schools, 70 trips in all.

Analyst: How much are travel and per diem on average per trip?

Answer: Three hundred dollars.

Analyst: OK, 2 trips to 35 schools = 70 trips; 70 trips × $300/trip = $21,000. So the full cost of your first step, college relations visits, is $87,538 in labor expense and $21,000 in direct costs, a total of $108,538 for Step 1. Now, what would happen if you decentralized?

Answer: [The division recruiters look at one another and smile.] No way do we want to be in the wining and dining college dean business. We're perfectly happy to leave that centralized.

Analyst: So, the cost of Step 1 is $108,538 either way. What's the next thing that happens—the next step in hiring a minority engineer?

Answer: If we stay centralized, one of the three of us visits each of the 35 schools to talk to college seniors who will be graduating the following spring.

Analyst: Which of you visit the schools? How much time do each of you spend on these visits?

Answer: Well, we share the work about equally and make two two-day trips to each of the 35 schools.

Analyst: OK, two trips × 2 days/trip × 35 schools = 140 days. I'll take your average salary, $30,000, or $346/day × 140 days = $48,462. What's your average travel and expense cost (T&E) on these trips?

Answer: All are about the same as the college relations visits, $300.

Analyst: OK, so 70 trips × $300/trip is another $21,000 direct costs for this step. Your total cost for exploratory interviews is $48,462 in labor costs, plus $21,000 in direct costs, or $69,462. Now what happens if you decentralize?

Answer: Each of the four divisions has to send a fairly high-level person on two trips to the 35 schools. But because there would be a gang of us going, I think we'd divvy up the interviews so we'd each spend only one day at each school.

Analyst: OK, 2 trips × 4 divisions × 1 day/school × 35 schools is 280 days on the road. Now how much does a "fairly high-level person" make?

Answer: $35,000.

Analyst: OK, the full cost of a $35,000/year person's time is $404/day × 280 days = $113,077 in labor costs for this step. Now you're also talking 280 trips. What's your T&E expense likely to be per trip?

Answer: Well, a lot of those trips would be doubled up. Anyone who went from our West Coast region to the South would visit several schools per trip. Also, I suspect we will do a lot more local recruiting, which won't cost anything. Everything considered, I can't imagine it would cost us any more than the $300/trip that it costs corporate.

Analyst: OK, 280 trips × $300/trip is $84,000 in outlay cost. The total cost of doing exploratory interviews if you decentralize is $113,077 in labor costs, plus $84,000 in outlay costs—a total of $197,077.

             What happens next? What's your third step in hiring a minority engineer?

Answer: Interview reports come to headquarters.

Analyst: Who is involved in that? How much time do they spend? For example, do you have to spend time writing up the interview reports?

Answer: No, we do it on the road during the time we spend interviewing. All that happens is that at headquarters a secretary files them.

Analyst: [Making a judgment call.] I don't think this step is worth costing separately. That secretary's time is what your three-times overhead multiplier is paying for. What's the next thing that happens? What's the fourth step in hiring a minority engineer?

Answer: Interview report files are reviewed by division staff repre-
            sentatives in weekly meetings at headquarters.

Analyst: How many division representatives are there?

Answer: Twelve—three from each division.

Analyst: How much do these people make?

Answer: $25,000 a year.

Analyst: How long is the meeting?

Answer: Two hours.

Analyst: How many meetings are there a year?

Answer: Fifty.

Analyst: OK, a staffie making $25,000/year costs $288/day. If 12 reps
            meet 2 hours/day at 50 meetings, you spend 12 people ×
            2 hours/8 hour-day = .25 day × 50 meetings = 150 person-
            days on this task; 150 days × $288/day is $43,200 in labor
            costs for this step. Are there any outlay costs involved?

Answer: No, everything takes place at corporate office.

Analyst: What happens if you decentralize?

Answer: No change—the division representatives are already at
            headquarters.

Analyst: OK, so Step 4 costs $43,200 either way. What's the next
            thing that happens? What's the fifth step?

Answer: The division representatives contact the applicants for a sec-
            ond interview.

Analyst: Who's involved in that? How much time do they spend?

Answer: Well, it's not really the reps who contact the applicants.
            Secretaries schedule the interviews. They spend a few days
            on the phone, I guess.

Analyst: OK, this step is not worth costing separately either; we'll
            leave it in overhead. What's the next thing that happens?

Answer: Applicants are interviewed at headquarters. We bring them
            in, give them a nice dinner and a tour, and then each can-
            didate has five interviews with fairly senior corporate ex-
            ecutives.

Analyst: How much does a "fairly senior corporate executive inter-
             viewer" make?

Answer: $35,000 a year.

Analyst: How many applicants do you invite?

Answer: Four hundred.

Analyst: How long is the interview?

Answer: One hour.

Analyst: OK, 400 interviewees × 5 interviews × 1 hour (⅛ of a day)
             = 250 person days. A $35,000/year person costs $404/day,
             so labor costs for these interviews cost $101,000. What are
             the direct costs involved in this step?

Answer: We reimburse applicants for their travel and expenses. Their
             costs have to be about the same as ours, $300 per trip.

Analyst: OK, 400 applicants × $300/day per applicant = 120,000 in
             direct costs. Your total cost for final interviews at head-
             quarters is $101,000 in labor costs, plus $120,000 in direct
             costs = $221,000. Now, what happens if you decentralize?

Answer: Well, instead of having corporate types do these interviews,
             we'd have senior division representatives come to head-
             quarters to do the interviews.

Analyst: How many people would come from the divisions?

Answer: Four.

Analyst: How much would they make?

Answer: $35,000 a year.

Analyst: How much time would they spend on these trips to head-
             quarters?

Answer: Probably 20 days each. Each of the four of us wouldn't need
             to see all 400 applicants, because we'd already have a pretty
             good idea who we wanted to talk to from the preliminary
             interviews. We wouldn't mind corporate folk interviewing
             them too, as long as we have the final say.

Analyst: OK. As far as I can see, the labor costs would be the same.
             Interviewers from the divisions make the same amount cor-
             porate interviewers do: $35,000/year. Division people would

spend 4 people × 20 days = 80 days doing interviews. The total interviewing time of 250 days won't change, so the labor cost for the decentralized option will also be $101,000. But division people will have outlay costs in coming to headquarters to do the interviews. How many trips would you make?

Answer: Well, given 20 days, two trips each—ten days is about the maximum anyone would want to be away from home.

Analyst: What would the travel and per diem cost per trip?

Answer: Well, airfare would be $300. For the 20 days we had to stay at corporate, we'd get per diem of $75/day.

Analyst: OK, if 4 division people take 2 trips each, that's 8 trips × $400/trip = $3200 total air fare, plus 4 people × 20 days × $75/per diem = $6000. Total outlay costs for division people to come to corporate for final interviews is $3200 air fare + $6000 per diem = $9200. The total cost for the decentralized option is $221,000 centralized cost plus $9200 = $230,000.
            What's the next thing that happens—your seventh step?

Answer: Applicants are offered jobs. We make up our minds about whom we want to hire while we are doing the final interviews, and we tell the secretary to crank out the acceptance letters.

Analyst: I think I'm hearing that this step is not worth separate costing.

Answer: Right, all that's really involved is the secretary hitting a button on a word-processing machine and printing out identical letters.

Analyst: Are there any other hiring costs?

Answer: Yes, we give hirees an average of $3000 relocation expenses. We hire about 100 of the 400 candidates who make it to the final interviews.

Analyst: OK, 100 new hires × $3000 relocation = an additional $300,000. Now if I total up both the centralized and decentralized columns, I get a cost of $742,300 to recruit 100 minority engineers if you stay centralized, as opposed to [$879,100] if you decentralize. In fact, the decentralized option is *not* "four times" the centralized option. It's only $136,800 more. Only two of your steps really change: having division people go out and do preliminary interviews, which does cost $127,600 more, and having them come to corporate headquarters to do final interviews, which costs only $9,200 more.

We now can answer the cost-benefit question we started with: How many additional engineers would you have to retain to justify the costs of the decentralization? How much does an unhappy minority engineer make at the time he or she leaves the company?

Answer: Well, they tend to quit after about one year, when they're making $25,000 a year.

Analyst: Human resources accounting studies show that, at minimum, employees are worth the amount they are making when they leave. In this case, each engineer who leaves the firm is a $25,000 loss. If you divide the $136,800 cost of decentralizing recruitment by $25,000 you find that if you can retain five to six additional engineers a year, the decision to decentralize will pay for itself. This is a number that you can track over the next year to see whether the benefit of decentralizing in fact justifies its cost.

Several points can be made about the inquiry process used in this case. First and most important, by asking the right questions, you can very quickly extract reasonably sophisticated cost-benefit data from people who do not think they know *any* of the costs involved. Granted, you are asking for estimates and recollections of people's salaries and time spent on various activities. While these "guesstimates" are not as good as having time sheet data (an argument for keeping time sheets!), my experience is that guesstimates *are* surprisingly accurate—rarely more than 2% to 3% off when compared with calendar data. People *do* know how they spend their time and are very good at estimating how much others get paid.

If you have any doubts about the accuracy of your costs, cost several similar events and find the average cost. You can even use simple statistics to test the accuracy of your average cost. (The way to turn suspect guesstimates into an honorable *statistic* is to get several values and report their mean and standard deviation.)

Second, the inquiry process is very simple and straightforward if you stick to the costing worksheet format. Be sure you get the steps in sequential order. If you start to jump around among steps, people involved, times, and costs, you will very quickly get lost. The columns in the calculation worksheet are set up to prompt you to ask the right questions: the first step? Second, third, and so forth? Then for each step: the people involved, the number of people, their costs, and the time they spend to calculate total labor costs; then for outlay costs, the expense, the number of units, the cost per unit, the total expense.

If you are comparing two options—for example, centralized versus decentralized or a current way you do something versus a proposed new way—calculate the cost for both options, step by step. This will help you to see where costs differ between alternatives: which steps save you or cost you money, and where your opportunities are for cost savings.

Probe if you get vague answers, for example, "a fairly high level person." A "fairly high-level person" is not costable. You must probe and ask, "How much does a 'high-level person' make?"

You must make judgment calls on whether or not to cost minor steps in the process. If a step costs less than 3% to 5% of the total and/or its costs are included in overhead (e.g., secretarial support), you can omit it. This was done in the hiring minority engineer example for Step three (collecting interview reports), Step five (calling applicants for a second interview), and Step seven (calling or writing applicants to offer them jobs). These steps do not take enough time or cost enough to be worth costing separately. It can be assumed that clerical functions are accounted for in the full cost multiplier.

Turning Costs into Benefits

As you will see in the following chapter, *calculating the costs of human resource and other professional services is the key to calculating their BENE-FITS*. Benefits are very often shown by comparing the cost of two ways of doing something, then claiming the difference between them as a cost-saving benefit. Calculating the costs of "people problems" (e.g., grievances, accidents, employee relations conflicts) is the way you show the benefits of reducing these problems. Your ability to find the *cost* for any program or activity will enable you to find the *benefit* for any program or activity.

APPLICATIONS

Training and Consulting Programs.   Calculating the costs of training programs and consulting projects is relatively straightforward because both follow a known sequence of steps (e.g., the "Instructional Systems Development" [Branson, Rayner, and Cox., 1975] steps for training or the Kolb-Foreman [1970] model for consulting). Table 3.11 summarizes these steps with typical labor and outlay costs for each step. You should, of course, tailor these steps to fit your own process, using the costing worksheet or Lotus 1-2-3 spreadsheet or BASIC programs to calculate costs. Similar tables are provided in Chapter 4, "Calculating Benefits: Basic Strategy," for hiring and other personnel services.

"Overhead Accounting."   Some organizations (especially those required to do so by government procurement rules) break overhead costs into overhead, selling, marketing and "general and administrative" (G&A) expenses and/or calculate overhead on bases other than direct labor (e.g., products, materials, space square footage, or specific manufacturing activities). Separate accounting for general and administrative and selling overhead is particularly common in professional service firms which do business with the federal government, essentially because the government does not want to be charged for marketing activities and general business expenses unrelated to government work. General and administrative costs do not change delivery professionals' costs per person day or billing rates, just account for costs in a different place. A typical worksheet for full costs including general and administrative overhead looks like this:

1. Direct labor   (1)
2. Plus: fringe costs @ fringe % × (1):   (2)
3. Subtotal: Direct labor + fringe costs: (3)= (1) + (2)

TABLE 3.11

Typical Steps and Costs in Training and Consulting Programs

TRAINING			CONSULTING		
Step	Labor Costs	Outlay Costs	Step	Labor Costs	Outlay Costs
1. Initial "Scouting," "Contracting," and Planning Meetings with Client	• consultant • client	• T&E	1. Initial "Scouting," "Contracting," and Planning Meetings with Client	• consultant • client	• T&E

2. Needs Assessment
  a. interviews
  b. surveys
  c. data analysis
	• consultants
	• client respondents
		• T&E
		• consultant (external)
		• surveys
		• computer time
			2. Diagnosis	• consultants
				• client respondents
					• T&E
					• consultant (external)
					• surveys
					• computer time

3. Course Design	• consultants • clients (review)	• T&E • materials • consultants (external)	3. Intervention Design	• consultants • clients (review)	• T&E • materials • consultants (external) • facilities

(continued)

TABLE 3.11 continued

TRAINING

Step	Labor Costs	Outlay Costs
4. Curriculum Development	• consultants • clients (review)	• T&E • materials • consultants (external)
5. Trainer Training	• consultants • trainer • trainees	• T&E • materials • consultants (external) • equipment • facilities
6. Training	• trainers • trainees	• T&E • materials • consultants (external) • equipment • facilities • opportunity costs(?)
7. Follow-up Technical Assistance	• consultants • trainers • trainees	

CONSULTING

Step	Labor Costs	Outlay Costs

4. Data Feedback/problem solving/implementation planning meeting	• consultants
	• clients
	  - manager
	  - members
		• T&E
		• materials
		• consultants (external)
		• facilities

5. Implementation	• consultants
	• clients
	  - manager
	  - members
		• T&E
		• materials
		• consultants (external)
		• facilities

6. Follow-up Technical Assistance	• consultants • clients	• T&E • materials • consultants (external)

8. Evaluation

- consultants
- trainers
- trainees

- T&E
- surveys
- computer time

9. Final Report

- consultants
- client

- T&E
- word pro-cessing

7. Evaluation

- consultants
- clients

- T&E
- surveys
- computer time

8. Final Report

- consultants
- clients

- T&E
- word pro-cessing

4. Plus: Overhead costs @ overhead % × (3):   (4)

5. Subtotal: Direct labor + fringe + Ohd costs: (5) = (3) + (4)

6. Plus: Direct costs: (6)

7. Total labor, fringe, Ohd, and direct costs: (7) = (5) + (6)

8. Plus: G&A costs @ G&A % × (7):   (8)

9. Total costs: (9) = (7) + (8)

10. Plus: Profit @ profit % × (9):   (10)

11. Total price (per project, person-day, etc.):   (11) = (9) + (10)

General and administrative overhead is added in "on top of" all other costs, including direct outlay costs, on the assumption that arranging for a trip, consultant or equipment costs the time of an administrative person. Profit is then added to total costs to figure the total price a person or firm has to charge per day or for a project to cover all of its costs and make its desired profit.

Fultz (1980) provides an excellent discussion how professional service firms account for different types of overhead when dealing with government auditors and procurement offices.

Components of a typical professional service group's overhead rate are shown in Table 3.12. When I'm asked by an organization to establish accounting standards for internal service groups, I ask the firm's comptroller for the data shown in Table 3.12 for representative professional service cost centers (e.g., training, curriculum development, wage and salary planning, labor relations, organization development, and legal services).

Table 3.12 shows the direct and indirect costs that go into cost center with full cost and overhead multiplier calculations.

1. *Direct Labor Expense.* Salaries of professionals delivering services.

2. *Fringe Benefits.* Added to direct labor expense, in this case, 20%.

3. *Travel and Expenses.* Charged to overhead (i.e., travel costs that could not be billed to a client).

4. *Relocations.* In this company, personnel cost centers were charged by the firm's relocation office for moving expenses.

TABLE 3.12
Calculating Overhead %'s and Full Cost Multipliers from Cost Center Data

1983 Budget Unit Charge Breakdown (Hourly Basis)

	Cost Center 1 $	Cost Center 1 %	Cost Center 2 $	Cost Center 2 %	Cost Center 3 $	Cost Center 3 %	Cost Center 4 $	Cost Center 4 %	Cost Center 5 $	Cost Center 5 %
Direct Labor Costs										
1. Direct Labor Expense	15.22	36.3	15.40	34.3	14.21	33.1	15.56	36.4	15.56	36.4
2. + Fringe @ 20%	3.04	7.3	3.08	6.8	2.84	6.6	3.11	7.3	3.11	7.3
3. Subtotal: Labor + Fringe (1) (2)	18.26	43.6	18.48	41.1	17.05	39.7	18.67	43.7	18.67	43.7
Indirect Overhead Costs										
4. Travel & Expenses	0.77	1.8	1.11	2.5	1.32	3.1	1.39	3.3	1.39	3.3
5. Other Expense e.g., Supplies	1.04	2.6	1.75	3.9	2.34	5.4	2.78	6.5	2.78	6.5
6. Relocations	0.61	1.4	0.83	1.8	1.76	4.1	-	-	-	-
7. Occupancy	2.03	4.8	2.75	6.1	3.35	7.8	1.39	3.2	1.39	3.2
8. Equipment' -- Depreciation	1.70	4.1	3.18	7.2	2.30	5.3	-	-	-	-
9. Cross Charges Purchasing, Graphics, etc.	3.44	8.2	2.83	6.3	3.40	7.9	2.58	6.0	2.58	6.0

TABLE 3.12 continued

	Cost Center 1		Cost Center 2		Cost Center 3		Cost Center 4		Cost Center 5	
	$	%	$	%	$	%	$	%	$	%
Indirect Overhead Costs										
10. Cost Center Admin[2] -- Mgmt Staff	4.84	11.5	4.20	9.4	2.89	6.7	10.00	23.4	10.00	23.4
11. Site Admin -- Dept Mgmt & Staff	3.50	8.4	3.78	8.4	3.22	7.5	5.94	13.9	5.94	13.9
12. Corporate Admin -- Div & Corp tax	5.72	13.6	5.99	13.3	5.37	12.5	-	-	-	-
13. Subtotal (4-12): Overhead	23.65	56.4	26.42	58.9	25.95	60.3	24.08	56.3	24.08	56.3
14. TOTAL COST/HOUR	41.91	100.0	44.90	100.0	43.00	100.0	42.75	100.0	42.75	100.0
Overhead Percentage (13) ÷ (3)	129.5%		143.0%		152.2%		129.0%		129.0%	
Overhead Multiplier (14) ÷ (1)	2.75x		2.91x		3.02x		2.75x		2.75x	

Averages

• OHD percentage = 136.4%
• Direct Labor Multiplier = 2.83X

[1] Includes System Manager, operators, and maintenance salaries, plus 20% fringe.
[2] Includes Manager's, Supervisors', and Secretaries' salaries, plus 20% fringe.

5. *Occupancy.* Office space, lights, heat, maintenance, cleaning, and the like.

6. *Equipment.* Depreciation expense, plus the computer system manager's, operators', and maintenance workers' salaries and fringe.

7. *Cross-charges.* From other service groups for purchasing, graphics, and so forth, services that cannot be billed to clients.

8. *Cost Center Administration.* The cost center manager's, supervisors', secretaries', and other support people's salaries, plus fringe benefits.

9. *Site Administration.* The cost center's share of department management and staff salaries, plus fringe benefits and overhead.

10. *Corporate Administration.* The division and corporate headquarters "tax" (sometimes called "home office overhead allocation") for higher-level managers, staff and secretaries' salaries, fringe, and overhead, up to and including the chairman of the board.

This organization was somewhat unusual in explicitly breaking out the overhead costs of various higher levels of management: cost center, then site, then division and corporate. Table 3.12 breaks out the costs of each part of overhead on an hourly and percentage basis. The total hourly cost for cost center 1 is $41.91, or, on a yearly basis (2080 hours), $87,173 per professional. The overhead percentage for cost center 1 is the "overhead costs" subtotal 13, $23.65 ÷ the "labor + fringe" subtotal 3: $18.26 = 129.5%. This 129.5% overhead is the amount added to labor + fringe to find the full cost per hour: $18.26 + (129.5% × $18.26 = $23.65) = $41.91.

The full cost multiplier is the total cost per hour, $41.91 ÷ direct labor expense, $15.22 = 2.75×. This is the amount by which the cost center must multiply professionals' salary costs/hour paid to recover all their costs of doing business.

I estimated this firm's service groups' overhead rate to be the average of the five cost centers: 136.4%, and its full cost multiplier: 2.83. The overhead rate is greater than the U.S. average of 115%, but its full cost multiplier is less than the standard multiplier of 3, because the firm's fringe benefits at 20% were substantially below the U.S. average of 35%.

CHAPTER 4

Calculating Benefits

BASIC STRATEGIES

This chapter shows you how to calculate the benefits of any human resource program or service. The following key concepts will be discussed:

Any *cost* or *problem* is an opportunity to show a *benefit*.

Benefits are calculated the same way costs are.

Time savings produce the most benefits: anything that saves time or helps people use time more efficiently has a dollar value.

BASIC STRATEGIES: REVENUES AND COSTS

All benefits come from the two ways you make more money in business, that is, (1) increase revenues by raising prices or increasing volume, and/ or (2) decrease expenses.

Increasing Revenues

Pricing. Opportunities for service people to show benefits by affecting pricing decisions are relatively rare but do exist.

EXAMPLE. *Benefits of negotiation training for salespeople, lawyers, and purchasing agents:*

Karrass (1973, p. 15) has shown negotiating skills can improve unskilled bargainers' performance as much as 260%: poor negotiators accepted contract settlements of $198,000, where skilled bargainers got $518,000. Training or consulting that increases sellers' average price per unit sold can claim the average dollar gains per person (or group) multiplied by the number of people (or groups) trained or advised. In this case, a single trainee concluding a single more effective negotiation produces a $320,000 benefit.

Sales. Knowledge workers' own "sales," direct charges for their services, are by far the easiest and most direct proof of their dollar value to their firms. If internal clients are willing to pay market rates for your work, and your billing receipts equal or exceed your cost center's budget, others will have difficulty arguing your services are not worth what is freely paid for them. As will be discussed in Chapter 6, "Increasing Productivity," cross-charging for services is the sternest and best test of their cost effectiveness.

Tracking sales before and after changes in salesperson selection methods or in sales training or sales management programs can show these interventions return dollar benefits.

EXAMPLE. *Benefits of better salesperson selection:*

A retail sales firm had three problems with its sales force: lagging sales, a new-hire turnover rate of 40% a year, and unmet affirmative action goals. The firm hired only people with ten years of sales experience. In the company's area, these were mostly older white males.

The firm decided to experiment with a new competency-based sales selection method (Goleman, 1981; Spencer, 1983). This method identified a number of characteristics, for example, achievement motivation and accurate empathy, which predicted superior sales performance.

The firm selected 30 new hires, including a number of women and minorities without prior sales experience, using the competency criteria. As a control, it hired another 30 using its old approach.

At the end of a year, salespeople hired on competence criteria had a turnover rate of 20% and sales of $5000 per week, versus $4200 per week for those hired under the old method. No race or sex differences in performance were seen. Given gross margins of 50%,[1] each new salesperson's $800 additional sales per week produced a 50% × $800 = $400/week benefit for the firm. Over a year the new sales selection system earned the firm $600,000 ($400/week additional revenue × 50 weeks × 30 people = $600,000).

The 50% reduction in turnover provided another benefit: at a replacement cost of $20,000 per person, retaining six additional salespeople saved the company $120,000 per year.

---

[1]Gross margin (sales less direct selling expense, e.g., sales commissions and cost of goods sold) is the fairest benefit to claim for increased sales. Commissions and costs of goods sold are considered "in-outs"—you take in this part of the sale but pay it right out again to vendors or salespeople. The remaining gross margin from the sale is the real benefit to the firm.

FIGURE 4.1A
Selecting Retail Salespeople

COST: = $30K

BENEFITS:	COMPETENCY SELECTION GROUP	CONTROL GROUP	NET BENEFIT	
TURNOVER:	6 left @ 20K replacement cost = $120K	12 left @ 20K replacement cost = $240K	$120K cost avoidance	= $120K
SALES:	$250K/yr/person	$210K/yr/person	$ + 40K revenue × 50% gross margin = $20K × 30 people	= $600K

NET BENEFIT: $720K

As shown in Figure 4.1A, total benefits for the improved selection system, which cost $30,000, were $720,000, a cost-benefit ratio[2] of 1:24, or a return on investment of 2300%.[3]

Figure 4.1B shows the sales performance of the two groups during their initial "learning curve" time on the job. For the first three weeks, new hires with prior sales experience sold more than the competency-selected group. From this point on, competency-selected new hires did better. The area *A* between the two curves is the dollar value of ten years of sales experience—and the most the firm should spend on training

[2]Cost-benefit ratio = benefits (return)/cost (investment).

[3]Return on investment = benefits (return) − cost (investment)/cost (investment).

FIGURE 4.1B
Sales Learning Curves: Selection on
Competence vs. Traditional Method

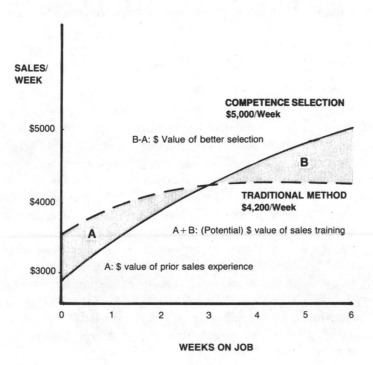

competency-selected new hires. The areas $B - A$ is the dollar value of the competency selection system. Areas $A + B$ are the potential benefit of competency-based sales training for people lacking sales experience or competencies.

Increased sales benefits can also be shown by reducing new products' time to market. A major problem in high-tech firms is getting announced products out on schedule. Late products usually mean sales lost forever. Customers switch orders to competitors, or short product life cycles render products that miss their market "windows" obsolete and unsaleable. Services that can produce reduced time-to-market sales benefits include:

Team-building and communications workshops with engineering design teams

Conflict resolution work with feuding engineering, marketing, and manufacturing groups

Planning to reduce the number of, or time to respond to, engineering change orders

EXAMPLE. *Sales benefits from reducing time to market for want of a key engineer:*

The personnel department of a major computer company refused to approve the hiring of a highly specialized microchip engineer (one of only six in the world) because his salary would create a $15,000 "red circle" exception to the firm's salary standard for design engineers. For want of this engineer, the firm's next major product was six weeks behind schedule. A call to the marketing department revealed that first-year sales for the product were expected to be $240 million, $20 million a month! Given this firm's gross margin of 65%, quibbling over $15,000 had already cost the firm $19.5 million (6 weeks = 1.5 month lost sales × $20,000,000 sales/month × .65 gross margin). A "damaging precedent" analysis shows that even if every one of the 80 other engineers at that salary level also demanded and received a $15,000 raise (highly unlikely), the maximum cost is still only 80 people × $15,000 raise/person = $1,200,000, peanuts compared with the benefit of getting the product to market on time.

Production. Production increases can be shown for many types of services; for example:

Training in production methods

Process consultation with maintenance groups

Introduction of quality circles

The dollar benefits of increased production by individuals, work groups, or plants can be documented and claimed.

EXAMPLE. *Benefits of organizational development (OD) with unionized workers in a southern paper mill:*

A strike threat and horrendous labor relations problems (320 grievances a year) led management to contract for an OD intervention. The OD effort involved surveying unhappy workers, data feedback and problem-solving meetings with managers and workers, training, and creation of ongoing worker-manager quality circles. ("OD" to the workers meant "overtime and donuts" because meetings were held after working hours and donuts were always served.)

After some weeks of griping about poor supervisory practices, workers identified several maintenance problems that had caused frequent breakdowns of the 50-year-old mill's assembly line. Special attention to key gear boxes resulted in a 10% increase in production: 35,000 tons of paper worth $40 profit a ton, a yearly benefit of $1,400,000. Total cost of the OD intervention was $90,000. The OD consultant cheerfully claimed the 1:15 cost benefit. (Additional benefits from improved labor relations, an averted strike, and reduced grievances are discussed below.)

Collections.   Direct revenue benefits can also be shown from better accounts receivable and bad debt collection skills.

EXAMPLE.   *Benefits of communications training for utility customer service representatives:*

A large utility company found its customer service representatives—the people you call to scream at when you get an outrageous bill—were not good at dealing with irate customers. Angry customers don't pay their bills on time—or don't pay them at all. At a time when the prime rate was 18%, the utility had $20 million in overdue receivables (a yearly interest expense of $3,600,000) and a non-payment rate of 3% (a yearly loss of $600,000). Complaint desk workers were given communications skills training: active listening ("You feel *angry* because your gas bill doubled last month . . . "), and transactional analysis ("Stay adult, don't blow your stack and scream back at the customer."). It worked. Irate customers do respond to kindly, sympathetic bill collectors. Trained people increased late bill payments 5% (a 5% reduction × $20,000,000 receivables = $1,000,000 revenue gain per year—at minimum, 18% interest × $1,000,000 collected = $180,000 interest expense saving) and reduced non-payments 10% ($600,000 unpaid × 10% collected = $60,000 revenue gain per year). The training, which cost $50,000, produced a benefit of at least $230,000—a cost-benefit ratio of 1:4.6 or a return on investment of 360%.

(These workers also had a turnover rate of 300% a year and a host of people problems: absenteeism, stress illnesses, employee complaints— all additional opportunities for showing benefits.)

Decreasing Expenses

Most benefits from human resource programs come from "cost avoid-ance," reducing costs in:

Labor (time and people)

Materials and other outlay costs

Capital expenses, for example, equipment down time

Benefits from reducing turnover, various expensive "people-problem events" (e.g., grievances, accidents, and disability days), and poor mo-rale are found by calculating the costs of these events.

Labor (time and people)

Reducing the person-hours or days needed to perform certain organi-zational functions (e.g., time wasted in useless meetings) is the easiest way to show dollar benefits.

EXAMPLE. *Benefits from fewer unproductive staff meetings:*

A senior manager making $46,000 a year held an hour-long staff meeting every morning, 50 weeks a year, with eight of his immediate subordi-nates. These subordinates made an average of $34,000 a year. Both the manager and his subordinates agreed that these meetings were often worthless, and requested assistance from an internal organizational con-sultant. This consultant spent two hours teaching the group basic prin-ciples of meeting management: preparation of a specific agenda with information and decision items, time limits for each item on the agenda, and the like. At the end of this session, the manager and his subordi-nates agreed that they could do with *one* well-prepared meeting a week.

Interviewed six months later, the manager and his subordinates agreed they now got more done in the one meeting a week than they previously had in five meetings a week.

Table 4.1 shows a cost-benefit accounting for this very simple training/consulting effort. Total costs, calculated by adding the full cost of

TABLE 4.1
The Manager's Unproductive Staff Meeting

<u>Cost</u>

Manager: $\frac{\$46,000}{260}$ $177 x 3 (FCM) = $531/day ÷ 8 hrs = $66/hr.

Subordinates: $\frac{\$34,000}{260}$ $131 x 3 (FCM) = $393/day ÷ 8 hrs = $49/hr.

Consultant: $\frac{\$28,000}{260}$ $108 x 4 (FCM) = $430/day ÷ 8 hrs = $54/hr.

<u>Cost</u> of Intervention Meeting

Manager:	2 hrs. x $66/hr. =	$ 132
Subordinates:	8 x 2 hrs. ea x $49/hr. =	784
Consultant:	2 hrs. x $54/hr. =	<u>108</u>
Total Cost		$1024

Benefit

Saving of 4 meetings a week x 50 weeks = 200 meetings

Manager:	1 hr. @ $66/hr. = $66	
Subordinates:	8 x hr. @ $49/hr. = <u>392</u>	
Cost of Meeting	$458 x 200 meetings =	

TOTAL BENEFIT $91,600

Cost benefit ratio: $\frac{\$91,600}{\$1,024}$ = 1:90

the labor of the manager, his subordinates, and the consultant for the two-hour training session, are $1024. The benefit of saving four meetings a week for 50 weeks (200 meetings), at the cost of the manager's and his subordinates' time, is $91,600: a cost-benefit ratio of 1:90.

A skeptic might object: "That may be the full cost 'opportunity' value of these people's time, but it's 'funny money.' You haven't saved any *real* money. For all you know, those people just slept an hour later, or spent the time they saved drinking coffee. *You have to pay them anyway.*"

There are two answers to this:

First, you have to assume that people's time is worth what it costs their firm. If time is freed from less productive activities, it will be spent on more productive tasks—what the firm is really paying them to do. You can check on this by asking each person, "What did you do with the time you saved?" Very often, this question will turn up additional benefits.

Second, you *don't* "have to pay them anyway." *Time savings always add up to people (i.e., head count) savings.* Underemployed people can be, and ultimately will be, transferred to more productive activities or let go. (In the case above, the work group was reorganized so that only seven subordinates reported to this manager. One managerial salary was saved.) The full cost of time saved represents the *opportunity* the firm has to save *real* outlay dollars *if* management is willing to make the hard decisions to cut staff and overhead.

Training and consulting efforts that simplify work or reduce paperwork can claim the benefits of time saved.

EXAMPLE.   *Benefits of reducing the length and number of memos:*

Sixty managers were trained in a one-day effective-writing course that taught them how to write succinct memos, an average of one-and-one-half pages versus three pages before the course, and when not to write a memo at all.

An unnecessary memo is a double curse: it wastes not only the time of the person who writes it, but also the time of all who must read and respond to it. Including trainers' and managers' time and materials, the course cost $40,000. A sample of managers followed up after the course said they saved an average of two hours a week writing and correcting memos. An average of five addressees saved 30 minutes a week reading managers' memos. At an average hourly full cost of $62.50, the 60 managers saved 2 hours × $62.50/hour × 60 people = $7500 a week, a yearly saving of $375,000. Their subordinates, at an average cost of $40.00 an hour, saved $40/hour × .5 hours = $20.00 per person × 5 people × 50 weeks × 60 managers = another $300,000. Total opportunity cost savings from reduced memoing was $675,000.

Many management problems result in "wasted time" costs that, if documented and prevented, can be claimed as benefits.

EXAMPLE. *Benefits from reducing delays, "waiting around doing nothing" time:*

Inventory problems caused a commercial aircraft manufacturer to have large ribbed sections of aircraft wings "held for materials," sitting on a shop floor waiting for a part to arrive. The result in a nearby hangar, where the rib went for the next step in assembly, was that three union machinists making $18 an hour ($54/hour full cost) spent an average of three days sitting around doing nothing, waiting for the rib section to arrive. Each delay at this one step in the assembly process cost $54/hour × 8 hours × 3 days × 3 people = $3888. (The "ripple effect" of delays on succeeding steps was doubtless much greater.) "Held for materials" delays in this firm numbered in the hundreds. Potential benefits for consulting on inventory management, or labor relations to permit machinists to be assigned to other productive tasks without violating work rules were obviously very great.

The dollar value of time is a common denominator and currency for almost everything that happens in an organization. Selling savings can be calculated for less time per sales call; word-processing benefits for less time per letter; savings in service costs for less time per service call. Any training or consulting effort that results in saved time can claim the dollar value of this time as a benefit.

The dollar value of time can be used in many creative ways to estimate costs and benefits. For example, time values can be used to calculate the dollar benefits of training programs and "morale" from subjective estimates of employees' productivity.

Table 4.2 shows one way of estimating the dollar benefits of produc-

TABLE 4.2
Calculating the Value of Productivity Increases from Supervisor Estimates

A. BEFORE the training or other program, ask the supervisor:

1. How much does trainee/employee make (salary/yr.)? $20K
   (full cost overhead multiplier)   x 3
   full cost of person's total work time   = $60K   (1)

2. What percentage of total working time does the person spend on tasks that will be affected by the program?

Task 1:	% Time on task		Full cost of total time (1)		Cost of time on task	
	50%	x	$60K	=	$30K	(2)

(Task 2, 3, . . .)

3. How productive is (or was) person in performing tasks (100% = fully productive, equal to average experienced worker)? Circle the appropriate figure on the following scale.

Task 1:

0%   10%   20%   30%   40%   50%   (60%)   70%   80%   90%   100%   Above 100% (3)

(task 2, 3, . . .)

4. Please calculate the baseline value of person's time spent on tasks.

Task 1:	Cost of time on task (2) $30K		Baseline % productivity 60%		Baseline value of time on task $18K	(4)
		x		=		

(Task 2, 3, . . .)

B. AFTER the training or other program, ask the supervisor:

5. How productive is the person now in performing:

Task 1?

0%   10%   20%   30%   40%   50%   60%   70%   (80%)   90%   100%   Above 100% (5)

(task 2, 3, . . .)

TABLE 4.2   continued

6. Please calculate the after-program value of time spent on tasks.

	Cost of time		After-program		After-program value	
Task 1:	on task (2)	x	% productivity (5)	=	of time on task	
	$30K		80%		$24K	(6)

(Task 2, 3, . . .)

7. Please calculate the average increase in productivity (after program - baseline: Item 5 - Item 3) among all participants for each task.

	After-program		Baseline			
Task 1 average increase:	Productivity		Productivity			
	80%	−	60%	=	20%	(7)

(Task 2, 3, . . .)

8. Please calculate the total value of increased productivity (after-program value - baseline value: Item 6 - Item 4) for each task among all participants.

	After-program		Baseline			
Task 1 total value:	Value or Time		Value of Time			
	On Task		On Task			
	$24K	−	$18K	=	$6K	(8)

(Task 2, 3, . . .)

9. State the findings of Items 7 and 8 as follows: "As rated by their supervisors, employees increased productivity on Task A by 20% percent (7). The value of this increased productivity was $6K (8) per person." Total benefits of training 120 people x $6K increased productivity/person = $720,000.

tivity gains from valuing time. First find the full cost of trainees' total time per year (1) and time spent on a task (or tasks) affected by training (2). Then ask supervisors to estimate trainees' productivity on a scale from 0 to 100% (or above 100%, where 100% is defined as the maximum productivity experienced workers can sustain if doing their best), before (3) and after (5) training. Findings can be stated: "Based on supervisor estimates, training increased participants' productivity (5) − (3) = (7) percent. This increase in productivity has a dollar value of (6) − (4) = (8) per trainee; and the total benefit of the course is (8) × the number of trainees."

EXAMPLE. *Benefits of increasing productivity of maintenance workers:*

Maintenance workers earning $20,000 a year spent 50% of their time trying to repair an advanced PBX (telephone switching system). The value of their time on this task was 50% of their full cost, $60,000: 50% × $60,000 = $30,000. Managers estimated workers' before-training productivity at 60%. Two months after training, managers' estimates of workers' productivity had increased to 80% (e.g., average repair time per PBX was reduced 20%). The value of this productivity increase is 20% × $30,000 = $6000 per worker. The total benefit of the course is $6000 × the number of workers who completed it.

Learning Curves. The cost of a new employee's "learning curve," and the benefit of reducing unproductive learning-curve time by better selection or training, can be estimated similarly, as shown in Figure 4.2 and Table 4.3. First, find the full cost of an average new hire's time (1). Calculate the value of a new hire's time during each third of his or her learning period by dividing his or her full cost (1) by 3. Next, ask supervisors to estimate the time it takes a typical new hire to become 100% productive, defined as the average productivity of experienced employees in the job (2). Next, ask supervisors how productive an average new hire is during each third of his or her learning period (4a, b, and c). The value of lost productivity during each third of the learning period is the employee's percent productivity multiplied by the cost of his or her time during the period. The total cost of learning-curve time (4e) is the full cost of the person's time for his or her total learning period (1) less the sum of productive time during the three learning periods (4d).

The benefit of a new-hire training program, or better selection system (6c), is the difference between average learning-curve productivity value of time per person with the new system (5d), less those incurred with the old system (4d) times the number of new hires selected or trained (6b).

FIGURE 4.2
Benefits of Reducing
Learning Curve Costs

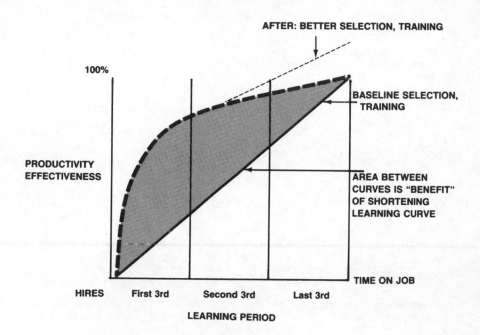

Morale. The costs and benefits of good and bad morale can be estimated from estimates of employee productivity. Think of a time when you were in a work group in which morale was terrible and people spent their time complaining, plotting behind closed doors to "get" one another or save themselves from political conflicts. How much work got done? Most people will answer, "Not much." This subjective estimate can be quantified by asking people to rate their work groups' productivity on a 0% to 100% scale, where 100% is defined as the maximum productivity the work group could sustain if it were doing its best. This calculation is shown in Table 4.4.

A group in crisis might give an average productivity rating of 40%. If this group has six people, making an average of $30,000 a year, the full cost of the group's time is total payroll: $30,000/person (1) × 3 (full cost multiplier) (2) × 6 people (3) = $540,000 (4).

TABLE 4.3
Calculating the Value of Reducing Learning Curve Time

1. Full cost of new hire's time:

Salary/Year ×			Ohd Multiplier =		Full Cost/Year	
$20K AI			3	BI	$60K	CI = AI*BI

2. Learning Curve Period:Years   1   C2
3. Cost of Time during each third of learning period $20K   C3 = (CI*C2)/3
4. Baseline

Third of Learning Period	Time Cost ×	% productivity		=	$ Value of Time	
4a. 1st	$20K ×	20%	B4	=	$ 4K	C4 = B4*C3
4b. 2nd	20K ×	50%	B5	=	10K	C5 = B5*C3
4c. 3rd	20K ×	80%	B6	=	16K	C6 = B6*C3

4d. Total productivity value of
   time during learning period $30K   C7 = @ Sum (C4 ... C6)

4e. Learning curve loss   − $30K   C8 = − C1 + C7

5. After

Third of Learning Period	Time Cost ×	% productivity		=	$ Value of Time	
5a. 1st	$20K ×	70%	B9	=	$14K	C9 = B9*C1
5b. 2nd	20K ×	95%	B10	=	19K	C10 = B9*C1
5c. 3rd	20K ×	100%	B11	=	20K	C11 = B9*C1

5d. Total productivity value of
time during learning period $53K   C12 = @ Sum (C9 ... C11)

5e. Learning curve loss   − $7K   C13 = − C1 + C13

6. Benefits
   6a. Dollar gain/person $23K   C14 = C12 − C7
   6b. Number of people   20   C15
   6c. Total benefit $460K   C16 = C14* C15

At 40% productivity, the dollar value of the group's time is .40 (5) × $540,000 (4) = $216,000 (6). The cost of poor morale is $540,000 (4) − $216,000 (6) = $324,000 (7).

The benefit of improving morale can be calculated in the same way. For example, OD consultants might run a conflict-resolution/team-building intervention with this group. A month after the intervention, they could ask work group members to rate the work group's productivity again on the 0 to 100% scale. If productivity was rated an average of 55%, the dollar value of the work group's time would be .55 (8) × $540,000 (4) = $297,000 (9). The benefits due to the consulting inter-

TABLE 4.4
Calculating the Value of
Improving Morale from Time Values

1.	Average Salary of Workgroup Members	$30K	A1
2.	Overhead Multiplier	3	A2
3.	Number of Workgroup Members	6	A3
4.	Total Value of Workgroup Members' Time	$540K	A4 = A1*A2*A3
BEFORE			
5.	Perceived Productivity of Workgroup (0%-100%)	40%	A5
6.	Value of Workgroup Effort	$216K	A6 = A4*A5
7.	Loss due to morale at less than 100%	$324K	A7 = A4 − A6
AFTER			
8.	Perceived Productivity of Workgroup (0%-100%)	55%	A8
9.	Value of Workgroup Effort	$297K	A9 = A4*A8
10.	Loss due to morale at less than 100%	$243K	A10 = A4 − A9
11.	Dollar Value of After vs. Before Morale Improvement	$81K	A11 = A9 − A6

vention is the gain in dollar value of time: $297,000 (9) after consulting − $216,000 (6) baseline = $81,000 (11). Note that at 55% productivity the work group is still doing far less than its best. The consultants have more work to do.

The dollar value of time can be used to quantify the benefit of increasing "discretionary effort," defined as the difference between "the minimum work (productivity) needed to get by" and "the most work (productivity) one has to give." Motivation training, changes in incentives or compensation, and many consulting efforts can be evaluated in this way.

Materials, Energy, and Other Outlay Costs

Travel, Per Diem, and Purchased Services. Human resource interventions can lead to material and other outlay cost savings that can be claimed as benefits. Examples include: reduced waste or scrap on assembly lines due to better quality control procedures identified in quality circles; and savings in gasoline and spare parts costs resulting from better planning and vehicle maintenance developed in a problem-solving workshop.

EXAMPLE: *Benefits of fewer dressing changes in a teaching hospital:*

A one-day conflict-resolution workshop was held with a group of surgeons and postoperative ward nurses. The policy at this particular hospital stated that nurses on the departing shift always left patients with clean dressings. But the nurses complained that doctors invariably arrived for rounds at the end of the 7:00 A.M. to 3:30 P.M. nursing shift. Nurses would apply clean dressings only to have them removed by doctors who wanted to inspect wounds. Consequently, nurses on this shift found themselves staying an additional 30 minutes a day on overtime to reapply dressings. In addition, patients complained of the pain and inconvenience of having their dressings removed and reapplied within so short a time.

The nurses felt that their relationship with doctors was poor, which resulted in low morale and a high turnover rate in the nursing staff. They also cited quality control problems. In two instances a nurse had to leave to pick up her children at 3:30 before she had time to reapply a dressing. She left the reapplication to an aide who was not fully trained. The aide applied the dressing over a penrose drain, resulting in two severe infections.

The doctors were blissfully unaware of any of these problems until a consulting firm surfaced them in a group discussion. The consultants helped doctors and nurses arrive at a practical agreement: Doctors would call from the operating theaters and notify nurses before launching their rounds so that nurses wouldn't apply fresh dressings pointlessly; the later nursing shift agreed to reapply any dressings the doctors removed so that the early shift would not have to stay late.

Everyone was pleased with this solution, but in retrospect the whole thing seemed so simple: were there any tangible benefits the hospital could show for the $1500 it paid the consultants? Following the inquiry strategy suggested, I saw two immediate opportunities for showing benefits: time (the nurses' overtime) and materials (the cost of the wasted dressings being applied).

I asked: ''How much do nurses make on overtime, and how many nurses stay late for how long?'' The answer was that five nurses making $18 an hour on overtime stayed an average of one-half hour a day. So: $18 × .5 hours × 5 nurses = $45/day.

I then asked: "How much does a dressing cost, and how many, on average, are unnecessarily replaced each day?'' The answer was that each dressing cost $30, and an average of 15 were replaced each day— a total additional cost of $450 a day.

A total cost of doctor-nurse miscommunication and nurses' admirable but inefficient policy was therefore $495 a day. In this teaching hospital, which operated 365 days a year, the dollar benefit of that $1500 consulting intervention was a savings of $45/day (labor) + $450/day (materials) = $495/day × 365 days = $180,675, a

$$\frac{\$180,675 - 1500}{\$1500} = 11,945\% \text{ return on investment.}$$

Three additional benefits *could* have been pursued in this case.

Census (Hospital Beds Filled on a Given Day, i.e., Sales). Patients pained by frequent, insensitive removal of dressings might choose to have their next operation in a different hospital. If a patient-satisfaction questionnaire correlated with census, you could estimate the dollar value of improved satisfaction from the change in the average number of beds occupied per day multiplied by patient cost per day.

Impact on Turnover. If turnover among experienced postoperative nurses making $25,000 a year was indeed being influenced by the dressing problem, a saving of *one* nurse in a year would have paid the consultants' bill almost 17 times over.

Quality Control. If better coordination between doctors and nurses prevented one or two complications a year (e.g., a severe infection causing avoidable amputation of a limb—and producing a malpractice suit), the dollar value of avoiding this unhappy event could be claimed as a saving.

Capital Equipment and Facilities Utilization and Down Time

Reducing the costs of major capital assets (e.g., computers, assembly lines, or aircraft) that are not functioning can be a major source of benefits. For example, when a computer in a bank or brokerage-house accounting office goes down, work must be performed by hand, often with very expensive temporary personnel and overtime. The number of hours the computer is down can be translated directly into costs for the organization. Training or consulting work that *reduces* the number of hours per year that the computer is down can claim the dollar value of these hours as cost-avoidance benefits. Nonprofit organizations without revenues can value capital assets by dividing their amortization cost per year by the number of hours or days (or other unit measures) they are budgeted to be on-line.

EXAMPLE. *Benefits of reducing down-time of capital equipment and turnover of mechanics:*

The officer in charge of a military air group was very concerned about its number of "hangar queens" (aircraft unable to fly). Air squadrons under his command were missing 20% of their deployments because of inoperable aircraft. These aircraft (helicopters) were inoperable because there were no mechanics to fix them. There were no mechanics because the junior enlisted technicians who repaired the aircraft were being fired for having traces of THC (marijuana) in their urine. By the time each of these mechanics was qualified to repair a helicopter engine, the military had invested approximately $30,000 in his or her recruitment and training. Each mechanic who was fired cost the military $30,000, in addition to the lost value of expensive aircraft unavailable when needed. In this case, helicopters cost $6 million each and had a useful life of eight years. Aircraft amortized value per year was $750,000 ($6 million ÷ 8 years = $750,000/year). Each helicopter had 600 budgeted flying hours a year. The value of each flying hour was thus $750,000 ÷ 600 hours = $1250/hour. At 20% below their budgeted utilization rate, helicopters were flying 600 − 120 (600 × 20%) = 480 hours a year, at a cost of $750,000/year/480 hours = $1563/hour.

The solution in this case was simply a change in personnel policy: instead of firing mechanics for drug offenses, refer them to an "amnesty" drug and alcohol counseling program already available at little cost. (The military did check the obvious quality control issue raised by pilots: "I ain't going up in no chopper fixed by no dopers!" Aircraft inspections showed mechanics who had used drugs made no more errors than nondrug users.)

The results in three months in one squadron were three mechanics saved, which, at $30,000 each, provided a turnover cost saving of $90,000. The squadron had a 10% increase in operational readiness: in a year, a net benefit of 48 more flying hours per helicopter at a new cost $750,000/year ÷ 528 flying hours = 1420/flying hour, a utilization value of 48 hours × $1420/hour × 9 aircraft/squadron = $613,440. The total benefit was $703,440: the $90,000 value of the mechanics saved plus the $613,440 value of helicopters flying versus sitting in the hangar.

The basic strategies for valuing labor time, productivity value of time, outlay, and capital costs can be combined in countless ways to show benefits for human resource and knowledge worker products and services. The following chapter provides examples for a variety of human resource services.

CHAPTER 5

Calculating
Benefits

APPLICATIONS

This long chapter, intended as a reference, provides examples of benefit calculations for human resource services:

Staffing and turnover
   Separation and outplacement
   Recruiting: internal and external
   Selection
   Relocation
   Career planning
   Equal opportunity/affirmative action
Absenteeism
Wage and compensation planning
Performance appraisal
Employee and Labor Relations: Grievances
Safety: accident fatalities and injuries
Employee assistance
   Health and wellness: smoking, alcohol, diet, exercise, and stress
   Company cafeterias and stores
   Day care
Organization development: team-building and structural changes
Personnel services: payroll and record keeping
Training
Public and community relations
Morale
Human resource asset accounting

Benefits may be shown in two ways:

(1) *efficiency*—Show you can deliver your existing services for less; and

(2) *effectiveness*—Show more benefits for your services.

Efficiency benefits come from cutting costs: labor (people and time), material and other outlay expenses, and capital.

Effectiveness benefits can come from increasing revenues *or* decreasing costs of operations or problems your services affect, for example, turnover, conflicts, grievances, accidents, and health.

These examples are in no way exhaustive. The objective is to stimulate your creativity in spotting opportunities to calculate benefits for your programs and services.

TURNOVER AND STAFFING: EXIT AND ENTRY

Turnover costs and benefits are the dollar value of a series of events in the exit of an employee and the entry of a replacement person. Typical steps, labor time and outlay costs for turnover and staffing, are shown in Table 5.1. You can develop a costing worksheet for exit and entry in your firm by entering the appropriate steps, labor and outlay costs, in the Table 3.8 template.

Exit (separation and/or termination) steps and costs are shown under "Exit," in Table 5.1. Labor time of the manager and exiting employee is spent, if the person is being fired, in a series of (1) counseling, feedback, problem-solving, and warning meetings, and in (3) termination of the employee. The manager may spend additional time (2) documenting performance problems to create an audit trail in case a formal complaint or lawsuit results from the termination. Personnel staff usually conduct (4) an exit interview. Administrative time (5) is spent processing the person's departure and notifying various departments, such as payroll, security, and the credit union. Direct outlay costs may include separation pay, increased unemployment tax, theft losses of materials and supplies, and legal fees plus settlement costs if the employee sues or files a complaint. An additional labor cost is (6) the reduced productivity of the employee prior to separation. Many employees exhibit a "reverse learning curve"—they slack off, or are absent more often—in the weeks or months before they leave or are terminated. The dollar value of lost productivity should be added to the exit cost. Outlay or opportunity costs of lost productivity can include the cost of lost sales or production, delays, quality problems, and overtime or temporary hire costs.

Work group productivity (5) may also be reduced when key people leave (see Figure 5.1A). Co-workers may be demotivated if they feel a fellow employee is being treated unfairly. (Alternatively, if a trouble-maker leaves, co-workers may become more productive.) The more people who leave a work group, the greater the disruption and adverse impact on the group's productivity (see Figure 5.1B). Impact of turnover on co-workers can be shown by estimating the value of lost productivity: total work group payroll/month times (100% − perceived productivity %) times the number of months productivity is reduced.

The cost of (7) a position being vacant is estimated the same way: labor costs are found by multiplying the total work group payroll for the short-handed period by the percent estimate of lost productivity. (A

TABLE 5.1
Turnover and Staffing: Exit and Entry Costs

I. Exit

	COSTS	
Step	**Labor**	**Outlay**
1. Counseling, warning meetings	• Manager(s) • Employee	
2. Documenting performance problems	• Manager(s) • Employee • Personnel Staff	
3. Termination meeting	• Manager • Employee • Personnel Staff	
4. Exit interview	• Employee • Personnel	• out-placement fee
5. Administrative: payroll, security, credit union, unemployment hearings	• Personnel (legal, etc.)	• severance pay • unemployment benefits • losses: theft of tools, supplies • law suits (legal fees and settlement)

(continued)

TABLE 5.1 continued

COSTS

Step	Labor	Outlay
6. Lost productivity during separation period, e.g., absenteeism	• Individual • Team	• lost sales, production delays, scrap, quality problems • overtime, temporary worker costs
7. Cost of position being vacant	• Team	• lost sales, production delays, scrap, quality problems • overtime, temporary worker costs

II. Entry

Step	Labor	Outlay
1. Recruiting/Communication of job opening: job description, job posting, advertising, college (and other source) relations	• Manager • Personnel staff	• advertisements • travel and expenses
2. Pre-employment Administration	• Personnel staff	• tests
3. Interviews	• Personnel staff	• travel and expenses (recruiters and applicants)
4. Hiring-decision meeting	• Managers • Personnel staff	• signing bonus • agency fees • referral bonus
5. Post-employment administration	• Personnel • Employee	• relocation: moving, temporary living, etc. • medical exams
6. Orientation	• Personnel • Manager • Employee	
7. Training	• Trainers • Employee	• training materials
8. Learning curve	• Employee • Team	• lost sales, production, delays, accidents, scrap, quality problems

FIGURE 5.1 A
Individual Productivity Losses in Months Prior to Separation

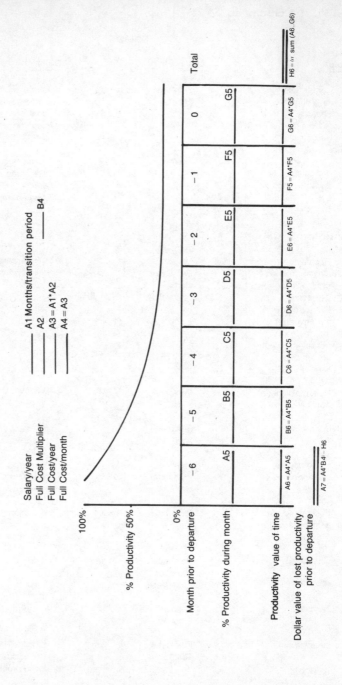

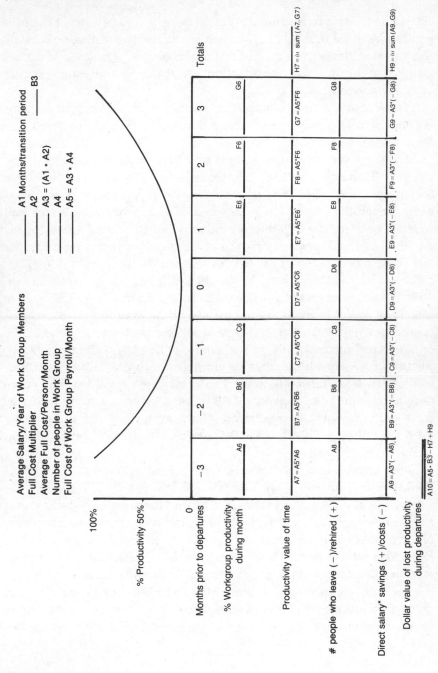

FIGURE 5.1 B
Workgroup Productivity Losses/Gains from Turnover

Average Salary/Year of Work Group Members   A1 Months/transition period
Full Cost Multiplier   A2   B3
Average Full Cost/Person/Month   A3 = (A1 * A2)
Number of people in Work Group   A4
Full Cost of Work Group Payroll/Month   A5 = A3 * A4

	−3	−2	−1	0	1	2	3	Totals
Months prior to departures								
% Workgroup productivity during month	A6	B6	C6	D6	E6	F6	G6	
Productivity value of time	A7 = A5*A6	B7 = A5*B6	C7 = A5*C6	D7 = A5*C6	E7 = A5*E6	F8 = A5*F6	G7 = A5*F6	H7 = ((sum (A7..G7)
# people who leave (−)/rehired (+)	A8	B8	C8	D8	E8	F8	G8	
Direct salary* savings (+)/costs (−)	A9 = A3*(−A8)	B9 = A3*(−B8)	C9 = A3*(−C8)	D9 = A3*(−D8)	E9 = A3*(−E8)	F9 = A3*(−F8)	G9 = A3*(−G8)	H9 = ((sum (A9..G9)
Dollar value of lost productivity during departures								

A10 = A5+ B3− H7 + H9

* Assume severance benefits = fringe benefits and overhead costs "fixed" i.e. incurred during time salaried positions are vacant

100%

% Productivity 50%

0

121

simpler method is to assume the vacant position is worth what the firm would pay to fill it, e.g., the full cost per day of the exiting or replacement person times the days the position is vacant.) Outlay and opportunity costs of lost sales, production, overtime, or temporary worker costs are added to labor costs.

Typical entry (hiring, placement, training, and learning-curve) costs are shown in Table 5.1 (under ''Entry'') and in Table 3.10 (the case ''Hiring a Minority Engineer'').

Total turnover costs at minimum equal an employee's direct salary per year (Flamholtz, 1974, p. 228; Gross, 1982). My analyses (see Table 5.2) suggest this is low, at least for higher-level professionals and managers. Separation costs average 20% to 25% of departing employees' full cost per year, mostly in reduced productivity before they leave. For example, if a $35,000 a year employee is 75% productive during his or her last three months, the dollar loss to the firm is the person's $105,000 full cost/year × .25 year × .75 = $19,678. Hiring costs equal 30% to 40% (.3 salary) of first-year salary, whether paid to a recruiter or done internally as, for example, in the case of hiring minority engineers discussed in Chapter 3. Learning-curve costs for professionals equal 50% of new hires' full cost (50% × 3 × salary = 1.5 salary) Cullen, Sawzin, Sisson & Swanson, 1976. Learning curves for technical and sales professionals can be significantly longer. For example, typical learning-curve time for computer sales people is 18 months before a new hire sells as many computers as an experienced sales person. Total cost of computer sales new hires is $180,000, $10,000 per month, *six* times new hire salaries of $30,000/year.

Total turnover cost, as shown in Table 5.2, is approximately 2.4 times the salary of a managerial or professional person who leaves.

Key steps, policies, and services affecting turnover and staffing bear further discussion. *Separation, ''qualified''* and *voluntary versus involuntary turnover* policies, and *outplacement* services affect exit costs and benefits. *Recruiting, internal promotion versus external hire* policies, *selection,* and *relocation* affect entry costs and benefits. *Career planning* services offer benefits in reducing turnover, readying people for internal promotion, and increasing productivity and morale. *Equal opportunity/affirmative action* programs represent a special case of turnover and staffing efforts targeted on minority personnel.

TABLE 5.2
Estimated Full Costs of Turnover
of a Professional or Managerial Person

Full Cost = 3 x Salary = 3S

Exit Cost = @ 20% full cost	.20 x 3S = .60S
Hiring Cost = @ 30% of direct salary	.30 x S = .30S
Learning Curve = cost @ 50% of full cost	.50 x 3S = 1.5S

Total Cost of Turnover of a Professional or Managerial Employee	2.4S: 2.4 x Salary

Separation.   Separation decisions involve a cost-benefit trade-off. The cost of firing a poor performer is the total turnover (exit plus entry) cost. The benefits are suggested in Table 5.3:

1. The lost value of the person's lower productivity; plus

2. The incremental managerial and personnel costs of dealing with the person; plus

3. The dollar value of co-workers' lost productivity due to lower morale and motivation from having the problem person around; plus

4. Any additional outlay opportunity expenses;

5. All multiplied by the number of years the employee is likely to stay in the position.

EXAMPLE.   *Costs and benefits of firing a poor performer.*

A civil-service work group was plagued by an extremely disruptive employee. This person did little work (her manager estimated her productivity at 20%), yet was demanding a promotion. She repeatedly filed nuisance grievances claiming discrimination with union representatives. She also complained to radical political groups, legal aid agencies, her congressperson, several layers of civil service ombudspeople, and the press. Charismatic and articulate, she spent most of her time recruiting allies from among the department staff, urging them to subvert or openly defy superiors. As a result, the department was in a continual state of turmoil. Work backlog was growing and senior personnel were working an inordinate amount of overtime. The manager reported he spent fully 20% of his time (8 hours a week) dealing with hassles created by the disruptive employee. Other department personnel said the same.

An OD consultant was brought in to help the manager and conduct conflict-resolution meetings with the work group. No changes in job or task design resulted, but department employees felt morale greatly improved. Co-workers saw clearly how difficult the disruptive employee was to work with and that many of the problems she attributed to her superiors were a product of her own behavior. One employee noted: "Before, you wouldn't have believed the amount of time people spent whispering, plotting behind closed doors, and office politicking. Now, if this person comes around with her latest gripe or conspiracy theory, she gets politely brushed off so we can get on with our work." The consultant ultimately helped the manager find a politically acceptable way of transferring the disruptive employee.

Table 5.3 shows the annual costs and cost-saving benefits of firing the disruptive employee.

TABLE 5.3
Estimating Costs and Cost-Saving Benefits of
Firing a Poor Performer

	Salary		x	FC Multiplier		=	Full Cost	
• Employee full costs:	$20K	A1		3	B1	=	$ 60K	C1 = A1*B1
• Manager full costs:	$40K	A2		3	B2	=	$120K	C2 = A2*B2
• Personnel staff full costs:	$30K	A3		3	B3	=	$ 90K	C3 = A3*B3

TABLE 5.3 continued

I. Cost of Poor Performance:

Employee % Productivity		$ Value of lost productivity/year
20%	A4	$48K $\quad$ C4 = (1-A4) *C1

II. Increased Managerial Costs:

	Additional hours spent with employee/week	
Manager	8 $\quad$ A5	$24.00K C5 = A5/40*(C2)
Personnel Staff	5 $\quad$ A6	$11.25K C6 = A6/40*(C3)

III. Impact on Co-Workers

Co-worker/ team % productivity	×	# Co-workers	= $ value of lost productivity/year
.75 $\quad$ A7		8 $\quad$ B7	= $120K C7 = C1*(1-A7)*B7

IV. Other costs
(Suits, lost sales, production, etc.)

Cost/incident	×	# Incidents/Year			
_____ A8		_____ B8	=	0	C8 = A8*B8

Total cost poor performer/year	$203.25K	C9 = @ sum (C4 . . . C8)
Number of years poor performer likely to stay in job	1	C10
Total benefit of firing poor performer	$203.25K	C11 = C9*C10

125

1. The lost productivity value of the employee's time: 80% × her $60,000 full cost = $48,000.

2. Additional managerial and personnel staff time: for example, for the manager, 8 hours per 40-hour week × $120,000 full cost = $24,000 time spent on the problem.

3. Impact on 10 workers: 8 people making $20,000/year have a full payroll cost of 8 people × $60,000/person = $480,000. If these people are only 75% productive due to disruptive office politics, the dollar value of their cost productivity is (1 − .75) = .25 productivity loss × $480,000 payroll = $120,000.

4. Outlay and opportunity costs: in this case, the manager and personnel consultant avoided a discrimination complaint or lawsuit by transferring the disruptive employee. (This may not have been the best solution for the federal government, but it certainly was best for the work group and agency.)

Most firms will find it cost effective to let poor performers go as soon as they are identified, especially if they are troublemakers affecting other workers' productivity. Table 5.3 shows that the greatest cost of a poor performer is his or her negative impact on co-workers (in this case, $120,000).

Unionized and civil service organizations face the hardest decisions. The cost of firing a "tenured" civil servant who exhausts all legal and appeal options can exceed $100,000. Managers in these organizations may be tempted to "live with the problem" rather than face these costs, negative publicity, and political flak of taking action. Cost-benefit analysis can show when it is cost effective to make a hard decision, and can provide compelling data to other managers, hearing examiners, and arbitrators, showing why the decision should be made. In the case above, management could bear separation (e.g., complaint hearing and lawsuit) costs of up to $203,250 and still break even.

"Qualified" turnover.   Turnover events should be "qualified," that is, classified according to whether the employee who leaves is good or bad. The two categories should be costed separately. Ideally, good, productive employees stay and bad, unproductive employees leave. The most costly situation is when the good leave and the bad stay.

Unless there are special opportunity costs (e.g., lost sales due to the loss of a superstar), the dollar cost of a good employee leaving is often less than that suggested by the rule-of-thumb estimate (i.e., two-and-one-half times his or her salary). Separation costs are likely to be lower because good employees are more productive up until the time they leave, and usually go to other jobs, hence do not require outplacement services, get severance pay, or cause problems (complaints and suits).

Poor employees cost more to fire because they are less productive during the separation period (a reason for taking action quickly), require more outplacement assistance, and are more likely to cause problems. Often, however, the benefits of their leaving justify these increased costs. The cost-benefit trade-off for a poor employee is the benefit of the person's leaving less the turnover cost. As shown in the case of the disruptive employee in Table 5.3, this figure may be positive. Even if total turnover costs are 2.5 times salary (exit of the disruptive employee, entry hiring, training, and learning-curve costs of a \$20,000/replacement), turnover costs $2.5 \times \$20,000 = \$50,000$, as against the \$203,250 benefit of firing the poor performer.

Voluntary Versus Involuntary Turnover. Reducing staff by attrition or encouraging people to leave of their own accord—as opposed to having to fire them—is almost always cost effective. Separation costs are lower for voluntary turnover because fewer outplacement services are needed, severance and unemployment pay is less, and problems, complaints, and lawsuits are much less likely.

Outplacement Services. Efficient outplacement services can reduce unproductive employee time during the separation period and reduce the likelihood of complaints and lawsuits. Outplacement may also yield effectiveness benefits. Many firms, particularly service firms, find that employees who "leave happy" become valued clients, suppliers, or references. One consulting firm found that half of all employees who "left happy" brought the firm an average of \$50,000 in business over the next five years. Assuming a gross margin of 67% on this work, the expected value of outplacement services sufficient to be sure a person "left happy" was $50\% \times \$50,000 \times 67\%$ margin = \$16,750 per employee. Other benefits of humane outplacement services can include better morale, hence higher productivity of co-workers, and less costly hiring due to good will and good community relations. (See "Employee & Labor Relations.)

Recruiting.   Benefits in recruiting can be shown by reducing hiring costs, for example, by developing better sources of applicants with a high probability of being offered and accepting jobs and/or those with minimal learning-curve costs.

EXAMPLE.   *Benefits of hiring co-op students versus college hires:*

A high-tech firm compared the offer rate, acceptance rate, and learning-curve costs for co-op students with those for college hires. Co-op students had worked two or three summers in the divisions that offered them jobs. Eighty percent of co-op students were given an offer and 90% accepted. Co-op students' first-year productivity was estimated to be 90%.

Twenty percent of college hires were given an offer and half accepted. Estimates of college hires' productivity over the first 18 months was 25% during the first six months, 50% from six to 12 months, and 75% from 12 to 18 months. Total learning-curve costs for co-op students hired at $20,000 a year were 10% × $60,000 full cost = $6000. Total learning-curve costs for college hires averaging 50% productivity over 18 months was 50% × $90,000 full cost = $45,000. Co-op students cost $2000 to hire, and college students $6000, largely because many more college students had to be interviewed to get one new hire. Total cost for co-op students was $8000, versus $51,000 for new hires. The firm concluded that hiring co-op students was far more cost effective and expanded its co-op program.

Internal Hiring and Promotions Versus External Hiring.   Filling positions by internal hiring and promotion is likely to be more cost effective than external hiring, because (1) acquisition costs are significantly less (most managers know the candidate, requiring less interviewing and background-checking time), and (2) an internal person's learning curve is much shorter: he or she already knows the company, business, and often the work group and the job. Morale and motivation of other employees, hence productivity, may also be enhanced by internal hiring/promotion. The dollar value of this morale can be measured by the productivity value of time method or validated surveys, which relate "perceived opportunity for promotion" to employee performance (see "Morale," pp. 107 and 170). Benefits of internal hiring or promotion are similar to those of hiring co-op students who were already "internal" part-time and "promoted" to full-time employee status.

Two possible exceptions to the rule that internal hiring and promotion are most cost effective are: (1) when promoting a key person disrupts the productivity of the work group he or she is leaving, that is, the firm suffers the losses of "internal turnover"; and (2) when there are no qualified candidates to solve a particular problem in the firm.

Internal turnover losses rarely exceed benefits, because the person leaving is usually moving to a more valuable job. His or her contributions in the new position exceed losses in the former job. Occasionally, firms do make the cost-benefit decision to postpone a promotion so the promotable employee can finish a critical task, for example, a promotable design engineer who cannot be spared from a major product development effort. (A possible risk that should be added in weighing costs and benefits is that a promotable employee "held back" may quit. This can be avoided by explaining the reasons for delaying promotion and giving the employee the pay, and perhaps the title, that go with the new position during his or her remaining "special assignment" time in the old job.)

When a firm does not have qualified internal candidates for key jobs, it will be more beneficial to hire from outside. For example, a computer firm known for its engineering excellence but lack of marketing skill suffered major losses when marketing became more important in selling personal computers. The firm deliberately went outside to hire marketing experts to infuse the company with new blood, perspective, and expertise. The entry costs of bringing these new people in was doubtless greater than promoting from within. Benefits greatly outweighed these costs: the firm successfully repositioned its products and earned more than $100 million in the next three years. In this case, extraordinary opportunity costs and benefits had to be considered in deviating from the firm's internal promotion policy.

You can check the rule that internal hiring and promotion is more cost effective by costing internal versus external hiring events in your firm, using the costing worksheet in Table 3.8.

Selection. The value of a selection system is getting good hires while rejecting people who would be poor hires. A good hire is more productive and more likely to stay on the job. Bad hires are less productive and more likely to leave. The effectiveness of a selection system is its "hit rate," the number of good hires divided by the total number of hires. Sophisticated statistical models exist for estimating the benefits or utility of improved selection procedures. (See discussion under "Advanced Topics.") These models can be approximated by the simple calculation shown in Table 5.4.

The dollar value of a good hire is the difference between good and bad hires' average salary times percent productivity times years in the job. The total value of the selection system is the number of good hires times this good-hire differential. Table 5.4 provides a format for comparing an existing selection system with a new, improved selection system, for example, calculating the dollar value of increasing the selection hit rate by 10%

Relocation. Firms that send employees and their families overseas to relative hardship locations such as the Middle East, find that as many as a third do not adapt and instead return prematurely to the United States. Relocation "fails" are very expensive. In addition to the outlay costs of sending an employee and family overseas, then moving them back home, there are separation costs, particularly:

Reduced productivity—time and attention spent trying to cope with the environment rather than doing the job before giving up and returning.

Administrative and counseling expenses to help the employee resume his or her career at home.

The cost of the position being vacant and entry costs to replace the person.

You can estimate the costs of a relocation fail by costing an incident in your firm, using the costing worksheet in Table 3.8. My analyses suggest an international relocation fail costs an average of $75,000.

Relocation fails are avoided by better selection, for example, by picking people who have had substantial overseas experience and who thrive on the challenge of adapting to a new environment, by providing train-

TABLE 5.4
Estimating Benefits
of Improved Selection

Overhead multiplier _____ A1

Current selection system

	Number	Average Salary	Value % Productivity	Years in Job
Good hires	A2	B2	C2	D2
Bad hires	A3	B3	C3	D3

Percentage/probability of "good hire"
("Hit Rate") _____ D4 = A2/(A2 + A3)

$ Value of a "good hire" _____ D5 = A1*((B2*C2*D2)—
(B3*C3*D3))

$ Value of current selection system _____ D6 = D5*A2

$ Value of increasing "hit rate" __10%__ B7 _____ D7 = A2*B7*D5

New Selection System

	Number	Average Salary	Value % Productivity	Years in Job
Good hires	A8	B8	C8	D8
Bad hires	A9	B9	C9	D9

Percentage/probability of "good hire" _____ D10 = A8/(A8 + A9)

$ Value good hire _____ D11 = A1*((B8*C8*D8)—
(B9*C9*D9))

$ Value of new selection system _____ D12 = D11*A8

Summary

Improvement in "hit rate"	D13 = D10-D4
Increased dollar value per hire	D14 = D11-D5
Total benefits of new system	D15 = D12-D6

ing, and by offering support and orientation "hand holding" during the initial stressful period of moving and settling in. (Few people get much work done if they are worried about their families or possessions [Tung, 1982].)

Career planning.   The benefits of career planning and counseling are most easily shown by reduced turnover, increased productivity, and the number of internal promotions versus external hires required to fill higher-level jobs. Employees who are in a job they like and perform well, or on a career path to jobs they will like and perform better, are less likely to leave and more likely to be productive. Literature on goal setting suggests career counseling and planning programs that get employees to set good goals and define specific action plans for performance improvement can increase productivity 19% (Latham and Locke, 1979). The availability of internal people for promotion saves the difference between internal and external hiring costs.

Career planning and counseling is particularly important in organizations in flux. When requirements are changing, career paths are not obvious and many people are in a state of transition.

EXAMPLE.   *Benefits of a computer firm's "job fair" career planning program:*

A major computer company found that fully 20% of its professional staff were "in transition," or "on the shelf," looking for new jobs or project assignments within the firm. These people took an average of three months to find another position. At one site with 3000 professional employees, this meant 600 people making an average salary of $35,000 a year, a full cost of $35,000 × 3 = $105,000/person × 600 people = $63 million/12 months = $5,250,000 per month in lost productivity.

Career counselors put together a "job fair," a computerized job posting and job-person matching system that any in-transition employee could use to identify other available jobs in the company. The system solicited opening descriptions from managers, helped employees analyze their interests and skills, write and transmit resumes, and arrange interviews. The job fair system cost $1 million to develop. Career counselors justified this expense on the basis that if they could save *one week* of employee time in internal job search, this would save $63,000,000/52 weeks = $1,211,538/week—more than enough to pay for the system.

Equal Opportunity/Affirmative Action.   Equal Opportunity/Affirmative Action (EO/AA) programs are a special case of staffing and turnover for minority groups. Efficiency benefits of doing EO/AA well are minimum entry costs to reach goals or compliance standards and minimum turnover costs. Costs (and cost-avoidance benefits) of poor EO/AA practice include: loss of government business sales and revenues due to failure to meet standards; lower productivity; costs of discrimination complaints and suits; and possible loss of sales and management time required to deal with boycotts, picketing, and the like. The dollar costs of these problems are calculated the same way as other turnover examples.

Cascio (1982) notes: "Human Resource Management executives have a financial responsibility to see that affirmative action does not result in declining productivity or become an expensive social exercise. There is simply no good reason to lower *bona fide* occupational qualifications in order to select minorities or women, when, with a little more effort and a wider search, qualified minorities and women can be recruited." Tokenism has many costs: lower productivity, resentment of co-workers, reverse discrimination suits, and increased separation costs and problems.

Certain affirmative action efforts, for example, for older workers, offer special benefits. Older people with roots in the community are much less likely to turn over. Driessnack (1979) observes that 83% of college graduate hires leave within the first three years of employment, as opposed to only 10% of recruits aged 50 or older, who stay for an average of 15 productive years.

ABSENTEEISM

Consider the following event: your secretary is absent for the day. What is the cost of this event or the benefits of preventing it from happening? You might think the cost is nothing: he or she gets paid anyway. Or you might think: the firm is paying for his or her time and not getting any work for this pay, so the cost is the secretary's salary for the day. You might further figure that even though he or she is absent, the firm is still paying for his or her vacation, health insurance, pension, unemployment insurance, and other fringes, so the real cost is direct salary plus fringe. Then you might look at the empty desk and think, even though he or she isn't there, the firm still has to pay for the desk, the rent or depreciation on the typewriter, the rent on the square footage he or she should be occupying, lights, heat, cleaning, and all other office expenses. This is his or her full cost. Now, assume you still have to get a report out, and hire a temporary for the day. The temporary's cost is an outlay expense: you actually have to pay an agency $10 an hour, or $80 a day, for the temporary's time. But now that the temporary is sitting at the desk, using the typewriter and the square footage, should you still include overhead in the cost of his or her absence?

There is no agreed-on answer to these questions. In each case, you must ask: What is the real cost to the firm? How much would you have to charge for the report to cover your secretarial costs? In this case, the firm does pay the absent secretary's salary and fringe, and the overhead costs of desk, typewriter, and other office expenses, plus the cost of the temporary. You would have to charge this amount for the report to pay your expenses.

(Note, however, if a temporary or regular worker stays and works overtime, you do not need to add fringe and overhead costs on top of the one and one-half times direct salary because these expenses do not increase: they are already paid for by the full charge on the person's regular time.)

The major costs of absenteeism are:

The cost of the time of the absent employee.

The cost of managerial time spent coping with the absence: rescheduling work, reassigning other workers to fill in for the absent person, hiring temporary workers, arranging for overtime, and counseling or warning the absent worker upon his or her return.

Any out-of-pocket outlay or opportunity costs caused by the worker's absence: lost sales or production, productivity losses of co-workers due to the absence of a key person, quality problems, delays, missed deadlines, overtime, or costs of temporary workers.

Absenteeism runs about 3% of total time paid in American industry and costs an estimated $35 billion a year in lost pay and fringe benefits. Cascio (1982) and Fitz-Enz (1984), using direct (not full) costs, estimate absenteeism costs at $620 per person per year ($80 per absence incident) for employees making an average of $18,000 a year with fringe benefits and managers making $25,000 a year with fringe benefits.

My analyses (see Table 5.5) suggest the full cost of absenteeism in service groups runs quite a bit higher. A manager making $30,000 a year is assumed to spend about one-half hour dealing with the problems caused by an absent employee making $15,000 a year (Cascio, 1982; Fitz-Enz, 1984; Kuzmits, 1979). Outlay and opportunity costs assume that for every four days of work lost, the firm will hire a temporary worker for one day at $10/hour, an expected cost of .25 × $80 = $20 per absent day. Total cost of an absence is thus $207.48/day. An absenteeism rate of 3% per year means the average employee will be away from work 7.8 days. In a firm of 100 people, this means an absenteeism cost of $161,834, and a cost per employee per year of $1618.34.

As with other personnel problems, benefits in reduced absenteeism costs can be shown in two ways: (1) reduce the number of absenteeism incidents, and (2) reduce the cost per incident. Employee assistance programs to help workers cope with life stress, strict tracking and warning about absenteeism, and incentives for perfect attendance can reduce absenteeism incidents and costs. For example, in Table 5.5, if a 100-person firm could reduce absenteeism 10%, from three to 2.7% a year, it would save 78 absent days, worth $16,183.44 per year, and reduce absence costs per employee by $161.83. (Table 5.5 provides a version of the costing worksheet in Table 3.8, formatted to calculate baseline ("before") versus "after" absence frequency and unit costs and to summarize cost saving benefits.)

Cost of absenteeism can be reduced by flexible scheduling and by maintaining a group of "float" workers who can fill in for absent people, eliminating lost sales, production overtime, and quality and other outlay and opportunity expenses. Float workers are not free, however; their costs are either part of overhead or are billed to a work center as temporary workers from an outside agency would be. See Chapter 6, "Increasing Productivity," for ways of using part-time workers to reduce labor costs.

TABLE 5.5
Costs and Benefits of Reducing Absenteeism

A	B	C	D	E	F	G	H	I	J
		Labor Costs			**Outlay and Opportunity Costs**				
Person	Salary/Year	Full Cost/Day	Time	Total Labor	Expense	# Units	Cost/Unit	Total Expense	Total
BASELINE									
Employee	$ 15K	$173.08	1 Day	$173.08	Temporary Worker	.25	$80	$20	
Manager	$ 30K	$346.15	.05/Day	14.40					
Cost/Absent-Day				$187.48				$20	207.48 (J3)
AFTER									
Employee					Temporary Worker				
Manager									
Cost/Absent-Day								$20	207.48(J6)

	Baseline	After	Benefit Saving
Absenteeism Rate/Day =	.03 A4	.027 B4	.003 C4 = A4-B4
Number of Employees =	100 A5	100 B5	B5
Days Paid/Year =	260 A6	260 B6	B6
Total Absent Days =	780 A7 = A4*A5*A6	702 B7 = B4*B5*B6	78 C7 = A7-B7
Total Absenteeism Cost =	$161,834.40 A8 = A7*J3	$145,650.96 B8 = B7*J6	$16,183.44 C8 = A8-B8
Cost/Employee/Year =	$ 1,618.34 A9 = A8/A5	$ 1,456.51 B9 = B8/B5	$ 161.83 C9 = A9-B9

WAGE AND COMPENSATION

The simplest way of showing wage and compensation benefits is to compare a firm's actual with budgeted payroll costs or actual payroll costs with industry averages for competing firms. Compensation groups with payrolls below budget or below industry average can claim the difference as a benefit of good wage and compensation and administration.

A measure of compensation group efficiency is the full cost of the group's payroll as a percentage of total firm payroll. (One standard is that personnel should be 1% of payroll and compensation planning 10% of personnel or .1% of total payroll.) Effectiveness measures include turnover and productivity, and the avoidance of pay discrimination complaints and suits. If a firm's wage and compensation plan is not in line with industry norms, good people will leave and be harder to recruit, and bad people will stay and probably be overpaid. Similarly, if productivity is not rewarded with compensation, productivity will decrease.

A common method of assessing whether an individual or group's pay is in line with that of comparable people or groups is a "distribution pattern." There are two types of distribution patterns: (1) by relative percentages of workers in different performance or pay groups; and (2) actual productivity: pay per unit output.

Figure 5.2 shows the distribution pattern of workers ranked by performance level and pay grade.

Division Two has a relatively normal distribution: 10% of the workers are rated marginal, 20% below average, 40% average, 20% above average, and 10% superior. If pay is in proportion to these performance ratings, Division Two has a total direct-salary payroll of $2.5 million and an average of $25,000.

Division One has a performance and pay distribution skewed to the left. A greater percentage of workers are ranked marginal, below average, or average, and are paid accordingly. Division One has a total payroll of $2,350,000, and average salary of $23,500. Pay in this division may be an accurate reflection of productivity or unrealistically high management expectations. Below average pay is an obvious benefit—here a saving of $1500/person, or $150,000 for Division One over the Division Two average. This saving may be a false economy if Division One has

FIGURE 5.2
Compensation Distribution Pattern: Percentage of Workers
Ranked by Performance or Pay Grade

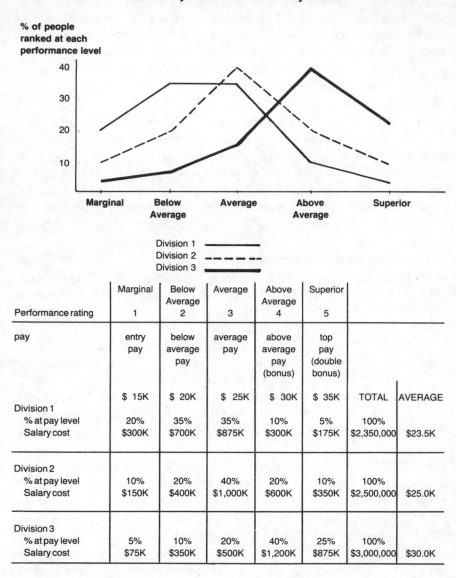

% of people ranked at each performance level

Performance rating	Marginal 1	Below Average 2	Average 3	Above Average 4	Superior 5		
pay	entry pay	below average pay	average pay	above average pay (bonus)	top pay (double bonus)		
	$ 15K	$ 20K	$ 25K	$ 30K	$ 35K	TOTAL	AVERAGE
Division 1							
% at pay level	20%	35%	35%	10%	5%	100%	
Salary cost	$300K	$700K	$875K	$300K	$175K	$2,350,000	$23.5K
Division 2							
% at pay level	10%	20%	40%	20%	10%	100%	
Salary cost	$150K	$400K	$1,000K	$600K	$350K	$2,500,000	$25.0K
Division 3							
% at pay level	5%	10%	20%	40%	25%	100%	
Salary cost	$75K	$350K	$500K	$1,200K	$875K	$3,000,000	$30.0K

a high turnover of more productive people: compensation savings will be offset by high turnover costs.

Division Three has a salary structure skewed to the right—a common problem in "top-heavy," or aging, organizations. Here, few people are rated marginal or below average, and 65% are rated above average or superior and paid accordingly. Division Three has a total direct-salary cost of $3 million and an average of $30,000 per person. The benefit of bringing Division Three back into line with the Division Two average would be a saving of $500,000 per year in direct-salary cost.

Figure 5.3 shows the distribution pattern of productivity against pay in dollars per hour for retail clerks. A new hire, Person One on the graph, makes $6 an hour and is relatively unproductive, completing 25 transactions per hour at a cost per transaction of 24 cents. At peak productivity, Person Three on the graph, a clerk making $10 per hour, can

FIGURE 5.3
Compensation Distribution Pattern: Productivity (Pay per unit output)

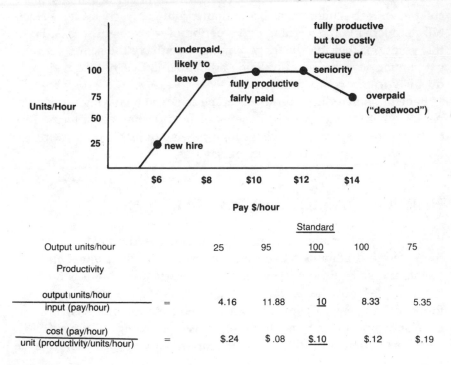

		$6	$8	$10	$12	$14
				Standard		
Output units/hour		25	95	100	100	75
Productivity						
$\dfrac{\text{output units/hour}}{\text{input (pay/hour)}}$	=	4.16	11.88	10	8.33	5.35
$\dfrac{\text{cost (pay/hour)}}{\text{unit (productivity/units/hour)}}$	=	$.24	$.08	$.10	$.12	$.19

complete 100 transactions per hour at a cost of ten cents per transaction. Person Two, making $8 an hour and completing 95 transactions per hour, or 8 cents per transaction, is more productive than he or she is being paid for. Highly productive people who feel themselves underpaid are likely to turn over: leave for another, better-paying job. Person Four is fully productive 100 transactions per hour, but because of seniority has become too costly: at $12 per hour his or her pay has increased but productivity has not. Person Five is clearly overpaid. This person's performance has dropped to 75 transactions per hour, yet because of seniority he is being paid at the highest level, $14 per hour, a labor cost of 19 cents per transaction.

A rational compensation scheme would raise Person Two's pay to retain a good performer, try to cap Person Four's pay, and encourage Person Five to retire or move on.

Overpayment—that is, increases in pay beyond increases in productivity—is a common problem in union and civil service environments, for example, for teachers and postal clerks. A high-seniority teacher may make much more than an entry-level teacher, yet not teach any more children or teach children any better than a younger teacher. Clerks reach full productivity in a learning-curve period of six to eight weeks. From this point on, their productivity remains essentially the same, yet they get annual raises and cost-of-living adjustments that reduce their productivity-to-pay compensation ratio.

Benefits from reduced turnover can be achieved by paying productive people what they are worth. Benefits of holding pay equal to productivity and retiring workers whose high pay is not justified by their productivity can result in direct payroll savings.

PERFORMANCE APPRAISAL

Benefits of performance appraisal include increased employee productivity, reduced administrative expense, and fewer discrimination complaints and suits. Properly conducted, a performance appraisal not only tells a worker how he or she is doing, but helps the worker solve performance problems, set specific goals for performance improvement, and develop action plans to attain these goals. According to Avner (1983), managers estimated productivity of employees who had performance appraisals improved 1.25% more than subordinates who did not have good performance appraisals. A 1.25% performance improvement for a worker making $20,000 a year, having a full cost of $60,000 a year, produces a benefit of 23 additional hours of productive work worth $750 for a person working 1840 hours a year. Given the literature on goal setting, which indicates that just setting goals increases performance productivity an average of 19% (Latham and Locke, 1979), Avner's data are reasonable, even conservative. To have the best chance of realizing these benefits, performance appraisal quality standards should include measurable goals and action plans for improvement, signed by both boss and subordinate.

Effective performance appraisals may also reduce administrative costs. In one firm, managers' performance appraisals were reviewed by personnel staff for completeness, equity, and approval of any pay raises given or not given. Before performance appraisal training, managers had to redo half their written performance appraisals. This process took three hours, one hour of the manager's time at $38 an hour and two hours of a compensation specialist's time at $60 an hour, a total cost of $98 per performance appraisal reviewed. For 100 managers managing an average of seven subordinates each, this meant 350 performance appraisals had to be redone, at a cost of $98 each, a total of $34,300. After training in how to conduct and document performance appraisals, the personnel department reported: "We don't even look at managers' appraisals anymore; we haven't had any problems." Benefits of this training: the entire $34,300 savings in administrative costs.

Complete and accurate performance appraisals also provide protection against pay discrimination complaints. Avner (1983) estimates good performance appraisal documentation reduces legal expense 40%, a savings of two suits at $25,000 per suit, or $50,000 per year.

EMPLOYEE AND LABOR RELATIONS

Effective handling of employee and labor relations problems can produce significant savings in employee, manager, and personnel-specialist time.

I have costed employee relations problems in several firms (see Table 5.6) and found that if a manager deals with an employee effectively when

TABLE 5.6
Benefits of Managers Handling Employee Relations Effectively

Manager handles effectively

Step 1: Manager-Employee meeting

Who	Full cost/hour	Time	Total Labor
Manager	$38/hour	.50/hour	$19.00
Employee	$12/hour	.50/hour	6.00
			$25.00

End!

Total if manager does handle effectively	$25/incident

Manager does not handle effectively–issue goes to personnel

Step 2: Employee goes to personnel

Employee	$12/hour	.75/hour	$ 9.00
Personnel Counsellor	$30/hour	.75/hour	22.50
			$31.50

Step 3: Personnel-Manager-Employee Meeting

Employee	$12/hour	.75/hour	$ 9.00
Manager	$38/hour	.75/hour	28.50
Personnel Counsellor	$30/hour	.75/hour	22.50
			$60.00

Step 4: Personnel checks with manager and employee

Employee	$12/hour	.20/hour	$ 2.40
Manager	$38/hour	.20/hour	7.60
Personnel Counsellor	$30/hour	.40/hour	12.00
			$22.00

Total if manager doesn't handle effectively	$138.50/incident
	5.5 x more expensive!
Total if manager handles effectively	$25.00/incident
Savings Benefit if manager handles effectively	$113.50/incident

the problem is first raised, the issue is resolved in one person-hour (half an hour of the subordinate's time, half an hour of the manager's time), and the process stops there.

If the manager does *not* handle the problem effectively, the process continues for four to nine times as many person-hours. For example, if employees do not receive satisfaction from their manager, they go screaming to personnel. The counseling session with a personnel staff person takes 45 minutes of counselor and employee time, adding another hour and a half. Then the personnel counselor calls the manager and the three meet for another 45 minutes, adding another two and a quarter hours. Usually, the personnel person checks back with both the employee and the manager, adding another half hour.

Table 5.6 shows the benefits of competent handling of employee relations problems for a manager with a full cost per hour of $38, an employee at $12 an hour, and personnel staff person at $30 an hour. If the manager deals with the problem effectively, the cost is $25. If the manager does not deal with the problem effectively, the cost is $55.10 in manager's time, $26.40 in employee time, and $57 in personnel staff time, a total of $138.50. The benefit of teaching managers to deal with employee relations issues is $113.50 per incident. This can justify a lot of management training.

Grievances

The full cost of a grievance can be calculated using the same inquiry strategy questions used for costing the dollar value of any incident.

EXAMPLE. *Benefits of reducing grievances—"Costing a Grievance":*

Labor relations specialists at a paper mill were concerned about the number of grievances being filed—80 grievances per quarter, or 320 per year. They figured these grievances must be costing the company a lot of money, but did not know how much. I used the inquiry strategy shown in Table 5.7. Note the standard probes: (1) what steps are involved; (2) who is involved in each step; (3) how much time (in this case in hours) does each person involved spend during the step; (4) how much does each person involved make; leading to (5) calculation of the full cost of the person's time at each step.

The expected value method is used to calculate arbitration costs. Only 5% of grievances go to arbitration, so each grievance carries a .05 probability of incurring the additional $2740 cost of arbitration. The expected value of any grievance incurring the additional arbitration cost is $137 (.05 × $2740).

TABLE 5.7
Costing A Grievance

(1) Step (What happens 1st, 2nd, etc.?)	(2) Who is Involved?	(3) How long-Time? (hours)	(4) Salary/year of each person involved	(5) Full cost calculation Cost/person/hour $\frac{(4) \times 3 \,(\text{OHD factor})}{260 \text{ days} \div 8 \text{ hours}}$	(6) = (3) × (5) Total Total Cost Per Step
1. "The hourly (worker) bitches to the foreman"	Worker Foreman	.25 .25	$15K $20K	$21.64 $28.85	$5.41 $7.21 $12.62
2. "Hourly bitches to shop steward"	Worker (Steward)	.5 .5	$15K (Paid by union)	$21.64	$10.82 $10.82
3. "Local union rep tells hourly how to write grievance"	Worker Union rep.	.5 .5	$15K $15K	$21.64 $21.64	$10.82 $10.82 $21.64
4. "Hourly writes up grievance"	Worker	.5	$15K	$21.64	$10.82 $10.82
5. "Union-Plant mgmt. meeting"	Worker Union Pres. Plant personnel rep.	.75 .75 .75	$15K $16K $25K	$21.64 $23.08 $36.06	$16.23 $17.31 $27.05 $60.59

6. "International union rep writes Division Personnel; Division Staff calls plant, researches and writes response, decides whether or not to go to arbitration"	Div Staff	8	$32K	$46.15	$369.20	$369.20
If no arbitration						
7. "Trip to meet with International rep in D.C., St. Louis or Oakland--deal with 4 grievances"	Div Staff	16	$32.K	$46.15	$738.40	
	Trip direct cost		$400		$400.00 $1138.40 ÷ 4 = 284.60 per grievance	
8. "Implement agreement"	PLant personnel rep.	2	$25K	$36.06	$72.12	$72.12
TOTAL PER GRIEVANCE IF NO ARBITRATION						$842.41
If arbitration (5% of Grievances go to arbitration).						
9. Legal preparation"	Corp Staff lawyer	16	$45K	$64.90	$1038.40	
	Div Staff	6	$32K	$46.15	$ 276.90	
	Plant Pers. Director	4	$25K	$36.06	$ 144.24	
	Labor Lawyer	4	$60K	$86.54	$ 346.16	$1805.70

145

TABLE 5.7 continued

(1) Step (What happens 1st, 2nd, etc.?)	(2) Who is Involved?	(3) How long- Time? (hours)	(4) Salary/ year of each per- son in- volved	(5) Full cost calculation Cost/person/hour $\frac{(4) \times 3 \text{ (OHD factor)}}{260 \text{ days} \div 8 \text{ hours}}$	(6) = (3) × (5) Total Total Cost Per Step
10. "Arbitration meeting"	Corp Staff lawyer	4	$45K	$64.90	$ 259.60
	Div Staff	4	$32K	$46.15	$ 184.60
	Plant Pers. Director	4	$25K	$36.06	$ 144.24
	Labor Lawyer (Arbitration Fee)	4	$60K	$86.54	$ 346.16
					$ 934.60

$2740.30

(To 8: "Implement Agreement")

- Additional cost per grievance if Arbitration $979.43

- Expected value (E(v)) = $\frac{\text{probability of occurrence} \times \text{cost of occurrence}}{\text{per grievance}}$

  = 5% × 2740.30 = $137.02

- TOTAL COST OF GRIEVANCE = $842.41 (no arbitration) + $137.02 (5% probability) of arbitration)

Summing the costs for all steps in a grievance process shows that the average grievance costs this organization $979. (Once again, this is information people had but did not know they had. Asking very simple questions, I was able to get the data to do this analysis on the back of an envelope in about 15 minutes.) At $979 per grievance, 320 grievances a year were costing the organization $313,280 a year.

The solution in this case was to do an organizational climate survey and conduct organization development problem-solving meetings with employees, primarily maintenance and production crews. The total cost of the organization development effort (calculated using the full-cost accounting methods described in Chapter 3, Calculating Costs) was $90,000.

The results of this intervention were that grievances were reduced to 25 a quarter, 100 a year, which at $979 per grievance gives a total cost of $97,900. The net saving of reducing grievances is $215,380 (the previous cost of 320 grievances per year, $313,280, less the new cost of grievances, $97,900).

A major unexpected benefit was a 10% increase in production because of less equipment down time. This second benefit resulted from identification and solving of maintenance and production problems in the OD problem-solving groups. The value of this increased production was $1.4 million, which with the $215,380 saving in reduced grievances produced a total benefit of $1,615,380. The cost-benefit ratio on this OD intervention was 1:18, or a return on investment of 1694% on the $90,000 investment.

Grievance reduction programs can lower grievance costs dramatically. For example, in one firm most grievances were filed on overtime and classification issues—who got how much overtime and who got to do which jobs. A grievance reduction effort essentially established trust in verbal contracts between foremen and workers. If a worker felt that he had not gotten overtime he should have received, and his boss promised, "Look, I'll get you those six hours sometime in the next ten days," the worker agreed not to file a formal grievance. Establishing trust took several weeks, but once workers saw that bosses lived up to their verbal contracts, grievances dropped virtually to zero—and workers became much more flexible in work assignments they would accept.

A rule of thumb in labor relations is that unionization increases payroll costs 25%: 10% in increased pay and 15% in increased management and labor relations time dealing with grievances, inflexible staffing due to work rules, time paid but not worked, problems in firing poor performers, and higher payroll costs due to seniority pay increasing faster than productivity.[1] Clearly, anything that human resource managers can do to pay employees fairly and conduct employee relations equitably, eliminating the need for unions, can create substantial benefits.

SAFETY: ACCIDENT FATALITIES AND INJURIES

Accidents causing worker deaths or injuries are clearly problem events all firms (and federal and local governments, e.g., OSHA) should try to prevent. Rinfort (1977) found that the average worker fatality cost industry $22,700 and the average injury $1910 and that safety related costs average 7% to 8% of worker payrolls in manufacturing firms during the years 1972–1974. More recent attempts to value human life in dollars, (for example, medical, funeral, and legal costs and the lost value of future earnings from premature death to retirement) give fatality costs of $176,000 to $260,000 (Rice and Cooper, 1967; Tayer and Rosen, 1976; Henderson, 1975; Zechhauser, 1975; Conley, 1976; Jones-Lee, 1976). Lawsuits for "wrongful death" can raise these costs into the millions.

Rinefort (1977, 1978) has calculated the dollar return on investments in human resource and management actions to promote safety and reduce worker deaths and injuries (see Table 5.8). Most cost effective were:

1. *Safety rules,* for example, specific directives for use of hazardous equipment
2. *Off-the-job safety activities,* for example, urging employees to wear seatbelts, guidelines for sports activities (warm-up before jogging), wellness programs

---

[1]Kochan (1980) reports unions raise labor costs from 12 to 16% in manufacturing, transport communications, and utilities, and up to 43% in construction. These costs *may* in some cases be offset by unionized workers 6 to 30% higher productivity (Freeman and Medoff, 1979).

TABLE 5.8

Cost-Benefit Analysis of the Relative Effectiveness of Safety Programs

Cost-Effective		Partially Cost-Effective		Cost-Ineffective	
Variable	Effect of $1 Expenditure Upon Injury Costs	Variable	Effect of $1 Expenditure Upon Injury Costs	Variable	Effect of $1 Expenditure Upon Injury Costs
Rules	− $58	Inspections	− $.81	Guarding	+ $ .64
Off-the-job	− $53	Meetings	− $.38	Staff	+ $ .80
Training	− $40	Span Control	− $.32	Equipment	+ $ 6.00
Medical	− $14			Interest	+ $10.00
Orientation	− $ 4			Physicals	+ $23.00
				Records	+ $32.00

Note: These values are an average of the initial B values (coefficients or multipliers of safety activity variables) in multiple linear regression equations for each group of survey respondents for which the value appeared. They are somewhat different than other reported relationships which are based on both B Values and R^2 values. (R^2 is the proportion of the variations between low and high work injury costs per employee explained by a variable.)
Source: Reinford (1978), p. 27.

3. *Safety training* about specific job tasks and equipment
4. *Medical services,* for example, availability of a corporate medical director or industrial nurse
5. *Safety orientation,* programs for new employees

Partially cost effective safety programs included:

6. *Inspection* of equipment or employees to be sure guard rails were in use and employees were wearing protective hard hats and goggles;
7. *Safety meeting* of management with employees to increase or maintain awareness of safety practices
8. *Span of control:* lowering the ratio of supervisors to workers to provide more management attention to safety practices

Not cost effective in reducing accidents costs were:

9. *Guarding:* fencing off or having human guards keep workers away from hazardous areas (e.g., high-voltage transformers or toxic chemicals)

10. *Safety staff:* "larger safety staffs were frequently not as cost effective as the smaller, leaner safety staffs found in some firms" (Rinefort, 1977, p. 35)

11. *Equipment:* Dollar investment in personal protective equipment is not *by itself* cost effective because issuance and use varies widely depending on enforcement of rules and safety training

12. *Interest:* Safety posters, publications, bulletin board reminders, safety contests, and incentives for accident prevention

13. *Physicals:* Medical surveying of employees for potential medical problems or "accident proneness" did not reduce problems, probably because firms which gave physicals had higher turnover and hired more inexperienced workers who were more likely to injure themselves

14. *Records:* expenditures on collection of data on safety hazards, accidents and injuries are not cost effective (perhaps because "firms with higher than average work injury costs . . . may emphasize government standards and regulations rather than injury prevention"; Rinefort, 1977, p. 35)

Clearly, human resource expenditures on safety training can prove highly cost-beneficial. You can establish the average cost of an accident in your firm using the costing worksheet inquiry process described in Table 3.8. Your firm's total cost of worker accident fatalities and injuries is the minimum it should invest in safety-related programs.

EMPLOYEE ASSISTANCE

Firms offer a variety of employee assistance programs. Benefits for these programs are shown by the usual strategy: efficiency benefits by reducing the cost to deliver services or products and effectiveness benefits from increased productivity or reduced labor time and outlay costs.

Health and Wellness.   Health and wellness programs include counseling for mental problems, stress management, smoking, dealing with drug and alcohol abuse, diet and weight, exercise, and general health (e.g., physical exams).

Benefits of these programs include reduction in medical benefit costs, sick days and disability claims, absenteeism, reduced time lost on the job, productivity increases, and reduced turnover. Cummings and Follette (1968) found that one counseling session reduced medical claims 60% and two-eight sessions reduced claims 75%. "Kennecott Copper Company estimated a return of 5.83 per $1.00 cost per year for its psychotherapy program . . . in reduced absenteeism, reduced hospital, medical, and surgical costs, and reduced costs of nonoccupational accident and illness" (Cummings, 1977, p. 768).

EXAMPLE.   *Benefits of a mental health counseling program:*

A 2600-person firm spent $29,000 on contracted counseling services at $60.41 an hour. Four hundred and eighty hours of services were used by 240 (9%) of the organization's employees, approximately two interviews per employee.

Assuming a replacement cost equal to the average direct salary of $20,000 a year, the firm figured that if it saved 1.5 employees a year in reduced turnover, the counseling service would justify its cost. Previous records showed that 10% of employees with mental problems turned over (approximately 24 of the 240 employees who sought counseling). In fact, personnel records showed that counseling had cut this number in half: 12 people had been saved, a benefit of $240,000 for the $29,000 counseling investment.

Personnel further calculated the percentage increase in counseled employee's productivity needed to pay for the counseling. For employees making $20,000 a year, a full cost of $60,000 a year × 240 people = a full cost of $14,400,000, a .2% increase in productivity, four hours a year, or one half of an absent day per person, would pay for the $29,000 spent on counseling services.

EXAMPLE.   *Benefits of reducing smoking:*

Table 5.9 summarizes data collected by Cascio (1982) on the annual costs of a worker who smokes: $4737 a year. The costs that go into this figure are:

TABLE 5.9

Additional Annual Cost of Employing Smokers and Allowing Smoking at the Work Place

Absenteeism	$ 310
Medical care	230
Morbidity and early mortality (discounted lost earnings)	765
Insurance (excluding health)	90
On-the-job time lost	1820
Property damage and depreciation	500
Maintenance	500
Involuntary smoking	522
Total cost per smoker per year	$4737

Note: All costs are in January 1981 dollars

Absenteeism. The absenteeism rate for smokers is 50% greater than for nonsmokers.

Medical Care. Medical care costs for smokers are $230 per person more for smokers than for nonsmokers.

Morbidity and early Mortality. Heavy smokers suffer a mortality rate 272% higher than nonsmokers. Early disability retirement is 5.43 times greater for smokers than for nonsmokers. The estimated per smoker loss to the firm is $765 (discounted lost earnings, a measure of replacement costs and lost investment in training.)

Other Insurance Costs. Smokers' accident, injury, and worker's compensation costs an additional $45; higher fire, life, and wage continuation insurance costs $45 more per smoker.

On the Job Time Lost. Smokers spent an estimated 30 minutes out of each eight-hour day reaching for, lighting up, smoking, and discarding cigarettes. This represents 18.2 days per year in lost productivity per smoker, an average cost of $1820. In the construction industry, particularly, the rule is: "Tools go down when smokers light up."

Property Damage, Depreciation, and Maintenance. Cigarette burns in furniture and carpets, and equipment malfunctions due to smoke contamination, add up to $500 per smoker per year. (In my firm, we have observed that smokers' word-processing disk drives are down three times as often.) Costs for maintenance and cleaning, washing interior windows and showcases, laundering drapes, repainting interior surfaces, and replacement of air-conditioning filters are 60% higher, $500 per year per smoker.

Involuntary smoking refers to the increased medical costs in absenteeism and decreased productivity of nonsmokers who are affected by smoke in the workplace, for example, allergy sufferers whose symptoms are worsened by inhaling others' smoke, or idle nonsmoking word processors whose disk drives are down because of smoke contamination. *New England Journal of Medicine* researchers found nonsmokers' impairment to be about one fifth that of smokers, for a total cost of $522 a year (White and Froeb, 1980).

Clearly, quit-smoking programs that help 75% of employees to stop smoking offer major benefits. For example, in a 100-person organization with 33% smokers (the national average), a stop-smoking program that helps 75% of the people stop would save 25 people × $4737/smoker = $118,425.

Data similar to the costs of smoking exist for other problems that may be addressed by employee assistance programs, for example, alcohol and drug abuse, stress, diet/overweight, lack of physical fitness, and so forth (Kiefhaben and Goldbeck, 1983).

For example, the average of eight studies of the costs of alcoholic employees, reported by Follman (1976), is $3000 increased cost per alcoholic employee in 1976 dollars (approximately $6000 dollars per person in 1984 dollars). Table 5.10 shows the annual cost for alcoholic employees versus all employees in the Oldsmobile division of General Motors: four times as many lost man-hours, three times as many sickness and accident benefits, twice as many grievances, 17 times as many disciplinary actions, ten times as many accidents.

A Control Data study found sedentary employees were hospitalized 57 days per year and had medical claims of $436.92, compared with .37

TABLE 5.10

**Annual Costs for Alcoholic Employees vs.
Non-Alcoholic Employees
Oldsmobile Division, General Motors**

	Alcoholic Employees	Control Group
Lost man-hours	47,182	9,440
Sickness and accident benefits	$33,329	$12,196
Leaves of absence	112	18
Grievances	26	12
Disciplinary actions	103	6
Accidents	51	5

hospital days per year and $321.01 claim costs for people who exercised. Canada Life Assurance found that employees who participated in company fitness programs had a 1.5% turnover rate, compared with 15% turnover for nonparticipants. Similar benefits reported by Berry (1981) for employee assistance programs offering a range of services (hypertension control, stress management, back treatment, breast cancer screening) include:

Kimberly Clark: 70% reduction in on-the-job accidents.

General Motors: 40% reduction in lost work time, 60% reduction in sickness and accident benefits, 50% fewer accidents and grievances.

Illinois Bell Telephone: 61.4% reduction in accidents and 31,806 disability days.

Kennecott Copper: 53% reduction in absenteeism, 55% in medical costs and 75% in weekly indemnity (sick and accident) costs—and a 478% return on investment in employee assistance efforts.

Clearly, where the costs of people problems addressable by employee assistance programs are significant, the benefits of effective employee assistance are easily demonstrated. Table 5.11 provides a worksheet and template for estimating the benefits of employee assistance programs. You are best advised to develop costs for types of employee problems for your own organization, because data from other firms' studies vary greatly. For example, estimates of costs per alcoholic employee range from $896 to $50,000 per year in studies reported by Follman (1976). (Differences are doubtless due to differing costing assumptions, direct versus full salary costs, types of costs included, etc.) Your strategy is to identify all costs that may be caused by the problem. Note in comparing cost data for problem versus average employees that problem employees may have both higher costs per unit or incident *and* more units or incidents than nonproblem employees.

The total difference between the costs of a problem employee and an average employee is the amount an employee with the problem costs the firm. The benefit of an employee assistance program that helps employees with this problem is the total cost times the number of employees in the organization with the problem times the cure rate. Cure rates reported for employee assistance programs are quite good. For example, Follman (1976) reports 14 studies that show the cure rate for company-sponsored alcohol treatment programs are 65% to 70%.

Company Cafeterias and Stores. The easiest way to show benefits for on-site services is to observe the amount of time saved by employees who use the service versus those who do not. For example, the usual rationale for providing a company cafeteria is to save employee time eating on the premises versus leaving to eat somewhere else.

EXAMPLE. *Benefits of a company cafeteria:*

A high-tech firm in a rural location opened an on-site cafeteria. Approximately half the firm's 400 people used the company cafeteria each day. (The others brought their lunch or didn't eat lunch.) Employees spent an average of 23 minutes of a 45-minute lunch period in the cafeteria. One spring the cafeteria was closed for a month for construction. About half the employees who used to eat in the cafeteria now drove three-and-one-half miles to a nearby town, where they had lunch at one of four diners or pubs. These employees now spent an average of one hour and 15 minutes on lunch, and not a few washed lunch down with

TABLE 5.11
Worksheet for Estimating
Benefits of Employee Assistance Programs

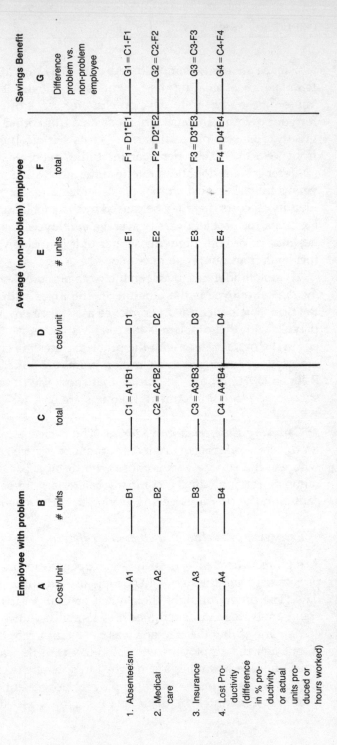

| | Employee with problem | | | Average (non-problem) employee | | | Savings Benefit |
| | A | B | C | D | E | F | G |
	Cost/Unit	# units	total	cost/unit	# units	total	Difference problem vs. non-problem employee
1. Absenteeism	A1	B1	C1 = A1*B1	D1	E1	F1 = D1*E1	G1 = C1-F1
2. Medical care	A2	B2	C2 = A2*B2	D2	E2	F2 = D2*E2	G2 = C2-F2
3. Insurance	A3	B3	C3 = A3*B3	D3	E3	F3 = D3*E3	G3 = C3-F3
4. Lost Productivity (difference in % productivity or actual units produced or hours worked)	A4	B4	C4 = A4*B4	D4	E4	F4 = D4*E4	G4 = C4-F4

5. Accidents	A5	B5	C5 = A5*B5	D5	E5	F5 = D5*E5	G5 = C5-F5
6. Property damage/depreciation/ maintenance	A6	B6	C6 = A6*B6	D6	E6	F6 = D6*E6	G6 = C6-F6
7. Employee relations problems: grievances, disciplinary actions	A7	B7	C7 = A7*B7	D7	E7	F7 = D7*E7	G7 = C7-F7
8. Turnover	A8	B8	C8 = A8*B8	D8	E8	F8 = D8*E8	G8 = C8-F8
9. TOTALS			C9 = (α sum (C1 ... C8))			F9 = (α sum (F1 ... F8))	G9 = C9-F9

Total cost (G9)

$ benefit/ employee helped	×	# employees* with problem	×	% cure rate	=	total benefit
A10		B10		C10		D10 = A10*B10*C10

a couple of beers, which probably affected after-lunch productivity. A fast estimate of the value of the cafeteria was 75 − 23 = 52 minutes/60 minutes of lunching time saved = .87 hour saved × a full cost of $28 an hour = $24.36 × 100 people = $2436 per working day. In a work year of 260 days the cafeteria saved $2436 × 260 days = $633,360—not to mention productivity loss to beer.

EXAMPLE. *Benefits of a company store:*

A company notions store was cost justified by observing the difference in the amount of time employees spent buying minor items (panty hose, snack foods) in the firm's lobby as opposed to having to walk three blocks to a shopping mall: 20 minutes per day per employee × approximately 200 employees who used the store every day = a savings of 4000 minutes or 66.7 hours per day. At an average salary of $15,000, employee full costs per day were $173 per day × 8.3 days = $1436 a day or $373,334 a year saved by the company store.

Day-Care Centers. The obvious benefit of day care centers is preventing absenteeism or turnover of valued female employees who otherwise might have to stay home to take care of a child. Day-care services are expensive and provide an interesting example of CBA as applied to the level of day-care service that should be provided and who it should be offered to.

EXAMPLE. *Benefits of a day-care center:*

A Catholic hospital wanted to figure out what level of day-care service it could provide its employees, whether the service could be self-supporting or would require a subsidy, and, if it required a subsidy, how the subsidy could be justified to the hospital's board of directors. The full cost of care was $12 an hour. The center thought it could charge $1.25 an hour, $11.25 a day, for nine hours of care.

The problem was that children of different ages require very different staff-to-child care ratios. Infants zero to 18 months require one caretaker for every four babies. At $12 an hour, this means that caring for a baby costs $3 an hour. Eighteen-month- to three-year-old children have a caretaker-to-child ratio of one to six; hence, care of each child in this age group costs $2 an hour. Three- to four-year-old children have a ratio of one adult to 10 children, hence cost $1.20 an hour per child to take care of. Four- to five-year-old children can have a ratio of one to 12, at a cost of $1 an hour. Five-year-old and older children have a staff-child ratio of one to 15, and cost only 80 cents an hour. Clearly, the day-care center will make a profit on children three years and older, but lose money on children less than three years old.

Day-care managers wondered how a subsidy out of general hospital revenues might be justified. For example, the subsidy for an infant, on which the center loses $1.75 per hour of care, would need to be $1.75 per hour × 9 hours per day × 230 days per year = $3622.50. Assuming replacement costs equal to first-year salary, this expense is easily justified for professional women. Women who cannot find adequate child care are out of the labor market for an average of 18 months. Subsidizing the care of a child of a female neurosurgeon, manager, or experienced lab technician is easily cost justified. If replacement costs are one-third direct salary, it pays the hospital to subsidize the care of infants whose mothers make more than 3 × $3622.50 = $10,867.50 per year. Justifying the cost for an $8000 a year cleaning woman who might cost only $1000 to replace is much more difficult.

Administrators' options were: (1) charge the actual cost of caring for kids at each age, discriminating against mothers with babies; (2) ration the service available by restricting the number of children under three the center would admit, letting the care of older children subsidize the care of younger ones; (3) offer subsidized care only to higher-salaried professional or managerial women, whose turnover cost would justify the subsidy; or (4) subsidize child care by adding day-care center costs to overhead, an option very difficult to implement given health care cost-containment pressures. (This case has no "right answer," but serves to illustrate the use of CBA to clarify policy options.) The hospital chose options (1), (2), and (4): raised the price per hour of care for babies (but not to actual cost), rationed the service to 30 infants, and charged off losses on infants to marketing on the assumption that loss-leader babies grow up to become profit-making clients.

Parties, Publications, Christmas turkeys. General "morale" services are the hardest for which to calculate dollar benefits. The argument for these services is that investments in employee morale, or "team spirit," will pay off in increased productivity and reduced absenteeism, turnover, and special problems, such as "shrinkage" (theft) from retail stores. Approaches for showing benefits include tracking levels of employee satisfaction by survey (e.g., "I feel the firm really cares about me," "I enjoy reading the company newsletter") with various levels of service, for example, experimenting with putting out an employee newsletter once a month versus once a week to save money. If employees do not notice the reduction in service, the efficiency cost saving is justifiable.

Another approach is to experiment with offering a service at some sites and not at others to see if the expected morale or productivity differences result. For example, one retail outlet sent birthday cards to all employees on their birthdays, had summer and winter parties, published an employee newsletter, and gave all employees Christmas turkeys. A new store employing similar people had none of these services. In fact, company loyalty and "family feeling," as measured by employee surveys, was 3% higher in the highly served store, while turnover and shrinkage were 1% lower. (Unfortunately, productivity was higher in the store without services, because higher turnover produced clerks with less seniority and hence lower pay.)

ORGANIZATION DEVELOPMENT CONSULTING

Organization development (OD) consulting services include a variety of techniques: team-building, conflict-resolution, survey guided development, and goal- and role-clarification workshops, and specific consultation on organization procedures and structure. The easiest benefits to show for OD are: (1) reduction in time and people needed to complete tasks by groups working together more smoothly or working with improved procedures; (2) head-count savings from reduced overlap or duplication of effort, as a result of improved organization structure; (3) increased productivity and quality; and (4) increased morale.

EXAMPLE. *Benefits of team building for computer installation teams:*

A computer firm's installation teams included marketing, hardware, software, telecommunications, and service engineers. Teams installed computer systems averaging $1 million in value. Team members came from different organizations, geographically far from one another. Each person had a different agenda, for example, sales and customer-tending versus ensuring that customer facilities were properly air-conditioned to prevent future equipment breakdowns. Installation time from customer order to the time equipment was up and running was scheduled to take three months. In fact, installations averaged five months because installation team members had problems communicating and cooperating with one another.

The firm's internal OD consultants conducted a three-day series of team-building, conflict-resolution, task-planning, and problem-solving meetings with a typical team. The five team members and their consultant all made approximately $42,000 a year, a full cost of $485 a day. The cost of the OD effort was six people × three days/person × $485 per day = $8730.

The benefit was that the team met its three-month deadline, saving two months (40 days) of five people's time, a total saving of 200 days × $485 per day = $37,000 in time savings. An additional benefit was speeded up collection of the $800,000 balance due from the computer customer. (Customers paid 20%, $200,000, at the time they placed the order, but were notoriously reluctant to pay the balance until the equipment was up and running.) Ten percent interest on $800,000 for two months is $13,333. One time in ten, customers who did not have their equipment up and running canceled their order and went with another computer company. Each lost customer cost the firm $576,000 ($1,000,000 less a 5% order cancellation fee = $950,000 × 60% gross margin = $576,000). The expected value of this loss is an additional 10% × $576,000 = $57,600 in cost-avoidance benefits claimed by the OD consultants. Total benefits of the OD workshops were $37,000 in time savings, $13,333 in interest costs, and $57,600 in lost revenues = $107,933 on an $8730 investment in consulting.

EXAMPLE. *Benefits of reducing overlap and duplication in personnel hiring:*

A large manufacturing firm had four plants within a 90-mile radius. Each plant had its own temporary hiring office: a manager, personnel specialist, secretary, and data-entry clerk. Each office recruited about 1500 assembly-line workers, secretaries, and laborers per year, 90% from agencies. Each office took personnel requisitions from client departments, called agencies, screened personnel, and handled payroll, payments to agencies, and administrative paperwork. Offices paid about $1700 per month, $20,400 per year for time-sharing computer services.

Managers of the four temporary hiring offices met occasionally and felt they were competing with each other, duplicating one another's efforts, and frequently dealing with the same "problem" personnel. (Temporary workers who had been let go for nonperformance at one site frequently showed up at other sites, got hired and then had to be fired a second time.)

An organizational consultant suggested restructuring the four offices to consolidate them in one location. Work-load estimates showed that this office would need only one manager and five staff. The consolidated office would have its own dedicated computer, costing $60,000. Table 5.12 shows the before and after structure and the cost savings in reduced head count, $588,600, a reduction in cost per hire of almost two thirds.

The consolidation offered other benefits as well. Plant managers initially resisted the reorganization because they were reluctant to lose "their own on-site hiring office." Probed, what they really feared losing was (1) good service, specifically the "response time" the hiring office took to fill a requisition, and (2) quality—the percentage of temporary hires that "worked out." Some temporary positions took five to six weeks to fill, and fully 50% of temporary people hired did not work out and were fired after three days for nonperformance. The average productivity of a temporary worker fired for nonperformance was 25% during the three days worked.

Response time. The OD consultant and employment managers were able to show that, in fact, response time would be *reduced* as a result of the consolidation because a single site would have access to a much larger labor pool. In the dispersed structure, one site often turned away good people another site could use. Employment managers found that 15% of the time one site turned away a good person that another site had an immediate need for, and that a temporary requisition took an average of four days to fill. A conservative estimate was that having knowledge of the total labor pool would save two days' hiring time per

TABLE 5.12

Benefits of Organizational Structure Consulting: Consolidating Temporary Personnel Hiring (6000 people/year)

BEFORE

Labor		Structure Site 1	Site 2	Site 3	Site 4	Total #	Cost (sal×3) ×full cost	Labor Total
Employment Manager 28K		1	1	1	1	4	$84K =	$336K
Personnel Specialist 20K		1	1	1	1	4	$60K =	$240K
Secretary 15K		1	1	1	1	4	$45K =	$180K
Data Entry Clerk 10K		1	1	1	1	4	$30K =	$120K

Headcount: 16

							Labor Total	$876K
Outlay Computer $1.7K/month		$20.4K	$20.4K	$20.4K	$20.4K		Outlay Total	$81.6K
							Total	$957.6K

Cost/hire = $957,600/6,000 hires = $159.60/hire

AFTER

Labor	Structure	Cost Total # ×full cost	Labor Total
Employment Manager 28K	1	1 × $84K = $84K	$84K
Personnel Specialist 20K	2	2 × $60K = $120K	$120K
Secretary 15K	1	1 × $45K = $45K	$45K
Data Entry Clerk 10K	2	2 × $30K = $60K	$60K

	6	Labor Total	$309K
		Outlay Total	$60K
		Total	$369K

Cost/hire = $369,000/6,000 hires = $61.50/hire

163

person × 900 people (15% × 6000 people hired) = 1800 days of position-open time. The value of an open position is worth what the manager is willing to pay for a temporary person to fill it. In this case, temporaries were receiving an average of $10 per hour, or $80 per person per day. Savings in reduced response time were 1800 person days × $80/person-days = $144,000 per year.

Quality.   Employment managers figured that consolidating their information system would enable them to identify the "bounce-arounds," bad performers fired by one site and then hired by another site. They figured they could cut the 50% failure rate to 30%, a savings of 20% × 6000 people hired, or 1200 poor hires. The cost of a poor hire, fired after three days and only 25% productive during the three days paid, is 3 days × $80 a day × 75% productivity loss = $180 per poor hire × 1200 poor hires avoided = $216,000 additional benefits. Total benefits of the organization consulting intervention were $588,600 in payroll, office, and computer costs, plus $144,000 in better service response time, plus $216,000 in better quality = $948,600.

Morale.   The method shown in Table 4.4 can be used by OD consultants to estimate the dollar value of morale and productivity improvements resulting from their work. (A statistical approach for relating changes in morale is discussed under "Advanced Topics" at the end of this chapter.)

BASIC PERSONNEL SERVICES: PAYROLL AND RECORD KEEPING

Benefits for basic personnel record keeping are shown by improving (1) efficiency: reducing costs per transaction, and (2) quality: reducing the number of "fails." Quality, it is said, is free, that is, quality *always* equals improved efficiency and productivity, because quality problems in human services, just as in manufacturing, invariably involve "scrap" or "rework": if you don't do it right the first time, you always have to do it over or fix it. Fixing a "fail," a mistake, or quality failure in service delivery, usually costs more than it does to do it right in the first place.

EXAMPLE.   *Costing a personnel record-keeping "fail":*

A personnel clerk in New Hampshire fails to enter an employee's new
address in time to mail his or her next paycheck to the right place. The
employee, now in Scottsdale, Arizona, finishes his or her first week on
the job, and on pay day—guess what? No paycheck! (Invariably, he or
she has to put down a deposit on a new apartment that evening.) What
happens? The employee goes screaming to his or her manager. The
manager and the employee go screaming to Personnel. The personnel
specialist in Arizona starts making frantic telephone calls to corporate
headquarters in New York. She next writes letters and memos, to trace
and document an "audit trail" for the lost paycheck. This process in-
volves numerous other people who have to stop what they are doing
to research what happened to the paycheck, then make telephone calls
and write memos and letters back. A "costing-the-fail" analysis using
the standard Table 3.8 inquiry strategy shows that this fail costs $2700.

Even simple fails that occur frequently in a large volume of routine
transactions can be very costly and hence provide great opportunities
to show benefits.

EXAMPLE.   *Benefits of improved work flow in reducing personnel
transaction costs and the number and cost of fails:*

A large insurance company processed 90,000 routine personnel transactions a year. Each transaction cost $10. A phenomenal 30% of these
transactions were fails: they were incomplete and had to be "kicked
back" to the employee or the employee's manager for additional information. Fixing each fail cost three times the original transaction cost,
$30 per fail. The cost of 90,000 transactions at $10 was $900,000. Fixing
30% of these transactions cost: 27,000 fails × $30 a fix = $810,000 additional cost due to poor quality—almost as much as the $900,000 cost
of the original transactions. The total cost of transactions was $900,000
to do it 70% right the first time, plus $810,000 to fix the 30% not done
right = $1,710,000.

The human resource productivity manager, by analyzing the work
flow and leaning on the firm's large EDP department to computerize
routine operations, reduced the cost per transaction to $3.33 and cut fails

in half, to 13,500 per year. Ninety thousand transactions now cost $299,700. The cost to fix fails dropped to $20. (Personnel's cost to fix fails was reduced to $3.33, but the larger part of the cost of the fail—employee and manager time—fell only $6.67 to $13.33 per fail.) Total cost of personnel transactions was now 90,000 transactions × $3.33/unit = $299,700 the first time, plus 13,500 fails × $20/fix = $270,000, a total of $569,700. Total benefits of the productivity manager's work was $1,710,000 (old system) − $569,700 (new system) = $1,140,300 in cost savings. At her salary of $35,000 a year, a full cost of $105,000 a year, this one project justified her cost to the firm for the next 11 years.

TRAINING

Benefits of training can include any of the examples discussed above: increased sales, greater productivity, better use of time, lower staffing and learning-curve costs, reduced people problems, and higher morale for both the trainee and the people he or she supervises. (A specific strategy for showing benefits from training, discussed in Chapter 8, "Designing Projects and Programs to Get Results," is to identify as precisely as possible the most costly/valuable problems the training will address ("value the problem"); target training to address this problem; get trainees to set goals to use what they have learned to reduce problem costs; and then follow up to document these benefits.)

EXAMPLE. *Benefits of secretarial training for laid-off blue-collar assemblers:*

A benevolent firm with a no-layoff policy realized in a poor economy that it had a number of idle assembly workers at the same time that it had a great need for secretaries. Many secretarial positions went unfilled for three to four months. Managers complained that *their* productivity was significantly reduced, for example, when a $40,000-a-year engineer had to type his or her own design specifications.

Personnel developed a four-week training program for laid-off blue-collar people to convert them to secretaries. This training program cost about $4600 a trainee ($400 a week in instructional costs × 4 weeks =

$1600 plus $150 a day full cost for assemblers making $13,000 per year × 20 days training = $3000).

Seventy-five percent of 40 people in the initial pilot class graduated and were judged successful (rated 85% productive by their managers) on the job three months later. Trainees' full cost of $39,000 a year × 85% productivity = $33,000 benefit per person per year. Benefits in three months were $33,000 × 3/12 year = $8250, almost twice the training cost per person. Managers reported that their productivity had been increased 25% (percent productivity with a secretary versus percent productivity without a secretary), mostly in time reallocated from clerical work—typing, filing, answering telephones—to their engineering jobs. A 25% increase in managers' productivity for three months was worth 25% × $120,000 full cost × 3/12 months = $6563 per engineer.

The personnel department also attempted a make-versus-buy acquisition cost analysis. They estimated that recruiting a competent secretary and getting him or her to 85% productivity, including agency fees, interviewing, and learning-curve time, was approximately $2500. They observed, however, that they hadn't been able to hire *any* secretaries, which was why many secretarial positions had been vacant for three to four months. Hiring a temporary secretary for three months would cost $80 a day for 65 days = $5200 per position filled. Training blue-collar assemblers who were being paid on layoff, a total loss to the firm, proved highly cost effective.

EXAMPLE. *No benefits from an "MBA Fellow" program:*

One that didn't work: A large firm had a special MBA Fellow program that put 25 high-potential employees through a prestigious business school. The firm paid all tuition, expenses, and employee release time to attend classes for two years. The program cost approximately $75,000 per employee. Fellows got many extra benefits: moonlight cruises on the chairperson of the board's yacht, all-expense-paid trips to Washington to meet with state senators and congressial representatives, dinners with business personalities about town.

One brave person in the firm's personnel department questioned the cost benefit of this program. (It was widely resented by other employees: people have a natural tendency to resent "crown princes and princesses" receiving special treatment.) She reasoned as follows: The real purpose of the MBA Fellows program was to produce a core of highly competent and politically sophisticated upper-middle managers. How else could the firm achieve this objective? Three options were obvious. One, the firm could simply hire proven upper-middle managers from competing firms. Second, it could hire MBAs who had financed their own education. Third, it could grow people internally, promoting motivated employees who by dint of hard work and competence, had risen from entry-level positions to middle management on their own.

Arguments for the Fellows program were that it would produce more and better managers than the alternative methods. The personnel person decided to check this. She looked first at performance appraisal ratings—and found that Fellows did no better in upper-middle-management positions than persons reaching these positions by the other three routes. She also looked at turnover—and found that a majority of Fellows stayed an average of six months after they finished their MBAs, then used their education to move on to better jobs elsewhere. The Fellows program was not effective in meeting its basic objective: producing superior upper-middle managers who stayed with the firm.

It follows that training programs for high-potential employees should be evaluated in terms of the percentage of people in fact promoted, how many are successful in the position they are promoted to, and their turnover rate.

PUBLIC RELATIONS AND COMMUNITY RELATIONS

Benefits for public relations and community relations, like those for employee relations efforts aimed at morale (e.g., parties, publications), can be difficult to show unless the efforts are focused on specific business objectives or problems.

Conversely, public relations programs designed specifically to increase revenues or decrease costs can show significant benefits. Good public relations can be shown to lead to an increased number of leads for sales or hiring. For these objectives, the benefits of public relations are evaluated much as advertising campaigns are. A firm can track the number of requests for service, qualified applicants, or the firm's stock price before and after a public relations campaign. For example, a consulting firm found that favorable mention in the business press resulting from *pro bono* work for arts organizations led to four new clients and $300,000 worth of business. Another firm found a community outreach program focused on identifying minority high school students interested in science resulted in a fivefold increase in qualified minority applicants for entry-level technical positions. This greatly reduced the costs needed to meet affirmative action goals. Public relations aimed at security analysts and investors may raise firms' stock prices.

Cost avoidance opportunities in public and community relations include reduced sabotage and vandalism—stores that maintain good community relations may not be looted or burned during riots—and the reduction in time of top management in dealing with community problems, picketing, boycotts, sit-ins, and the like.

EXAMPLE. *Benefits of a good community relations program:*

A food products firm was targeted by a national civil rights organization for picketing and boycott to pressure it to hire more minority employees. In fact, the firm had an excellent record of minority hiring and had been very supportive of minority community organizations, for example, by donating food and drink for many community functions.

The local minority community came to the firm's defense, and, in the words of one of the firm's executives, "threw the outside agitators right out of town." Management estimated it saved several hundred thousand dollars in time, security, and "defensive" public relations efforts—and possibly several million dollars in lost sales—as a result of its community relations efforts.

Advanced Topics

Sophisticated methods are available for estimating the benefits of better morale, improved selection methods, multi-year benefit flows, and the asset value of human resources. The statistics used by these methods are generally beyond the scope of this book. My purpose here is to describe these methods and provide examples and references, so you will know these tools exist and how to get more information if you need to use them.

Morale

A statistical method for estimating the dollar benefits from improvement in morale is shown in Figure 5.4. Morale measured by organizational climate survey scores is related to turnover, growth in sales and earnings, and productivity days in a number of work groups. The slope of the line of best fit between the organizational climate score and turnover shows a strong relationship: where morale is good, fewer people leave. Conversely, where organizational climate is poor, more employees leave, and sales and earnings are lower.

The slope of the line of best fit between results measures like turnover and productivity and morale on climate scores is called the "coefficient of determination," R, the square of a related statistic called a "correlation coefficient," r. These statistics relate the amount one variable (e.g., climate) changes to the amount another variable (e.g., growth in sales) changes. The amount each variable varies is measured in units of another statistic called a "standard deviation," abbreviated SD or σ. The percentage that the variable on the y axis, SD_y, will change if the variable on the $\times$ axis, SD_x, changes is its standard deviation, SD, $\times$ the coefficient of determination, r^2: $SD_y = SD_x \times r^2$.

The graph in Figure 5.4 indicates that an increase in the morale score on the survey from 3.60 to 3.85, one standard deviation, should result in an $R = (.50)^2 = .25 \times 5\%$ standard deviation = 1.25% decrease in turnover and a an $R = (.52)^2 = .27 \times 5\% = 1.35\%$ increase in sales.

Caution: statisticians warn that "correlation is not causality." In other words, instead of higher morale causing increased sales, sales may increase morale: people usually feel better when their firm is doing well. Alternatively, both higher morale and increased sales may be due to some third variable such as improvement in the general economy. Lag correlation methods, which test how much morale at one point in time predicts sales three months later, are available to sort out causality (see Taylor and Bowers, 1972).

The dollar-benefit value of increased morale is easily calculated from the firm's personnel and financial data. For example, using the data in Figure 5.4 for a firm with sales of $40 million, earnings of $4 million, and employing 1000 people making an average salary of $20,000, and a turnover rate of 15%, each SD of morale increase is worth:

FIGURE 5.4
Correlations of Organizational Climate Survey
Variables with "Hard" Organizational Outcomes

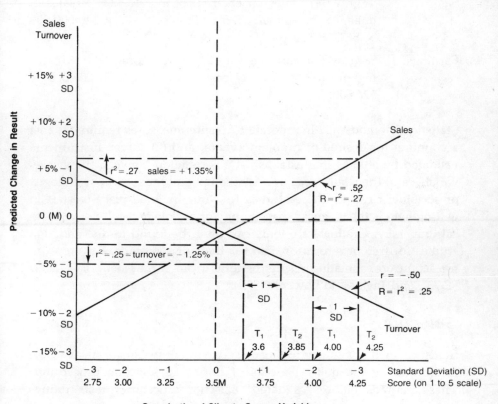

M = Mean Turnover Rate/Organizational Variable Score for all units surveyed

Correlations	Turnover	Growth in Sales	Return on Sales	Growth in Earnings
Organizational Climate Correlation coefficient	r = -.50	.52	.56	.34
Coefficient of determination	R^2 = .25	.27	.31	.12

171

Turnover: % turnover for each *SD* of morale x r^2 × number of employees × turnover cost/employee who leaves: 5% *SD* turnover × .25 × 1000 employees × 15% turnover × $20,000/employee = $37,500.

Sales: % growth in sales for each *SD* of morale × r^2 × sales in dollars × gross margin: 5% *SD* sales × .27 × $40,000,000 × 56% = $302,400.

Earnings: % growth in earnings for each *SD* of morale × r^2 × earnings in dollars: 5% *SD* earnings × .12 × $4,000,000 = $24,000.

Statistical methods relating morale to results measures require (1) cost accounting for desired or problem events, and (2) survey instruments validated by studies that establish the correlation between the survey variable and the result measure. Any competent industrial psychologist or sociologist can do these studies for your. A good place to start in getting help is the business, psychology or sociology faculty of your local university. Graduate students can often be found to do validation studies for free in return for data for their dissertations. For more information on estimating results benefits from survey data, see Likert (1973), and Taylor and Bowers (1972).

Selection

Statistical methods similar to those used to quantify climate are available for estimating the dollar benefits of improved selection procedures. These methods require "validated" selection procedures: tests, ratings by superior or peers, performance on assessment center exercises that have actually been shown to predict job performance. Tests have on average a maximum predictive validity of $r = .33$, a coefficient of determination of 10% of variance in performance (Ghiselli, 1966; Mischel, 1968). Ratings can have a predictive validity of $r = .4$, 16% of the variance in performance (Lewin and Zwaney 1976; Kane and Lawler, 1979). Assessment center selections have predictive validities of $r = .5$ to .6, 25% to 36% of differences in performance (McKinnon, 1975).

The meaning of these figures is shown graphically in Figures 5.5 and 5.6. The coefficient of determination, R or r^2, is the power of a score on

FIGURE 5.5

**Correlations of Test Scores with Job Performance
and Productivity**

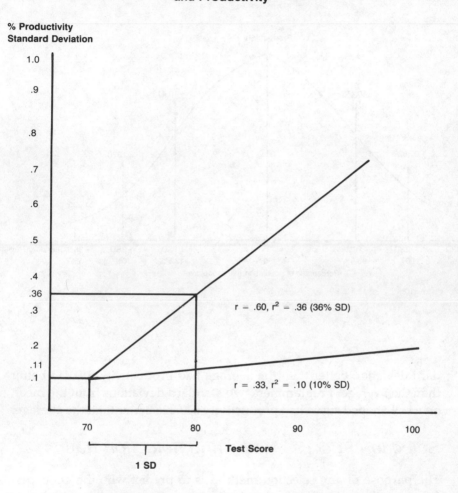

% Productivity
Standard Deviation

$r = .60, r^2 = .36$ (36% SD)

$r = .33, r^2 = .10$ (10% SD)

Test Score

1 SD

a test, rating, or exercise to predict actual hirees' performance on the job. One standard deviation on the test measure predicts 10% to 36% of the standard deviation on the performance measure.

Figure 5.6 shows standard deviations for computer programmer productivity reported by Schmidt, Hunter, McKenzie, and Muldrow (1979). Average programmers had a productivity of P. Programmers one stan-

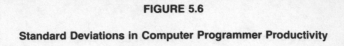

FIGURE 5.6

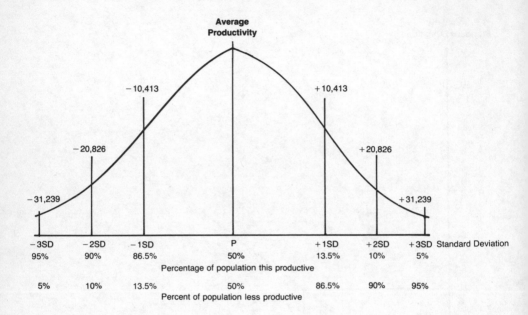

Standard Deviations in Computer Programmer Productivity

dard deviation better than the average had productivity $10,413 better than the average. Programmers two standard deviations from the mean on a bell-shaped curve had productivity $20,826 better than the average.

Selection Success Rates and Selection Ratios

The purpose of any selection method is to predict who the good performers will be. Good selection methods are most valuable when:

1. The success rate of most hirees is low:

$$\text{success rate} = \frac{\text{\# new hires who succeed}}{\text{\# new hires}}$$

If most hires fail, the probability of a bad hire and all related costs of reduced productivity and separation are high.

2. Selection ratios are low:

$$\text{Selection ratio} \quad = \quad \frac{\# \text{ hired}}{\# \text{ applicants}}$$

The firm elects to hire only a few from a large pool of applicants.

3. Tenure of employees is long, that is, you will be stuck with poor hires for a long time, as is often the case in civil service, union, and other politicized environments where it is very difficult to fire people.

4. The cost of a poor hire is high, either because the person's full cost is high, or the work he or she is doing is very valuable to the firm (e.g., a poor pilot or nuclear reactor operator).

No selection method is perfect. There can be one of four outcomes of selection: (1) selecting people who turn out to be good hires; (2) not hiring people who would turn out to be bad hires; (3) rejecting people who would have been good hires (a type 1 error); and (4) hiring people who turn out to be bad hires (a type 2 error).

If the success rate is low—that is, most people hired are likely to prove unsatisfactory—selecting the good people instead of the bad is very important. Alternatively, if the success rate is high—that is, most people hired will prove to be satisfactory anyway—selection is much less important. Similarly, if the selection ratio is high—you hire most people who walk through the door anyway—selection is less important. (When the military was short 30,000 junior officers, virtually all officers who were not grossly incompetent or morally unfit were "hired," i.e., promoted. Promotion or selection criteria were not important because almost everyone was going to be promoted anyway.) Alternatively, if you can be choosy and select a very small percentage of an applicant pool—in the extreme case, one person for an important job—selection becomes much more important.

The equation shown in Table 5.13 expresses these relationships mathematically. Schmidt, Hunter, McKenzie, and Muldrow (1979) studied the benefits of an improved aptitude test for selecting government computer programmers. The new test had a validity of $r = .76$ (very high for a test) compared to the old test, which had a validity of $r = .30$. Once hired, civil servants had an average tenure of 9.69 years. The standard deviation of hiree productivity was, as noted, $10,413. The selec-

TABLE 5.13

Estimating Productivity Gain Benefits from Improved Selection Methods

$$\text{Benefit} = tN (r_1 - r_2) SD_b\ \lambda\ - N \frac{(c_1 - c_2)}{\emptyset}$$

Computer programmer studies

Benefit	= productivity gain in dollars	
t	= tenure in years of average employee hired	9.69 years
N	= number of people hired a year	618 programmers
SD_b	= standard deviation of hiree's productivity	\$10,413
r_1	= correlation between selection measure and hiree productivity	.76
r_2	= correlation between old selection measure and hiree productivity	.30
λ	= cut off point on a normal curve for selection ratio (get from statistical table)	.2789
$\emptyset$	= selection ratio: # of people hired/total applicants	.20
c_1	= cost of new selection method	\$10
c_2	= cost of old selection method	0

Benefit for 618 programmers:

9.69 years x 618 people x (.76 - .30) x \$10,413 x $\frac{.2789}{.2}$ - 618 people $\frac{(10-0)}{.2}$ = \$40,098.592

Benefit for each programmer: \$64,884

Benefit per year = $\dfrac{\$64,884}{9.69 \text{ years}}$ = \$6,696/year

tion ratio was low: only two out of 10 programmers were hired. (λ, a statistic that can be looked up on a table (see Naylor and Shine, 1965, or Casio, 1982, pp. 231–239), relates the importance of the selection ratio to the performance standard deviation.) The cost of the new selection test was only \$10 more than the old test.

The benefit to the government of the new selection test was estimated by the equation to be $40,980,592; a dollar benefit for each programmer was $64,884 in improved performance over 9.69 years, or $6696 per year.

For more information on selection methods, see Chronbach and Gleser (1965), Cascio (1982), Schmidt (1979), et al. or Schmidt, Hunter, McKenzie and Muldrow (1979)), or any standard industrial psychology textbook.

Multiyear Benefit Flows

In most cost-benefit examples, we have looked at the costs and benefits for only one year. You might ask, how long can one assume a cost or benefit will continue, that is, how long should you account for it? How long you carry out benefits is a practical, "political science" question. Does it make sense to claim the $91,600 saved in the managers' unproductive staff meeting case for more than one year? I usually calculate benefits for one year because most American business budget, performance, and tax accounts are on a yearly basis. Other possibilities are the time the problem has existed, the time it is likely to persist, or the time the benefit income is likely to be received.

Technically, the way multiyear cost and benefit streams should be handled is called "discounted cash flow analysis." Discounted cash flow methods recognize that a dollar tomorrow is worth less than a dollar today. If $1 is put in a bank at a 10% interest rate, a year from now the dollar will have grown to $1.10. Conversely, $1.10 received a year from now is worth $1 today. The $1.10 has been discounted at the discount factor for a 10% interest or inflation rate, .91; to estimate its present value, $1.10 × .91 = $1.00. Discount factors can be looked up in any finance book or calculated by the equation $DF = 1/(1 + i)^y$, where i = the interest rate and y = the number of years in the future the benefit will be received.

Discounted cash flow accounts are shown in Table 5.14, for justifying a personnel computer system. The computer system costs $9000 to develop in Year 0, $3000 for hardware in Year 1, and $1000 a year in Years 2, 3, and 4 for data communications. There are no benefits in Year 0 because the system is still being developed. Benefits in Years 1 through 4 are $7500 a year ($3 savings per transaction × 50 transactions per week × 50 weeks per year). The net benefit (benefit − cost) × the dis-

TABLE 5.14
Discounted Cash Flow (DCF) or Present Value (PV)
Analysis of Multi-Year Costs and Benefits
"Justifying the Personnel Computer"

A	B	C	D	E	F
1 Year	0 B1	1 C1	2 D1	3 E1	4 F1
2 Benefit	$ 0 B2	$7500 C2	$7500 D2	$7500 E2	$7500 F2
3 Cost	$-9000 B3	$-3000 C3	$-1000 D3	$-1000 E3	$-1000 F3
4 Net Benefit	$-9000 B4 = B2 + B3	$4500 C4 = C2 + C3	$6500 D4 = D2 + D3	$6500 E4 = E2 + E3	$6500 F4 = F2 + F3
5 Discount Rate	.10 B5				
6 Discount Factor @ 10%	1 B6 = $1/(1+BS)^{B1}$	.91 C6 = $1/(1+B5)^{C1}$	.83 D6 = $1/(1+B5)^{D1}$	.75 E6 = $1/(1+B5)^{E1}$	.68 F6 = $1/(1+B5)^{F1}$
7 Discounted Value	$-9000 B7 = B4*B6	$4095 C7 = C4*C6	$5395 D7 = D4*D6	$4875 E7 = E4*E6	$4420 F7 = F4*F6
8 Net Present Value	$9785 B8 = @ sum (B7 . . . F7)				

*Lotus and most other spread sheet programs use an up arrow ↑ to indicate exponentiation, i.e. $1/(1+B5)↑B1$ B1 = $1/(1+B5)^{B1}$

178

count factor shows how much the net benefit is worth in present dollars each year in the future. The new system does not really pay for itself until the end of Year 2, when the $4095 net benefit in Year 1 plus the $5395 net benefit in Year 2 = $10,490, enough to pay the original $9000 investment in systems development and return a $10,490 − 9000 = $1490 profit. Over five years, however, the new system returns a $9785 net benefit ($18,785 in Years 1 through 4 less $9000 in Year 0) in present dollars on a $9000 investment, a return on investment of more than 100%.

Practically, discounting future benefits calculated on the dollar value of people's time often is not necessary because salaries and other elements of full cost go up with the rate of inflation. If you increase costs 10% a year for inflation and then deflate them at 10% to calculate present value, the inflation and discount factors cancel each other out. Simply extrapolating the numbers from the existing year will give you the same results. My rule of thumb is that most benefits for human resource and other professional service interventions pay for themselves in one year. Multiyear discounted cash flow analyses are usually not necessary.

For more information on multiyear benefit accounting, see Bierman and Smidt (1970), or any standard finance textbook.

Human Resource Asset Accounting

There are two ways to figure the economic value of people: (1) behavioral costing or expense methods; and (2) asset accounting. This book uses the "behavioral costing" or expense approach. It measures not peoples' asset values but the economic cost consequences of their behavior. Expenses, by accounting definition, are costs that occur within a given year. The behavioral costing approach adds up all the expenses of events such as turnover and treats them as costs in the year they occur.

The asset approach looks at people as if they were capital assets, like a building or machine tool. Assets, by accounting definition, have future value more than one year. Asset accounting approaches "capitalize" people and amortize their asset value over several years.

Arguing for the asset approach, Lickert (1967) asked managers to imagine they came to work Monday morning and found every position in the firm vacant. The firm had its present plants, offices, equipment, patents, and financial resources, but no people. How long would it take and how much would it cost to fill all of the present jobs, train replacements to present employees' level of competence, and develops them into the well functioning organization that now exists? Most managers reported it would take them several years and cost at least twice their firm's annual payroll. The "several years" suggests that present personnel had an asset value, that is, the behavioral cost of hiring and training them can be capitalized and expensed over several years.

There are at least six ways people have attempted to calculate the asset value of human resources (Flamholtz, 1974).

1. *Original/historical cost.* People are valued at what it cost to hire them. This approach gives people a "book value" similar to that of other assets on a firm's balance sheet. Original cost usually understates people's asset values. First, it rarely includes the learning curve costs of developing people and work groups to 100% productivity. Second, like physical asset book values, inflation rapidly makes original costs obsolete. The real cost of replacing a person is likely to be much higher now than it was originally some years before. Third, original cost values only input, what the person costs, not output, what the person produces or doesn't produce.

2. *Current/replacement cost.* People are valued at what it would cost to replace them. This approach, similar to the complete costing of a turnover incidents described in Chapters 3 and 4, corrects the problems with the "original cost" valuation method. It adjusts for inflation and includes the cost of individual and group learning-curve time needed to reach full productivity.

3. *Compensation.* People are valued at what they are currently being paid. This assumes a position is worth what the firm is willing to pay to have a person in it. Ignoring acquisition and learning curve costs, compensation seems a logical and defensible current valuation for an experienced employee.

4. *Adjusted present value of future compensation.* People are valued at what they are paid and will be paid over the time they are with the firm, adjusting for all possibilities. For example, some people will turn over at the end of one, three, or five years; and some will stay for 40 years until they retire. Some will not advance beyond their present positions,

hence will be worth less; some will become chairman of the board, hence worth a great deal more. To give an overall expected value, probability weights are applied to adjust for all possible outcomes. Future pay is discounted to give its present value. Flamholtz (1974, p. 184) shows that present compensation is a good surrogate measure of adjusted present value of future compensation. This has a nice economic logic to it: on average, people's future value is represented in what they are now being paid.

5. *Attitude and organization dimension methods.* A variety of approaches have been developed to estimate employee economic value from attitudes, subjective judgments of productivity, and perceptions of organizational climate.

Myers and Flowers (1974) find the dollar value of people by multiplying direct salaries by a weighted attitude score. Higher weights are given for higher job levels and longer tenure with the firm, on the assumption that the higher the person's position and the longer he or she has been with the company, the more influence he or she is likely to have on organization productivity. The dollar value of each person is his or her salary multiplied by the attitude weight times the attitude score on the attitude survey. Improvements in attitudes result in higher dollar values for people or groups. This approach has several problems. Level of position and tenure should be reflected in salary, so these additional weights are not needed. Myers and Flowers do not present any data to show that improved attitudes in fact result in different behaviors or lead to actual productivity results.

Another approach, called "global estimation," establishes the average dollar value of employee performance by asking managers to:

1. Rate the dollar value to the firm of an average employee in a given job (a value that economically ought to equal his or her direct salary).

2. Estimate the dollar value of a superior performer, a person whose performance is better than 85% of his or her co-workers in the job (i.e., one standard deviation better than the average).

3. Estimate the dollar value of a low-performing employee, one whose performance is in the bottom fifteenth percentile of all workers (i.e., one standard deviation less than average).

Schmidt et al. (1979) use this approach to estimate the dollar value of superior versus average computer programmers in the selection study described above.

Cascio and Ramos' (Cascio, 1982) Estimate of Performance in Dollars (CREPID) refines the global estimation method by rating each task an employee performs on the basis of time or frequency (0 to 100), importance (0 to 7), consequence of error (0 = no consequence, to 7 = extremely serious consequence), and level of difficulty (0 = workers have no responsibility, just do what they are told, to 7 = workers must take responsibility and make decisions for major groups of the organization).

A relative weight for each task is found by: (1) multiplying the tasks' ratings on frequency times importance times consequence of error times level of difficulty; (2) summing these scores for all tasks; then (3) dividing the score for each task by this total score.

The average employee's salary is divided by the relative weight for each task to find a dollar value of the task. Employees are then rated on each task, and this rating is multiplied by dollar value of the activity to get the net dollar value for the task. Dollar values for all employee tasks are summed to get the total dollar value for the employee in the job.

"Organizational-dimensions" approaches estimate a work group's value from scores on organizational climate surveys, following the method described for morale. Attitude or climate scores are correlated with economic performance or behavioral events having a known dollar value or cost. The value of the work group is the standard deviation of its climate score times the correlation coefficient between the climate score and an economic value (e.g., sales) multiplied by the value of one standard deviation on the economic value.

In my experience, simple global estimates of percentage productivity and time value of productivity give an estimate similar to those produced by more elaborate attitude weighting methods. Estimation of asset values from attitudes and subjective estimates of productivity are less convincing than behavioral costing of actual on-the-job events.

6. *Economic or "unpurchased goodwill" valuation methods.* The economic value of an asset is the return it produces or is expected to produce. Human assets as well as physical assets can be valued in terms of return on investment (ROI), where ROI = earnings divided by assets.

Flamholtz (1974) suggests that the economic value of human assets can be estimated by dividing human assets by total (physical and human) assets and multiplying by the present value of the firm's expected future earnings (see Table 5.15).

For example, a consulting firm employing 30 people making $30,000 an average of per year has a book value of $500,000. The firm's earnings are $400,000 per year, and these earnings are expected to continue for five years and to increase at the rate of inflation. The present value of expected future earnings is thus five years × $400,000 = $2,000,000. Valuing the consultants at their direct salary, human assets are 30 people × $40,000/person = $1.2 million. Total assets of the firm are $500,000 in physical assets (furniture, computers, etc.) + $1.2 million in (human assets) = $1.7 million total assets.

The contribution of the human assets to the firm's value is $1.2 million ÷ 1.7 million × $2,000,000 = $1,412,000.

The "economic value" method uses circular reasoning: you take a stab at estimating human assets and then get another value by multiplying the ratio of human to total assets by present value of future earnings. A simpler method, closer to the concept of "goodwill" in accounting, is to assume the present value of future earnings *is* (by definition) the value of a firm. Human assets by this method are simply the present value of future earnings less the value of physical assets $2,000,000 - 500,000 = $1,500,000.

In the consulting firm example, the people are worth $1,412,000 to $1,500,000, at least $200,000 more than the conservative estimate of their asset value found by valuing them at their current compensation: 30 people × $40,000/person = $1,200,000. This is true in most professional firms: the real asset value is the people.

"Unpurchased goodwill." People are valued by capitalizing the difference between their firm's return on investment and the average return on investment for the industry. For example, if Firm A has a return on investment of 15% and the industry average is 10%, Firm A must be doing something right. If Firm A's assets are $100 million and the industry average is also $100 million, something must be accounting for the additional 5% return (e.g., people, using their assets more efficiently than firms they are competing with).

The dollar value of these smarter people is found by capitalizing Firm A's assets at the average industry rate of return. If Firm A's profits are

TABLE 5.15

"Economic" and "Unpurchased Goodwill" Valuation of Human Resource Assets

• **Economic valuation** of a consulting firm's human assets

$$HA = \frac{HA}{HA + PA} \times PV$$

where

PA = Value of physical assets (PA) = $500,000

HA = Value of human assets (HA) (at current compensation)
      30 people x $40,000/year = $1,200,000
      Total assets = PA + HA $1,700,000

PV = Present value of firm's future earnings
      PV = 5 years x $400,000/year = $2,000,000

Asset value of firm's human resources

$$\frac{\$1,200,000 \text{ (human assets)}}{\$1,700,000 \text{ (total assets)}} \times \$2,000,000 \text{ (PV of earnings)} = \$1,412,000$$

Simple Solution $HA = \dfrac{HA}{HA + PA} \times PV$

$$HA (HA + PA) = HA \times PV$$
$$HA = PV - PA$$

Asset value of firm's human resources = $2,000,000 (PV) - $500,000 (PA) = $1,500,000 (HA)

• **"Unpurchased goodwill"**: Value added by human resources

Return on Investment (ROI) = $\dfrac{\text{earnings}}{\text{assets}}$

	Profits	Assets	ROI (capitalization rate)

Firm A $15 mil ÷ $100 mil = 15%

Industry Average $10 mil ÷ $100 mil = 10%

"Capitalization" of earnings at ROI rate $\text{assets} = \dfrac{\text{earnings}}{\text{ROI}}$

Firm A's assets "capitalized" at $\dfrac{\$15 \text{ mil}}{.10}$ = $150 million
industry average of 10%

Firm A's book value $100 million

Additional value of Firm A's human assets $ 50 million

184

capitalized at the industry ROI average of 10%, Firm A's assets are found to be $150 million, $50 million over Firm A's book value. The value of Firm A's human assets is this $50 million difference.

The problem with the "unpurchased goodwill" method is that it gives an uninterpretable result, a *negative* value for human assets, if the firm's rate of return is less than the industry average. This method may be most useful in making political and public relations points about the value added by your employees if your rate of return is higher than the industry average.

Economic and "unpurchased goodwill" evaluation methods may tell you the premium you should be willing to pay to acquire a professional service firm. Brokerage and insurance sales groups are in fact valued and purchased on the basis of present value of the earnings they can be expected to produce in the future.

For more information on human resource asset accounting, see Flamholtz (1974).

CHAPTER **6**

Increasing Productivity

This chapter will show you a variety of methods that have improved productivity in human resource and knowledge worker service groups.

KEY CONCEPTS

Measure everything—productivity metrics have great power to change behavior.

Keep time sheets, and bill time; manage internal service groups as if they were professional service firms.

Apply job-shop production management methods to administrative and service tasks.

Human resource and knowledge worker productivity-improvement strategies include: (1) improved utilization of people; (2) deletion of non-essential services; (3) work simplification; (4) use of job-shop management methods; and (5) use of technology.

The cost-benefit methods shown in Chapters 3, 4, and 5 underlie these strategies and are invaluable in choosing and justifying specific tactics.

IMPROVING UTILIZATION OF PEOPLE

People are the major cost in delivering any service. Productivity-improvement methods begin by increasing the utilization of people and time. These methods move from relatively crude broad-brush measures of service worker productivity to specific techniques for tracking and reducing time spent on specific tasks.

Value-Added and Comparative Staff System Measures

A rough measure of a firm's productivity is found by dividing its gross revenue output (sales less cost of goods sold) by the number of its employees (labor input). Figure 6.1, an excerpt from Prime Computer's annual report, shows value-added/employee data for six computer companies. Firms with value-added/employee ratios below those of competitors may be at a cost disadvantage and must ask whether they are using people efficiently.

Comparative (or common) staff system (CSS) ratios relate indirect "overhead" people (e.g., secretaries) to total employees or to employees who produce revenue (e.g., support staff to billable professionals in a consulting firm). The Army calls this the "tooth-to-tail" ratio: each

FIGURE 6.1
Value Added/Employee Data

People Resources

Prime's people are responsible for the company's ability to meet ambitious growth and profit goals. They have set these goals through the company's top down-bottom up planning methodology and have met the responsibilities that these goals imply.

During the past five years, the value added per Prime employee has consistently been one of the highest in the computer industry. And, during this time, Prime employees have increased their productivity at one of the fastest rates, as the figure following demonstrates.

Prime's management believes the reasons underlying this high productivity and continuing growth are three-fold.

First, in the selection of employees, their desire to seek responsibility is a major factor. Compensation and job satisfaction are encouragements to this end.

Second, Prime's innovative management development strategy provides younger managers both with a growth path and the benefits of working closely with experienced senior executives. Prime's senior management people have each managed considerably larger organizations than the group responsibility they undertook on joining the company.

A third major aid to productivity is that the company gives its people the tools needed for effectiveness. This is most apparent in the breadth of uses executed on the internal computer system network.

Technology to increase productivity includes such examples as:

- On-line, real-time transaction processing of inventory.
- On-line computer modeling for financial planning.
- Computer-aided layout of Prime's printed circuit boards that cut needed work-hours by 90%.
- An office automation system that speeds the creation, proofreading, editing and dissemination of documents, as well as enhancing the filing and accessing of information.

The results of this applied computer technology can be grasped by the mix of employees at Prime. In the typical financial department, clerical workers out-number professionals by 70% to 30%. At Prime, those percentages are reversed, with major cost savings and increased efficiency. Prime, in essence, works to put people in positions where all their skills can be used.

FIGURE 6.1 continued

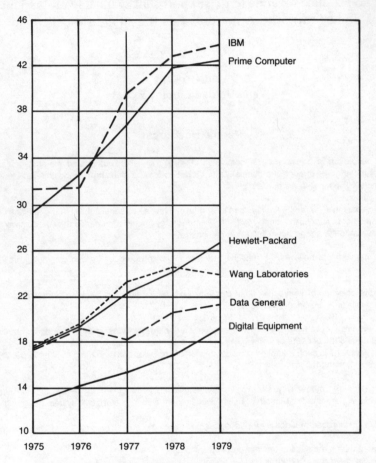

VALUE ADDED/EMPLOYEE*
(in thousands of dollars)

*Gross margin divided by average number of employees.

soldier who fights requires 10 support troops. Common Staff System ratios can be used to compare similar departments within a firm, or a firm with others in its industry.

Figure 6.2 shows comparative staff system ratios of human resource people to total firm employees.

FIGURE 6.2
Common Staff System (CSS) Productivity Ratios

A Productivity Ratio: Personnel Dept. Employees:: Total Employees

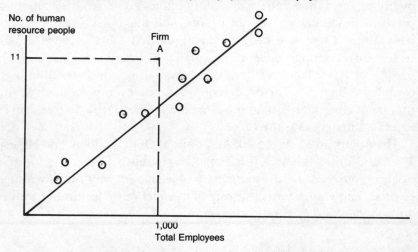

No. of human
resource people

Firm
A

11

1,000
Total Employees

A Productivity Ratio: Norm Index

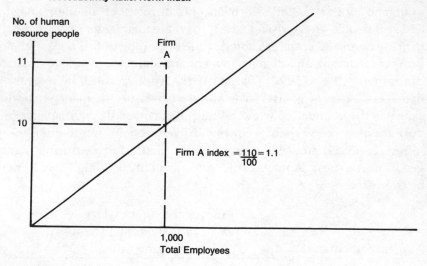

No. of human
resource people

Firm
A

11

10

Firm A index $= \dfrac{110}{100} = 1.1$

1,000
Total Employees

Having a CSS productivity ratio higher than other departments in your firm or other firms does not necessarily mean that you have a problem, but does call the question. Firms that differ significantly from industry averages must ask themselves if they are "fat." Having higher overhead costs than your competitors ultimately raises the cost of your products, lowers your sales or profits, and may force you out of business. Human resource people may argue that a higher level of effort results in recruiting better, more creative computer engineers, higher morale, or fewer labor relations problems—all of which result in higher overall productivity. The burden of proof, however, is on them to show that input costs higher than those of competitors really do translate into increased benefits for the firm.

The American Management Association (Oranti, Giblin, and Floersch, 1982) and other research firms regularly publish CSS ratios for all industry groups. A good productivity objective for any human resource or other knowledge worker group is to equal or better firm or industry value-added and CSS ratio averages.

Increase Managers' Span of Control

Many American firms have changed from "pyramids" to "light bulbs" in organization: the "fat"—swollen bureaucracies of middle managers and staff people—have risen to the top, where their larger salaries greatly increase overhead costs. As noted at the beginning of this book, "many firms are reducing middle management and staff 20% to 40% to increase productivity 30% to 50%" (BusinessWeek, April 25, 1983) by increasing managers' span of control. The simplest measure of managerial efficiency is the number of workers (output) managed by a manager (input), for example, a span of control of five-to-one or ten-to-one.

Ferebee (1981) suggests a productivity metric for measuring managerial effectiveness. A manager's "management cost ratio" (MCR) may be expressed as:

$$\frac{\text{management cost}}{\text{worker cost}} = \frac{\substack{\text{manager's direct salary} \times \\ \text{\% of time he or she spends} \\ \text{managing others}}}{\substack{\text{total salaries of employees managed} \\ \times\ (1\ -\ \text{\% of time spent managing others}) \\ \times\ \text{manager's salary}}}$$

For example, a $30,000 manager who spends 90% of his or her time managing five people has an MCR of:

$$\frac{\$30,000 \times 90\%}{\$100,000 + (10\% \times \$30,000)} = \frac{\$27,000 \text{ management cost}}{\$103,000 \text{ worker cost}} = .26$$

Ferebee argues that a firm's MCR should be between .20 and .30, which corresponds to an average span of control of four to six subordinates per manager.

Recent management practice suggests managerial spans of control can be increased with no loss—and perhaps even a gain—in quality and employee productivity.

Pushing responsibility down to lower levels not only results in significant savings in managerial time and people; it often motivates subordinates—who now have more "enriched," challenging jobs—to take initiative and improve productivity. Benefits of increasing managerial spans of control are calculated directly from the full costs of managers saved.

EXAMPLE. *Benefits of increasing managers' span of control:*

Xerox has increased the average manager's span of control from six or seven subordinates to 15 subordinates. At one facility, Xerox was able to reduce managers from 365 to 265. If these 100 managers were making an average of $35,000 a year times three (full cost multiplier), Xerox's full cost savings at $105,000 per manager × 100 managers = $10,500,000 (Main, 1984).

Increase Staff Applied Rates

There are three ways to increase applied rates: (1) set applied rate standards and give people feedback on applied rates by keeping time sheets; (2) increase marketing to utilize people fully; and (3) delete excess people when there simply is not enough work for them.

The simplest and most powerful method of increasing human resource and service worker productivity is to keep time sheets. All staff people should know their applied rate standard and receive regular feedback on their applied rates. Professionals in most service firms receive weekly printouts on their applied time and deviation from standards—and hear from their boss if their applied rate is below standard. Some firms even publicly post each professional's applied rate in green if it is at or above goal, yellow if it is 10% to 15% below goal, and red if it is more than 15% below goal. Such feedback has great power to get people's attention.

Again it should be emphasized that keeping time sheets is standard professional practice and need not interfere with creativity or flexibility. Time sheets do not mean heavy-handed bureaucratic management. Many professionals work odd hours: midnight to dawn; 36 hours straight, then not at all; at home or on the road. Time sheets don't control how work is done—only how much time is billable. Realistic applied-rate standards do not pressure people unduly; they actually help prevent burnout by helping professionals budget their time and balance work loads.

Effective marketing and scheduling can ensure enough work and an even flow of work to keep people utilized at their optimal applied rate.

Benefits of increasing applied rates are easily calculated from time savings and applied person-day costs.

EXAMPLE. *Benefits of increasing applied rates of Multinational, Inc.'s underemployed human resource management (HRM) people in Europe:*

A multinational firm had HRM offices in England, Spain, Italy, and Greece. Each office had 30 staff, a total of 120 people. The average salary of these HRM specialists was $20,000, hence a full cost of $60,000. Total cost of the HRM offices was $7.2 million (120 people × $60,000/person = $7,200,000).

The firm felt that its European HRM people were underutilized and asked me to investigate. A brief study of each office showed that the average applied rate for these specialists was 25%. (None of the offices kept time sheets, but people's applied times were easily reconstructed using the inquiry strategies described in Chapter 3, Calculating Costs.) An HRM person with a full cost of $60,000 per year at a 25% applied rate had a cost per applied person-day of $923.

The firm's lowest applied rates were in a drug and alcohol counseling office with three counselors and a patient load of eight patient-hours per *week*. A counselor with a 75% applied rate should deliver six patient-hours a *day* (8 hours per day × 75% = 6 hours per day.) In a five-day

week each counselor should see 30 patients (6 patient-hours per day ×
5 days = 30 patient-hours). Three counselors should deliver 90 patient-
hours per week. The eight patient-hours the service actually delivered,
divided by the 120 hours available, give a 6.7% applied rate and a full
cost of *$3444* per day, or *$431* per hour. Very expensive drug and alcohol
counseling!

I recommended that (1) the firm's HRM people be required to keep
time sheets, (2) a 75% applied rate be established as the standard, and
(3) all offices make a much greater effort to market their services to potential clients.

Six months later, one HRM office had been closed, deleting 30 people. Increased marketing had resulted in 100% more clients being served
by 25% fewer people. Applied rates had risen to 67%. Costs per applied
person-day had dropped to $344 per day. The net dollar saving for de-
leting the 30 excess people was $1.8 million (30 fewer people × $60,000/
person = $1,800,000).

Delivery of 100% more services with the remaining 90 people provided an additional benefit. Before, 120 people were paid for 260 days
but only 25% applied, that is, 120 people delivered 65 days of service
per year per person, 7800 total service days (120 people × 65 days). Six
months later, 90 people applied 67% delivered 174.2 days per year per
person, 15,678 total service days. Valued at the new cost per applied
person-day, benefits from increased utilization of HR people were
$2,710,032 (7878 additional days of service × $344/day). The net benefit
to the organization was $4.5 million.

Tracking and giving people feedback on applied rates and costs per
applied person-day has great power to shape behavior in the direction
of greater efficiency and productivity.

Transferring or deleting excess people (those who cannot keep up
their applied rates) immediately raises overall efficiency, lowers the average cost per applied person-day, and produces dollar benefits.

Keep People Off Fixed Overhead

Effective professional service groups keep people off fixed overhead
whenever possible, avoiding their fringe and overhead costs and having
to pay them when there is no work for them to do. Strategies for keeping people off fixed overhead include:

Control Head Count. Be tough on personnel requisitions by approving only those that produce benefits equal to their costs.

Rent Versus Buy People. Use temporary, part-time, and contract workers.

Buy Versus Make Products. Buy if making a product would cause you to add to staff.

Optimize Your Personnel "Inventory."

Control head count. Two strategies for resisting managers' requests for more full-time people are:

1. Approve requests only if the manager can show that the new hire will increase revenue three times the hiree's salary or that capacity utilization statistics (see "Work Simplification") show work units have increased enough to justify another person. Among other benefits, this discipline will quickly get managers thinking in cost-benefit terms, and you will see many fewer badly thought-out hiring requests.

2. Match requests for new hires with discussion of employees and jobs that are no longer needed. Managers may be willing to trade nonperforming people or low- or no-value jobs for a new person or slot. Poor performers are often found in jobs that have lost their value because these are the only places where they can be tolerated and remain invisible. Some tough personnel managers enforce a "fire one to hire one" policy.

   The personnel director of the most productive plant in his high-tech firm told me he had used these methods to approve only four of 64 personnel requisitions in the past year. He had saved, at an average new-hire salary of \$15,000, \$45,000 full cost × 60 people = \$2,700,000.

Rent Versus Buy People. Renting or contracting for help is almost always cheaper than adding to staff. Maintain a pool of "temporary" or part-time people (e.g., university graduate students, consultants, self-employed professional women at home raising children) who can be called upon when there is work for them but who do not become part of fixed overhead. A rule of thumb in many consulting firms is to maintain a temporary pool of people equal to one-third the number of permanent staff to provide flexibility in responding to periods of peak demand for work. Consultants are particularly cost effective in government or unionized environments, where it is very difficult to lay people off. You don't have to pay consultants when you don't need them, and they are much easier to fire or simply not hire than internal professionals.

Some firms are even encouraging internal staff professionals to become consultants by helping them set up offices at home and contracting with them for enough work to provide them with an income. *Business-Week* (1982) describes Rank Xerox's program for getting valued staff off fixed overhead: Middle managers and corporate staff in planning, purchasing and human resources functions are encouraged to resign as employees and become consultants to the firm. Rank Xerox helps former employees set up their own businesses, sells them office furniture and equipment at book value, and loans them a microcomputer linked to Xerox offices—but no longer pays them fringe benefits: medical and unemployment insurance, bonuses, pension contributions or social security taxes. Essentially, this transfers the firm's fringe and overhead costs to the employee. Self-employed consultants have more control over their own overhead and every incentive to keep overhead costs low. Rank Xerox expects as many as 25 percent of its corporate staff employees will become consultants, saving the firm 8–10 percent in overhead costs.

"Rank Xerox will realize its main savings by cutting such costs as office space, support workers, fringe benefits and national payroll taxes. These incidental expenses account for two-thirds of its cost of employing a worker" (*BusinessWeek*, August 30, 1982).

This strategy has benefits for both staff consultants and their firms. Advantages for staff include schedule flexibility, time to pursue other interests, and the opportunity to make much more money than corporate pay scales allow. Xerox pays staff consultants 95 percent of their base salaries for working two days a week, leaving them three days (60 percent of their available time) to sell to others. The advantage to the firm is the retention of experienced employees' expertise, which would be lost in a general cut of overhead personnel.

Note that the major saving is not salary but fringe and overhead costs of office space, equipment, and support staff equal to twice the salary: the real dollar benefits of avoiding the inevitable 3 × overhead multiplier.

A related approach is the increasingly popular practice of "leasing" workers. *Newsweek*, summarizes the overhead, paperwork, pension, and tax benefits available to small business from worker leasing (Gelman and Sandza, 1984):

The Boom in Worker Leasing

Companies always look for new ways to cut costs and reduce taxes, so equipment-leasing schemes have a certain appeal. Now, some enterprising businesses are experimenting with a variation on the theme: they are leasing workers. An owner simply dismisses his workers, then hires them back from an employee-leasing firm. He retains the right to hire and fire, but the leasing firm pays the workers and furnishes all benefits. The owner is freed of costly paperwork and rewarded with some attractive tax breaks. "I generally save employers enough to pay for my fee," explains Eugene Schenk, head of Staffco, a worker-leasing company. "And I've taken away all of the headaches."

The boomlet in employee leasing is the result of a provision of the tax law that went into effect this year. TEFRA, the Tax Equity and Fiscal Responsibility Act of 1982, allows employers to shift the burden of employee-pension plans to worker-leasing outfits. As a result, a small employer can now lease his workers from a third party and then set up any type of pension plan for unleased employees— including "top heavy" plans that give generous benefits to key employees and essentially serve as personal tax shelters.

The practice was pioneered by Contract Staffing of America, which began offering this novel approach to doctors and dentists in 1978. Because the arrangement did not have the formal approval of the Internal Revenue Service, the Tustin, Calif., firm hired former IRS Commissioner Sheldon Cohen two years ago to lobby Congress for legal recognition. Cohen persuaded Congress to legitimize employee leasing, and since then CSA has grown from 400 employees to 1,500, ringing up revenues of $26 million in 1983. Other leasing outfits have grown just as fast. By one estimate, more than two dozen employee-leasing firms now handle 20,000 workers for other companies, primarily small businesses in the West and Southwest. (Employee leasing makes little sense for large firms with their own personnel staffs, and it has yet to flourish in the heavily unionized Northeast.)

Mobility: Employee leasing has also proved to be popular among workers. As relatively large corporations, leasing companies can generally provide improved benefits at a lower cost per employee. In addition, employees gain mobility: they can switch jobs without a loss of benefits. That helped medical assistant Georgette Corpos-Holler when she decided to leave a physician who refused to give her a raise. "I asked for a transfer and CSA put me in another office," says Corpos-Holler. "If I was working privately I'd have had to quit."

Part of the popularity of employee leasing has nothing to do with pension plans: it is becoming an increasingly attractive option for firms that simply want to cut their administrative burdens. James Borgelt, general manager of Omnistaff, Inc., in Dallas, estimates that only 15 percent of his clients are motivated by the desire to skirt pension regulations. Nonetheless, Omnistaff's leased work force has jumped from 1,500 last August to 5,000 today. Walter Klein, for example, fired the 30 employees of his Klein Meat Co. in Ft. Worth, Texas, last October, instantly rehiring them from Omnistaff. He thereby dumped a crippling load of paperwork, and his staff got an improved benefits package. Employees never worried that they had been taken in by the switch: Klein was so eager to simplify his life that he transferred himself to the Omnistaff payroll as well.

Source: Gelman, E., with *Sandza* R., Newsweek May 14, 1984.

Identifying part-time people willing to work "minishifts" is a cost-effective way to handle surges in business. Minishift workers can be older people or women at home with children, both of whom do not want to work full time but do want to get out of the house, want to "keep an oar in" by doing productive work and can use the extra money. Minishifts often run from 10:00 A.M. to 2:00 P.M. so women can get their children off to school, put in four concerted hours of work, and get home before the children return from school. These workers are highly productive; firms get four hours of work for four hours of pay. (For eight hours of pay, most firms estimate they get six and one-half hours of productive work. Olson [1982] argues that white-collar workers average but four hours per eight-hour day, and that productivity programs can boost this 50% to six hours per day.) Most important, minishift and part-time people are not paid benefits, do not require additional office space or overhead support, and are easily laid off or not hired when there is no work for them. This sounds exploitive, but in fact it is a great deal for both firms and workers. Firms get a productive pool of employees off fixed overhead but available when needed; workers get an opportunity to work, flexible work schedules, and additional money.

Buy Versus Make Services and Products. Buy outside services and materials when it is cheaper than making them internally, especially if "making" requires adding staff to overhead.

EXAMPLE. *Benefits of buying versus making a training course:*

A firm putting 1000 people through a career-planning program purchased materials from a publisher at $100 per participant. The firm decided to create its own career-planning course so that it would not have to buy materials from the outside vendor. This firm's standard for curriculum development was 75 days of development time for each one day of course delivery. Development of a three-day course required approximately 225 days or one person-year. (An industry standard is ten days of development time and $10,000 for each day of management training delivered. Technical training requires much more development time: 75 to 100 days of development for each day of training.) Curriculum developers in this firm made $35,000 a year, which at full cost meant a $105,000 cost to develop the course in-house.

The firm decided to do a "make-versus-buy" analysis and put the course out for bid. A consulting firm offered to deliver a turnkey course for $45,000. (The consultant was 60% cheaper because it had a course that could be tailored to the client firm's specifications. Consultants are often cheaper because clients can "buy a consultant's learning curve," saving learning-curve costs of developing expertise from scratch.) The client firm would own all copyrights to course materials and could print them at a cost of $8 per participant.

The firm hired the consultant. The result was a saving of $60,000 in course development costs ($105,000 in-house costs less $45,000 contracted costs = $60,000). Alternatively, the firm saved $47,000 in materials costs the first year (the $100 per participant charged by the external vendor minus the $8 workbook printing cost = $92 × 1000 participants = $92,000 minus $45,000 consulting fee = $47,000). In this case, deciding to "buy" course development but "make" materials provided the optimum benefit.

Optimize personnel inventories. Operations research equations for determining optimum inventory levels can be applied to human resources. An "inventory person" is someone you don't have work for at the moment but may need in the future. The question is, how many such people can you afford to carry? The equation for optimum inventory level is:

$$\begin{array}{c} \text{optimum} \\ \text{staff} \\ \text{inventory} \end{array} = .5 \sqrt{\dfrac{\substack{2 \times \text{number of people needed per period} \\ \times \text{ acquisition cost/person}}}{\text{carrying cost per person/period}}}$$

This equation essentially trades off the cost of having to hire additional people when you need them against the cost of carrying people—and paying their salary and overhead costs when you don't have work for them.

For example, if it costs 30% of direct salary to acquire a professional, the optimum staff inventory for a ten-person group with a full cost multiplier of 3 × a given salary is:

$$.5 \sqrt{\dfrac{2 \times 10 \text{ people} \times .3 \times \text{salary}}{3 \times \text{salary}}} = .71 \text{ people}$$

or more generally,

$$\text{optimum inventory} = .22 \sqrt{\text{people needed}}$$

If it costs 2.4 × salary to hire a professional, the optimum staff inventory is:

$$.5 \sqrt{\dfrac{2 \times 10 \text{ people} \times 2.4 \text{ salary}}{3 \times \text{salary}}} = 2 \text{ people}$$

or more generally,

$$\text{optimum inventory} = .63 \sqrt{\text{people needed}}$$

The optimum staff inventory equation shows that as acquisition costs go up, the number of people you can afford to carry increases and that short-term layoffs rarely make economic sense. For example, if you have a three-month downturn in the summer and have to carry people for this period, the carrying cost is .25 year $\times$ 3 $\times$ salary = .75 $\times$ salary. If professionals cost 2.4 $\times$ salary to acquire, you can afford to carry:

$$.5 \sqrt{\frac{2 \times N \times 2.4 \times \text{salary}}{.25 \text{ salary}}} = 1.27 \sqrt{\text{people needed}}$$

or, for a ten-person group:

$$1.27 \sqrt{10} = 4 \text{ people}$$

(Sophisticated models for optimizing staffing levels are available. For more information, see Buffa, 1968 or Niehaus, 1979, 1980.)

DELETE INESSENTIAL SERVICES

In many firms, human resource services and other staff functions have grown up over the years like weeds. Typically someone long departed went to a transactional analysis workshop in 1969 and thought it the greatest thing ever seen, and the firm has been teaching transactional analysis ever since. Most service groups can use a thorough weeding of their products and services. The best method is to conduct cost-benefit analyses of all offerings and prioritize them on the basis of benefits. Elimination of noncost-beneficial and lower-priority products and services can greatly increase the overall efficiency of a service group.

Cost-Benefit Prioritization. Figure 6.3 shows a cost-benefit prioritization of the programs of one personnel department. Note that legally required programs are not cost-benefit analyzed: the "benefit" is negative, the cost to meet the requirement. (You may be able to show efficiency benefits by meeting the legal requirement for less.) Other programs are clearly ranked in terms of potential benefits. Expensive "marginal" and "not-worthwhile" programs costing $1,294,000 are candidates to be dropped.

In most service organizations, a cost-benefit analysis shows a classic Pareto distribution: 20% of the products and services provide 80% of the benefits, and the remaining 80% of the products and services provide 20% of the benefits. Ranking products and services on their anticipated cost benefits helps you see which 20% you should focus your efforts on and which 80% can be eliminated.

Portfolio Analysis

Another method of rating products and services is a strategic marketing technique called portfolio analysis.

EXAMPLE. *Benefit of a marketing approach to personnel:*

A manufacturing firm brought in an outsider to "clean up" the personnel function every two or three years. In one era it was a lawyer. The lawyer saw his job as keeping the firm out of trouble. He instituted all kinds of paperwork, with many approval forms and review levels that tied the firm in knots, increased overhead, and prevented personnel people from delivering services.

Next came a manufacturing manager with a mandate to "make personnel responsive to the line." This person succeeded in eliminating some of the lawyer's unnecessary paperwork. Not understanding personnel, she focused on programs that felt good and/or didn't get in the way, rather than providing real benefits.

Next to take over the personnel department was a finance manager. His mandate was to cut costs. Not understanding personnel, he cut— but not on any rational basis, because he lacked an objective way of telling which programs were cost beneficial and which were not.

Finally, a marketing manager was put in charge of personnel. This person adopted a very different and most interesting approach. She immediately initiated what marketing people call a product portfolio analysis. This technique, borrowed from strategic planning, puts products in one of four cells depending on their value and volume (see Figure 6.4).

FIGURE 6.3
Program Priorities Schedule

ACTION PROGRAM	Priority	Timing 1972	1973	1974	1975	1976	1977	Net annual dollar benefit	Cost/ benefit ratio (1:n)
LEGALLY REQUIRED PROGRAMS									
Labor Relations Strategy	x							($ 619)	n/a
Protect Right to Select Employees	x							($ 86)	n/a
Continue Validation of Selection Tests	x							$35,000	78.17
Redesign Personnel Data System	x							$ 273	1.78
Develop Part-Time Female Employment Approaches	x							$ 227	4.16
VERY DESIRABLE PROGRAMS									
Restructuring Service Force	1							$14,608	9.6
Service College Coop Program	2							$ 4,490	2.74
MODERATELY DESIRABLE PROGRAMS									
Service Job Enrichment	3							$ 9,920	24.3
Assessment Center	4							$ 4,946	15.40
Education & Training Center	5							$ 4,780	3.57

1. Legally required efforts come first

2. ... then, other programs are rated by overall feasibility category

3. ... and within feasibility category by net benefits

4. Priorities are indicated here

5. Starting from the lowest priority program, marginal efforts may be trimmed as required by the budget

6. In any case these programs are eliminated

Program and design development

Program implementation

Program	Priority	Cost	Ratio
Clerical Selection Program	6	\$ 1,799	19.94
Develop College Campus as Primary Employment Source	7	\$ 834	2.06
Interfunctional Moves & Fast Track Program	8	\$ 679	7.54
Selection Standards for New Sales/Tech. Rep. Types	9	\$ 520	11.6
Improve Economics of Field Employment Operations	10	\$ 472	1.42
Build Better Technical Recruiting/Selection Capability	11	\$ 222	2.48
Monitor Sales & Tech Rep. Selection Tests	12	\$ 211	9.05
MARGINAL BUT DESIRABLE PROGRAMS			
Implement Executive Search Function	13	\$ 177	1.67
Refine Career Path Guides	14	\$ 110	1.75
Continue National Trend Attitude Surveys	15	\$ 107	1.33
Reevaluate Overall Organization Approach	16	\$ 93	2.37
NOT WORTHWHILE			
Executive Retreat	x	(\$ 450)	n/a
Corporate Jet	x	(\$ 769)	n/a
Savings Plan	x	(\$ 75)	n/a

Source: Cheek, 1973

Products and services with high value delivered in high volume are clearly "stars," the 20% of people and programs that produce 80% of the benefits.

Services with high volume but relatively low value are called "cash cows." Most routine personnel services and training programs fell in this category. First-level supervisor training, for example, was a high volume but "ho-hum" product that reached many people but was not seen as making much of a contribution.

Programs with low value and low demand are called "dogs." Left-over "touchy-feely" services from the 1960s fell in this box.

Services with high potential value but in low demand are called "question marks" or "problem children." These were R&D efforts that could become the stars of the future but presently were in little demand and required time and cash investment to nurture. "Problem children" either grow up to be stars or never leave the high-potential-but-no-performance box and are reclassified as "dogs."

The marketing manager classified her people in these terms. "Question marks" were new hires, bright young people who needed development. "Stars" were persons who were in high demand and commanded high billing rates. "Solid citizens" were reliable workers who performed their jobs but did not add great value to the firm. "Deadwood" were people who did little work and had little potential.

This portfolio analysis led the manager to prune her product line back to emphasize the 20% of the services that provided 80% of the organization's value. Her strategy was to: (1) vigorously promote her stars, both people and programs; (2) support a reasonable level of R&D, nurturing future stars; (3) maintain her cash cows to meet legal requirements and to generate visibility and goodwill among clients she wanted to sell star services to (e.g., productivity methods as a follow-on to supervisory training); and (4) shrink her dog box by eliminating services of low value and demand, and terminating people with low applied and billing rates. She was able to reduce her staff from 40 to 32 persons (at full-cost savings of $280,000) and free remaining people to do more interesting projects that she (and they) claimed significantly increased their morale. By focusing her efforts on her star product—a productivity-improvement course that documented dollar savings—she greatly increased the credibility and visibility of the personnel department in the firm.

FIGURE 6.4
Product/Service Portfolio Analysis

- Pareto distributions: 20% of products/services provide 80% of revenue, value
  80% of products/services provide 20% of revenue, value

- Portfolio analysis graph

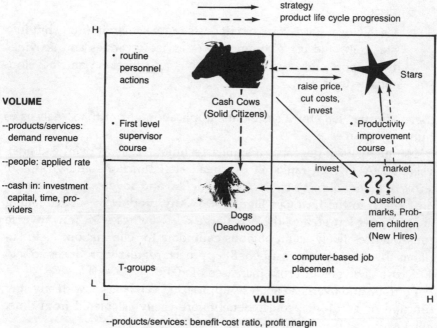

VOLUME

--products/services: demand revenue

--people: applied rate

--cash in: investment capital, time, providers

--products/services: benefit-cost ratio, profit margin

--people: billing rate

--potential, e.g., R&D efforts

--cash out: investment capital or time users

Implications:

- Evaluate your product line and "prune" it rigorously back to 20% that provide 80% of value

  -- <u>dogs</u>: kill (shrink dog box)
  -- <u>stars</u>: invest (expand star box)
  -- <u>?</u>: support a reasonable level of R&D: (nurture future stars); market to increase volume
  -- <u>cows</u>: maintain to generate visibility, goodwill, pay overhead; raise price or cut costs to increase profit

Figure 6.4 summarizes tactics for services and people in each of the portfolio cells.

1. Dogs. Kill low volume, low value services, lay off or retire deadwood

2. (?) problem children. Support and market to increase volume, grow into stars

3. Stars. Invest to expand volume and ability to charge a premium price

4. Cash cows. Raise price or cut costs to raise margin (i.e., shift into star cell), and use "commodity" service revenues and activities to support and train "?" new hires and research and development efforts

(See Odiorne, 1985 for a systematic application of portfolio analysis to human resources.)

Neuman (1975) describes a similar technique called "overhead analysis" (OVA), which ranks all overhead staff functions and groups in terms of potential cost savings (i.e., benefits) and adverse consequences (i.e., costs) to the firm (see Figure 6.5). Any product or service falling in the upper-left area of the box (large cost savings with few adverse consequences likely) is an obvious candidate for elimination. Neuman claims this very simple cost-benefit approach regularly produces 15% to 30% cost savings and profit increases of 100%.

Portfolio and overhead analysis approaches can be used with any staff function or group of people. Benefits are easily calculated from time, head count, and material savings.

Cross-Charge For All Services

Cross-charging or transfer pricing—actually billing other departments in a firm for your group's services or products—has long been standard procedure in manufacturing operations. Department A makes a motor controller. Depatment B makes a motor. Both A and B sell their products to Department C, which assembles a dishwasher or copying machine. Internal cross-charging for knowledge worker products and services—

FIGURE 6.5
Overhead Analysis

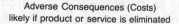

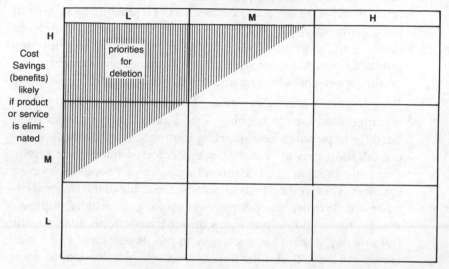

legal, market research, accounting, training, or consulting—is much rarer. It is, however, an excellent method for determining what services actually cost and getting feedback on which services internal clients think are really worth their cost.

Service groups can be set up as "cost centers" with the objective of breaking even, or as "profit centers" with the objective of making money above the cost of service delivery. Either fee-for-service approach makes internal service groups operate as if they were external professional service firms. As will be seen, this can greatly increase their efficiency, effectiveness, and productivity.

Effective cross-charging systems make clients pay what services actually cost and give them maximum freedom to decide whether or not to buy, what services to buy, and whom to buy them from. The following are degrees of "free market" for internal services:

1. *"Totally Free."* A client can buy services inside or outside the firm from whomever he or she chooses. This puts internal legal departments or training groups in direct competition with external law firms, training suppliers, or consulting firms. If the internal group's products are not seen as of equal quality or are not price competitive, it gets immediate feedback when clients go elsewhere. As in any free market system, this forces internal groups to find out what their clients want, improve quality, and become more cost efficient to meet the competition.

2. *Internal Clients Must Buy Inside, but Don't Have to Buy.* Firms wanting to encourage training often charge line groups an overhead fee to pay for a headquarters training department. Each line organization gets a "voucher," or dedicated budget for service (e.g., the right to send a certain number of people to training courses). This method provides some feedback to the training department. If many line people sign up for productivity-improvement courses and no one signs up for transactional analysis, the training department knows where to put its resources and which services to drop. If, despite the overhead charge, line groups don't send anybody to training, the training department has received very pointed feedback about the perceived value of its services. It can be sure that line groups will increasingly lobby to reduce the overhead charges, that is, to cut the training department's budget.

3. *Services Are "Free."* In many firms, human resources services are "free." Nothing, of course, is free. "Free" means that clients are not charged directly for service: human resource costs are buried in overhead. Clients have the choice of not using the service, perhaps giving the service provider some feedback. A more likely outcome is overuse. Free services are like free beer in the park. Free services encourage overuse and lack of accountability as to their real value.

4. *Services Are Mandatory.* This is least desirable. If everyone has to go to training or endure a specific consulting service, the firm gets no feedback at all as to whether the service is perceived as valuable. Mandatory services may be necessary when required by law or policy (e.g., affirmative action programs). Even with man-

datory programs, letting clients select the approach to affirmative action planning, and consultants they wish to work with to develop plans, is likely to result in more responsive and cost-effective service.

Variations on these degrees of free markets in buying internal services are possible. For example, services may be subsidized with service providers cross-charging for some of the real cost of the service. This is better than not cross-charging at all, but has the drawback of the services-are-free approach. Subsidized services not worth their real cost tend to be overused, distorting feedback as to what clients really feel is worthwhile. The subsidized part of the service cost is not free: it is simply buried in overhead, evading accountability for its real value.

Cross-charging for service rapidly "smokes out" which services clients really see as valuable and which they do not. Services clients are not willing to pay for can be deleted and cost-saving benefits claimed.

EXAMPLE. *Benefits of cross-charging in a corporate training center:*

A firm that felt it had a bloated training department started cross-charging for all training courses delivered. Enrollment immediately dropped 40%, and the number of courses offered by the department dropped 50%. By the end of one year, the training department had reduced its budget by 50% and its staff by 75%, saving $6 million. Only courses for which clients were willing to pay competitive rates ($200 a day) continued to be offered. Training staff decreased more than budget and enrollment because the department found it more cost effective to contract with external trainers and training firms for many of the courses offered, minimizing staff on fixed overhead. Most training center employees became purchasers and managers of external service providers. The only trainers left on the staff taught two first-level supervisor and mid-level-manager courses, for which there was high and steady demand.

Some firms are generating revenues and offsetting staff overhead by running professional service groups as profit centers selling services to other firms. *BusinessWeek* (January 16, 1984, p. 54) describes companies that have turned internal staff groups into for-profit consulting firms by "trying to transform staff people who have spent their lives as cost centers deep within the corporate womb into profit centers peddling their expertise to the outside world.'' (*BusinessWeek*, January 16, 1984.) Examples:

> Control Data Corp. has "spun out" 250 members of its corporate staff into a subsidiary called Business Advisors. This free-standing professional service firm provides a range of management consulting services: human resources, job structuring and compensation, marketing and strategic planning studies. Business Advisors employs another 1000 Control Data staff on a parttime basis, and sells its services on a competitive basis to units within the firm and to outside companies. Control Data managers believe free market competition will get them better staff services *and* lower overhead costs.
>
> American Telephone and Telegraph (AT&T) has similarly encouraged its Organizational Effectiveness Group to market strategic planning and organization design services to public and private sector clients. The Organization Effectiveness Group is expected to cover its costs and make a profit, and plans that 70 percent of its revenues will come from external clients within five years.
>
> Polaroid Corp sells human resource consulting, training and management development services.

This strategy of turning internal staff groups into for-profit consulting firms has additional benefits and possible risks for both staff and their parent firms. Advantages for staff include job security, the opportunity to earn more money, and professional growth from exposure to a wider range of organizations and problems. Firms benefit from new ideas staff pick up or develop in their outside consulting work. Possible risks include loss of control of critical services and information—and that staff who discover the market value of their expertise will leave, or pressure their parent firms to give them a share of the professional service firm's profits or equity—or spin them off altogether.

Clients of staff services have numerous options in negotiating fair and efficient charges for service. Clients should resist whenever possible automatic charges for services they use rarely or not at all, especially when charges are based on head count or budget, as opposed to actual problem incidents.

EXAMPLES. *Benefits of resisting automatic service charges:*

A plant that had never had an accident and was located eight minutes from a hospital emergency room was automatically billed $36,000 a year for nursing services. The nurse, who spent most of the day sitting alone in her cubicle reading magazines, had an applied rate of about 10%. Given the plant's accident rate and closeness to the hospital, the $36,000 fixed charge was justifiable neither in terms of services delivered nor in terms of contingency planning. The plant manager negotiated a small retainer of $4000 for a traveling nurse who spoke on employee wellness programs and saved $32,000.

A sales office that had never had a discrimination complaint was charged on a head-count basis $13,000 a year for affirmative action/equal opportunity consulting services. (None had ever been used.) The office negotiated out of this automatic charge by agreeing to pay a small retainer of $1000 per year to help support the corporate equal opportunity consultant but to purchase service on a per-day basis if ever needed.

WORK SIMPLIFICATION

What you can't delete, simplify.

Industrial engineering techniques long used in manufacturing settings can be applied to administrative and service operations. Three very useful methods are (1) baseline productivity metrics, (2) capacity planning staffing tables, and (3) work-flow analyses.

1. Baseline Productivity Metrics. Develop accurate productivity standards for each service or task procedure you perform, revisiting the productivity results measures you identified in Figure 2.6. We have defined productivity as:

Outputs/inputs: one unit of whatever product or service you produce divided by the time (in person-hours or days) it takes you to produce it:

$$\text{productivity} \quad = \quad \frac{1 \text{ unit of a product or service}}{\text{hours (or days) to produce 1 unit}}$$

or

Its reciprocal, *inputs/outputs:* for example, cost per unit output, the cost in time or money it takes you to produce some number of output units in a period of time, divided by the number of output units:

$$\text{cost per unit} = \frac{\text{total dollar cost}}{\text{number of units produced}}$$

$$\text{hours per unit} = \frac{\text{total available hours}}{\text{number of units produced}}$$

Figure 6.6 shows the steps in developing productivity metrics for a five-person career counseling office delivering 94 sessions per week.

    a. *Establish your baseline productivity index* in hours, days or cost per unit of service delivery. Pick a typical baseline period (a week, month, or quarter). Divide the total number of hours you or your work group had available to work during the

FIGURE 6.6
Productivity Metrics: Hours Per Unit (HPU)

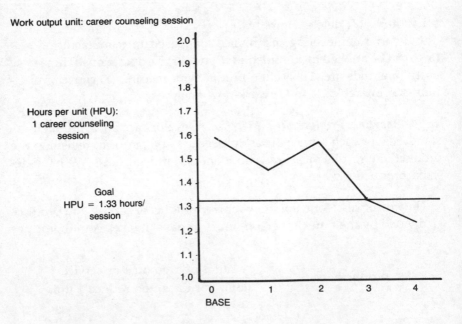

FIGURE 6.6
continued

		BASELINE	REPORTING PERIOD			
		A	B	C	D	E
		0	1	2	3	4
INPUT	(1) Applied rate	.75	.75	.75	.75	.75
	(2) Headcount	5	5	5	4.5	4
	(3) Available hours/person/week (1) * 40 hrs/week	30	30	30	30	30
	(4) Available hours (2) * (3)	150	150	150	135	120
OUTPUT	(5) Units of work output/week (counseling sessions)	94	102	96	98	92
PRODUCTIVITY	(6) Hours per unit: (4)/(5)	1.60	1.47	1.56	1.38	1.30
	(7) Productivity goal	1.33	1.33	1.33	1.33	1.33
	(8) % Variance from goal ((6) - (7))/(7)	20.3%	10.5%	17.2%	3.4%	-2.2%
	(9) % Improvement over baseline |(A6 - 6)/A6	0	8.1%	2.5%	13.8%	18.8%
	(10) Headcount at productivity goal ((5) * (7))/(3)	4.2	4.5	4.2	4.3	4.1
	(11) Headcount over goal (2) - (10)	.8	.5	.8	.7	-.1
COST BENEFIT	(12) Average salary	$25,000	$25,000	$25,000	$25,000	$25,000
	(13) Full cost/week ((12) x 3 x (2))/52	$7211	$7211	$7211	$6490	$5769
	(14) Cost/unit (13)/(5)	76.71	70.70	75.11	66.23	62.71
	(15) Saving over baseline cost/unit ((15) - (15A))	0	6.01	1.60	10.48	14.00
	(16) Saving/period (5) x (15)	0	$615	$154	$1027	$1288

215

period (i.e., total hours paid, less vacation, holiday, sick, and other unapplied time) by the number of units of service you delivered (e.g., compensation plans, OD efforts, training programs, etc.):

$$\text{hours per unit (HPU)} = \frac{\text{hours paid in period} \times \text{applied rate} \times \text{number of people}}{\text{units of work delivered}}$$

Thus for the career counseling group:

$$\text{hours per unit (HPU)} = \frac{40 \text{ hours/week} \times 75\% \times 5 \text{ people} = 150 \text{ hrs/wk}}{94 \text{ sessions}} = \frac{1.60 \text{ hours/}}{\text{session}}$$

   b. *Establish a productivity goal.* For example, the career counseling group figured that at an applied rate of 75%, counselors working 8 hours per day should deliver .75 × 8 hours = 6 hours of sessions per day. The group's hour per unit productivity goal = 8 hours/6 sessions = 1.33 hours per session.

   c. *Track HPU productivity in following periods* against the HPU productivity goal, as shown in Figure 6.6. Percent productivity improvement can be calculated for any period by subtracting HPU for the period from the baseline HPU and dividing by the baseline:

$$\text{percent productivity increase} = \frac{\text{HPU baseline} - \text{HPU in period}}{\text{HPU baseline}}$$

For example, in Figure 6.6, by the fourth period the career counseling group's HPU had bettered its goal and reduced its HPU to 1.3 hours per session. The counselors' percent increase in productivity was:

$$\text{percent productivity improvement} = \frac{1.60 \text{ (baseline)} - 1.30 \text{ (4th period HPU)}}{1.60 \text{ (baseline HPU)}} = 18.8\%$$

You can use productivity metrics to calculate other useful figures. *Optimum head count*, a key number for capacity planning and staffing, equals work unit volume per week (or other period) × HPU productivity goal divided by hours available per person per week (or other period):

$$\text{optimum head count} = \frac{\text{units/period} \times \text{hours per unit (HPU)}}{\text{paid hours/period/person}}$$

For example, if the average work load is 96 sessions per week, the career counseling group should employ:

$$\frac{96 \text{ sessions/week} \times 1.33 \text{ hours/unit}}{40 \text{ paid hours/person/week}} = 3.2 \text{ people}$$

This suggests that at five people the counseling group was overstaffed 5 − 3.2 = 1.2 people.

Cost-savings benefits can be calculated by comparing the actual cost per unit during a period with the baseline cost per unit. For example, if career counselors' average salary was $25,000, the group's full cost per week was $25,000 per person per year × 3 (overhead factor) × 5 people—52 weeks = $7211 per week. If during the baseline period the group delivered 94 sessions per week, baseline cost per session = $7211/94 sessions = $76.71 per session. By the fourth period, the counseling had reduced its weekly full cost to $5769 per week by reducing head count one person. In this period the group delivered 92 sessions per week, so cost per session was $5769/92 sessions = $62.71 per session, a saving of $76.71 (baseline session cost) − $62.71 = $14 per session × 92 sessions/week = $1288 per week.

Even when the time it takes to deliver a service varies widely (e.g., nonstandard staff studies or computer programming projects) HPU productivity metrics can be used. For example, a manager of eight computer programmers thought it would be impossible to develop productivity metrics for programmers because projects varied so much in scope: "Some take less than a day, others take months." In fact, she found that her eight programmers, working at a 75% gross applied rate (75% × 260 days per year ÷ 12 months = 16.25 days per month), had completed 34 projects in a three-month period. An average project took:

$$\frac{8 \text{ people} \times 16.25 \text{ days/month} \times 3 \text{ months}}{34 \text{ projects}} = 11.5 \text{ days/project}$$

In this case "days per project" instead of "hours per unit" served as a beginning productivity metric for this group. The programming manager was subsequently able to break large "many-month" projects into smaller, more predictable sub-project units and develop quite accurate productivity measures and estimating standards for planning projects. (Brooks, 1982, provides an excellent discussion of computer programming productivity metrics.)

Breaking big projects into their smallest common work units can help you develop productivity measures for complex services. For example, a training company offered a complex course that included five tests. Steps in delivering the course included mailing prework packages to participants and scoring and profiling test data. Putting the prework packages together took five hours per course, and each course was attended by an average of 20 participants. One test took 30 minutes per participant to score and profile, and three other tests took 15 minutes each per participant. (The fifth test was self-scoring.) The training company's test division wanted productivity metrics but didn't know what work unit to use—one course, one participant, or one test.

The best approach is to use "tests" as the smallest common work unit and build metrics for participants and courses from those for tests.

If prework for a course of 20 participants receiving five tests per participant (i.e., 100 tests total) takes five hours, the HPU for each test is

$$\frac{5 \text{ hours} \times 60 \text{ minutes/hour}}{100 \text{ tests}} = \frac{300 \text{ minutes}}{100 \text{ tests}}$$

$$= 3 \text{ minutes or } 3/60 = .05 \text{ hour per test.}$$

Scoring and profiling takes 30 minutes per participant for one test. Three tests take 15 minutes/participant: $3 \times 15 = 45$ minutes per participant. Total test prework plus scoring and profiling takes 3 minutes (prework) + 75 minutes (scoring and profiling) = 78 minutes (1.3 hours) per participant.

The training company now has a metric it can use to track productivity for courses, participants, and two types of tests. For example, a 20-participant course requires 20 people $\times$ 1.3 hours/person = 26 hours $\div$ 8 hours/day = 3.25 person-days to put together. If the company gets an order for 600 participants or 30 courses, it knows it must hire 3.25 days per course × 30 courses = 97.5 person-days (e.g., five temporaries for four weeks, 20 days × 5 people = 100 person-days), to deliver this volume of work.

Costing of a few wage and salary compensation plans, organizational development efforts, employee relations counseling sessions, or other services can tell you how long an average service should take and cost. This enables you to track and give people feedback on service delivery productivity. People and services that are consistently over budget are easily identified and corrected. Reduction in average costs for (over-budget) projects and services is an easily calculated productivity benefit.

2. Capacity Planning (Capacity Utilization). Knowing the time per unit of service enables you to plan and budget accurately for future service demand. If you know that it takes 30 hours to recruit an engineer and you have 50 positions to fill, you know you need to contract for or hire 1500 hours of recruiter time (about one additional full-time person for a standard 2080-hour year and 75% applied (2080 hours × 75% = 1560 available working hours). Forecasting service demand in terms of professional hours or days can help you optimize your staffing inventory.

Figure 6.7 shows a capacity planning/staffing table for the career-counseling-group productivity metrics developed in Figure 6.6. At an HPU of 1.33 hours per session, a counselor paid 40 hours per week can deliver 40 hours/1.33 hours per unit (session) = 30 sessions. The group may want to have one counselor available at all times, a "fixed" staffing requirement. Each additional 15 sessions demanded per week would cause the group to add an additional half-time person. In fact, the step increments could be less than 15 sessions or one half-time person. Following the "rent-versus-buy-people" principle, the group would be best off contracting for additional hours of counselor time as needed from an outside agency.

Capacity planning enables you to plan (and justify) additions to staff on a rational basis: work-load volume. Conversely, it gives you a rational basis on which to resist adding people to fixed overhead if managers requesting additional staff cannot show a need for them based on direct relation to work load.

Sources of productivity metric and capacity planning standards include

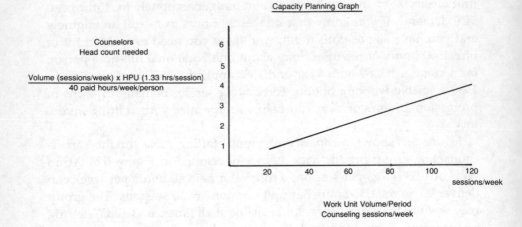

FIGURE 6.7
Capacity Planning Staffing Table and Graph

Staff requirement = $\dfrac{\text{work unit volume/period} \times \text{HPU standard}}{\text{paid hours/period/person}}$

Work unit: Career Counseling Sessions/Week

Capacity Planning Table

	If volume increases		Staff requirement is
	From	To	
Fixed requirement	0	30 sessions/week	1.0 person
	31	45	1.5
	46	60	2.0
	61	75	2.5
	76	90	3.0
	91	105	3.5
	106	120	4.0

Capacity Planning Graph

Counselors
Head count needed

$\dfrac{\text{Volume (sessions/week)} \times \text{HPU (1.33 hrs/session)}}{40 \text{ paid hours/week/person}}$

Work Unit Volume/Period
Counseling sessions/week

Your own service group's baseline or budgeted time and cost to provide the service

Performance of similar units within your own firm

Key competitors' performance

Industry averages

What external providers of the service would charge you for it

The best place to start is to get your own baseline data by costing three to five service delivery efforts and/or averaging data from past periods to find your average productivity cost and staff requirements per unit output.

Industry and competitive data are available from trade associations, such as survey reports published by the American Management Association and the American Society for Training and Development, trade press magazines and newsletters, and the general business press (e.g., *The Wall Street Journal*, *BusinessWeek*, and *Fortune*).

Data on competitors are available from proprietary surveys sold by various market-research and strategic-planning firms that specialize in competitor analysis.

For an external check on your efficiency, ask external providers of your product or service what they would charge for a training program, wage and salary compensation plan, computer program, market research study, or the like (i.e, do a make-versus-buy analysis). The average of three external service provider bids will give you a good fix on the market value of your service. If you provide internal services more cheaply than they could be bought outside, let this fact be widely known. If not, increase applied rates and productivity until you are cost competitive.

3. Work-Flow Analyses. A basic productivity-improvement technique is to flowchart all steps involved in delivering a service or administrative procedure. Figure 6.8 shows the symbols used to diagram work flows and the questions to ask about each step. Identify the time and dollar cost of each step; then see if you can simplify the work flow by deleting unnecessary steps, saving time and the dollar value of that time. Question each step in the work flow to see if it can be cut or made more efficient: Why do it at all? Can it be changed or combined with other steps? Can it be done by a less expensive person? The most time consuming and expensive steps, especially those that involve the time of higher-level, more expensive people, should be looked at hardest.

Often, simply laying out a work flow enables people to identify duplicated or unnecessary steps, for example, costly high-level approvals that delay work and take responsibility away from lower-level people whose job it is to see that things are done right.

A before-and-after flowchart of the steps required to approve an employee's expense account at Intel is shown in Figure 6.9. Intel was able to cut the time required to process an expense account from 23 minutes over a four-week period to 16 minutes over two days, a productivity increase of 30.4%. Such improvements may seem trivial, but small sav-

FIGURE 6.8
Symbols Used in Work Flow Diagrams

OPERATION	TRANSPORTATION	DELAY	CONTROL	STORAGE	DECISION
• Fill out a form	• Place document in basket	• Wait for signature	• Verify report	• Place in paper file	• Sort complete work from incomplete --If complete, pass on --If incomplete, send back to be redone (often combined with ● Operation or ■ control step)
• Look up a customer #	• Pass paperwork to another person	• Wait for approval	• Approve expenditure	• Input to computer file	
• Make entry in a log	• Walk to copy machine	• Wait in line	• Authorize requisition		
• Type a memo	• Deliver a package	• Wait for mail pick-up	• Check for completeness		

(DECISION symbol: If OK... / If Not...)

Questions to ask about each step:

QUESTION		ACTION INDICATED
• What is it and why do it?		Eliminate
• Where is it being done? Why there?		Place
• When/how often is it done?	Combine	
Why? Needed this often?	or	Time, Sequence, Frequency
• Who does it? Why?	Change	
Can a less costly person do it?		Person
• How is it done? and Why this way?		Simplify
Can it be shortened, simplified?		

ings in high-volume, routine administrative procedures can add up fast. The full cost of $12,000 per year of clerk's time is $12,000/year × 3 (overhead multiplier) ÷ 124,800 minutes/year = 29 cents/minute. A seven-minute saving per voucher × .29 = $2.03/voucher. Intel processes 33,000 vouchers per month × 12 months = 396,000 vouchers per year. At $2.03

FIGURE 6.9

Before and After Steps in Processing Expense Vouchers

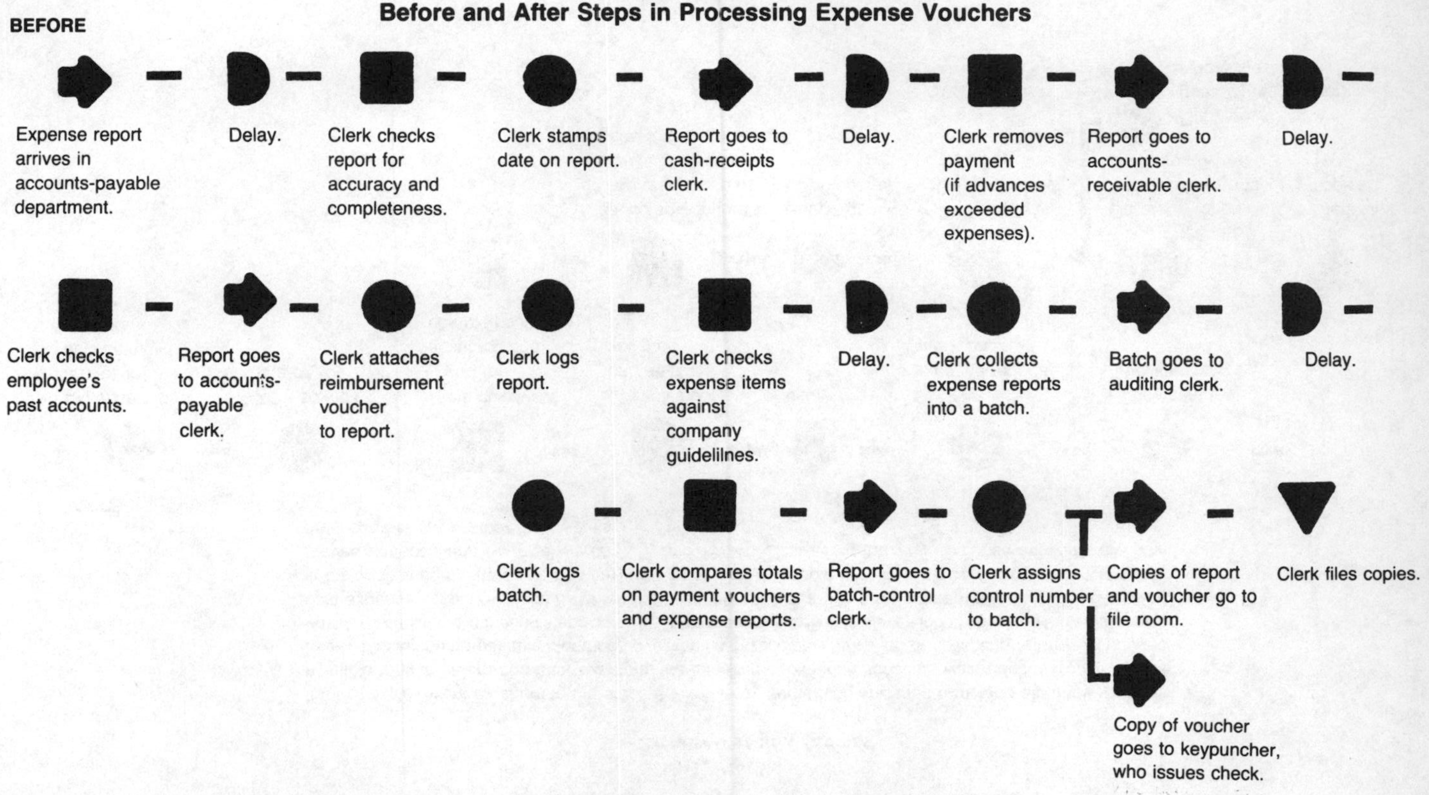

BEFORE

Expense report arrives in accounts-payable department.

Delay.

Clerk checks report for accuracy and completeness.

Clerk stamps date on report.

Report goes to cash-receipts clerk.

Delay.

Clerk removes payment (if advances exceeded expenses).

Report goes to accounts-receivable clerk.

Delay.

Clerk checks employee's past accounts.

Report goes to accounts-payable clerk.

Clerk attaches reimbursement voucher to report.

Clerk logs report.

Clerk checks expense items against company guidelines.

Delay.

Clerk collects expense reports into a batch.

Batch goes to auditing clerk.

Delay.

Clerk logs batch.

Clerk compares totals on payment vouchers and expense reports.

Report goes to batch-control clerk.

Clerk assigns control number to batch.

Copies of report and voucher go to file room.

Clerk files copies.

Copy of voucher goes to keypuncher, who issues check.

223

FIGURE 6.9 continued

The Expense-Account Express

Intel simplifies work by charting the steps it takes to do something and then removing as many steps as possible. In this before-and-after example, the handling of expense accounts was reduced from 25 steps to 14. The accounts-payable clerk took over the cash-receipts clerk's job of collecting refunds or unused traveler's checks, eliminating steps 5 and 7. The accounts-receivable clerk's job of checking the employee's past expense accounts (steps 8, 10, and 11) was eliminated; another department already did it. Checking items against company guidelines (14) was judged more trouble than it was worth. Logging batches (19) proved unnecessary. Four delays (2, 6, 9, and 18) were cut along the way. Expense accounts are now processed in days rather than weeks.

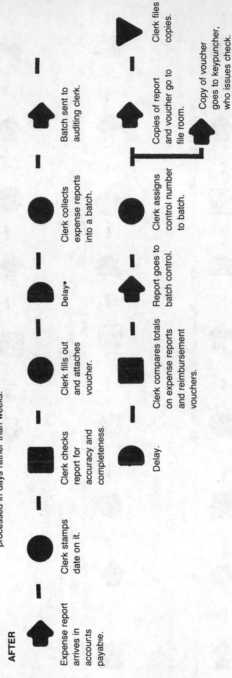

AFTER

Expense report arrives in accounts payable.

Clerk stamps date on it.

Clerk checks report for accuracy and completeness.

Delay.

Clerk fills out and attaches voucher.

Delay.

Clerk collects expense reports into a batch.

Batch sent to auditing clerk.

Clerk compares totals on expense reports and reimbursement vouchers.

Report goes to batch control.

Clerk assigns control number to batch.

Copies of report and voucher go to file room.

Copy of voucher goes to keypuncher, who issues check.

Clerk files copies.

per voucher, Intel gained $803,880 total savings benefits per year. Intel was able to reduce its accounts-payable staff from 71 to 51 people (Main, 1983; Bolte, 1982).

Work simplification flowcharting can be used to cost justify investments in computers and other capital equipment that simplify work flows.

EXAMPLE. *Benefits of computerizing personnel information:*

A major computer company did not use its own computers in managing its personnel system. Instead it had 165 personnel clerks entering an average of 50 data changes per week on sextuplicate carbon-paper forms. Figure 6.10 shows the inefficient flow process required to change any employee information item (e.g., a change in address). Personnel specialists filled forms out by hand, mailed one copy to corporate headquarters, and filed other copies in special files (e.g, equal opportunity logs) and a final copy in a master file. Each change took 11.3 minutes, which, at personnel specialists' full cost of 40 cents per minute, meant each change cost $4.52.

The firm gave the 165 personnel clerks computer terminals, which enabled them to enter data directly into a computerized personnel master file, eliminating all paper forms, physical files, and mailings. Each data entry took 3.8 minutes with the terminal, which at 40 cents per minute meant that changes now cost $1.52. The net saving was $3 per change × 50 changes per week × 50 weeks per year × 165 clerks = $1,238,000. Each terminal cost $5000 ($3000/year operating, transmission, maintenance, and $2000/year amortization of the system's development costs) × 165 terminals = $825,000. The cost benefit of work simplification by computerizing the system was 1.5 to one, or a return on investment of 50%.

Don't Write

The simplest work-simplification method is to save time and money by avoiding writing whenever possible. As shown in Chapter 4, "Calculating Benefits: Basic Strategies," written material invariably costs you twice: the time it takes to write something and the time it takes others to read and respond to it. People can talk and listen at a rate of 150 words

FIGURE 6.10
Work Flow Chart: Personnel Data Entry
After Computerization

WORK FLOW CHART

PAGE _1_ of _1_

DATE _____

ANALYST _____

TASK _____

PERSON 1*Cost/Min. = Salary/Yr. _____ × FCMLTPR _____ ÷ 124,800 min./yr. = $ _____ /min.

PERSON 2*Cost/Min. = Salary/Yr. _____ × FCMLTPR _____ ÷ 124,800 min./yr. = $ _____ /min.

PERSON 3*Cost/Min. = Salary/Yr. _____ × FCMLTPR _____ ÷ 124,800 min./yr. = $ _____ /min.

PERSON 4*Cost/Min. = Salary/Yr. _____ × FCMLTPR _____ ÷ 124,800 min./yr. = $ _____ /min.

STEPS: PROPOSED "With Computer"

#	Step	NOTES	QUANTITY	DISTANCE IN FEET	TIME IN MINUTES (A)	COST/MIN. (B)	COST = A × B (C)
1.	CHANGE PRESENTED TO PSS						
2.	PSS DULLS PROFILE ON TERMINAL SCREEN	"FILE" ELECTRONICALLY: ELIMINATE WALKING, PAPER FILES			.3	.40	.12
3.	PSS ENTERS CHANGE ON SCREEN	ENTER ON SCREEN, NOT PAPER! → FEWER ERRORS			1.0	.40	.40
4.	CHANGE UPDATED ON PMF FILE INSTANTLY	NO DELAYS - INSTANT: ELIMINATE PAPER, MAIL, DATA ENTRY→FEWER ERRORS					
5.	PSS FILES CHANGE IN DISK SUSODSE FILE				.5	.40	.20
6.	DELAY						
7.	PMF AUDIT REPORT RUN ON DATA						
8.	DELAY	EEO LOG MAINTAINED ELECTRONICALLY AUTOMATICALLY					
9.	PSS PRINT AUDIT REPORT ON TERMINAL	NO DATA CENTER MAILING COSTS					
10.	PSS CHECKS AUDIT REPORT FOR ERRORS	COMPARISON DONE ELECTRONICALLY → FEWER ERRORS			2.0	.40	.80
11.	IF ERROR REPEAT STEPS ② - ⑩			0%			
12.	IF OK: END	NO PAPER, NO FILING!					
13.							
14.							
15.	TOTAL			3.8		1.52	
16.							
17.							
18.							
19.							
20.							

TOTAL (A) PRESENT .... 11.3 .... 4.52

— (B) PROPOSED .... 3.8 .... 1.52

= (C) DIFFERENCE .... 7.5 .... 3.00

ANALYSIS → ACTION
ELIMINATE COMBINE PLACE SEQUENCE PERSON IMPROVE
WHAT WHERE WHEN WHO HOW

STEPS: PRESENT

#		FLOW DECISION	DISTANCE IN FEET	TIME IN MINUTES (A)	COST/MIN. (B)	COST = A × B (C)
1.						
2.						
...						
20.						

TOTAL (A) PRESENT

— (B) PROPOSED

= (C) DIFFERENCE

WORK FLOW CHART

PAGE 1 of 2

DATE _____
ANALYST LMS
TASK PERSONNEL STATUS DATA CHANGE

STEPS: PRESENT

PERSON 1 Cost/Min. = Salary/Yr. $16,500 × FCMLTPR _____
PERSON 2 Cost/Min. = Salary/Yr. _____ × FCMLTPR _____
PERSON 3 Cost/Min. = Salary/Yr. _____ × FCMLTPR _____
PERSON 4 Cost/Min. = Salary/Yr. _____ × FCMLTPR _____

STEPS: PROPOSED

PERSON 1 Cost/Min. = Salary/Yr. _____ × FCMLTPR 3 ÷ 124,800 min./yr. = $ .40 /min.
PERSON 2 Cost/Min. = Salary/Yr. _____ × FCMLTPR _____ ÷ 124,800 min./yr. = $ /min.
PERSON 3 Cost/Min. = Salary/Yr. _____ × FCMLTPR _____ ÷ 124,800 min./yr. = $ /min.
PERSON 4 Cost/Min. = Salary/Yr. _____ × FCMLTPR _____ ÷ 124,800 min./yr. = $ /min.

ANALYSIS — ELIMINATE, COMBINE, PLACE, SEQUENCE, PERSON, IMPROVE — WHAT, WHERE, WHO, WHEN, HOW

Step	STEPS: PRESENT "Without Computer"	DISTANCE IN FEET	QUANTITY	TIME IN MINUTES (B)	COST/MIN.	COST = A×B (C)	NOTES
1	DATA CHANGE PRESENTED TO PSS						
2	PSS WALKS TO FILE		1.0	.40	.40		
3	PSS PULLS PROFILE						
4	PSS WALKS TO DESK		4.0	.40	1.60		
5	PSS ENTERS CHANGE		.5	.40	.20		
6	PSS PUTS PROFILE IN "OUT" BOX						
7	PSS PUT PROFILE COPY IN SUSPENSE FILE		20%/÷2	.40	.08		*20% OF CHANGES
8	DATA IN EDD LOG						
9	DELAY						
10	PSS MAILS PROFILE COPY TO DATA CENTER		.1	.40	.04		THURS. NOON
11	DELAY @ DATA CENTER						24 HOURS
12	DATA INPUT BY EDP CLERK						
13	DELAY						0–5 DAYS — DATA CENTER COSTS?
14	PMF FILE UPDATE AND AUDIT REPORT PRINTED						
15	DELAY						
16	PMF AUDIT REPORT TO PSS						
17	DELAY						5–14 DAYS
18	PSS RECEIVES PMF AUDIT REPORT						
19	PSS PULLS SUSPENSE FILE		4.0	.40	1.60		
20	PSS COMPARE PROFILE COPY IN PMF AUDIT						

TOTAL (A) PRESENT
– (B) PROPOSED
= (C) DIFFERENCE

227

FIGURE 6.10 continued
Work Flow Chart: Personnel Data Entry
Before Computerization

WORK FLOW CHART

PAGE _2_ of _2_

DATE _____

ANALYST _LMS_

TASK _PERSONNEL STATUS DATA CHANGE_

PERSON 1° Cost/Min. = Salary/Yr. _____ ÷ 124,800 min./yr. = $ _____ /min.
PERSON 2° Cost/Min. = Salary/Yr. _____ ÷ 124,800 min./yr. = $ _____ /min.
PERSON 3° Cost/Min. = Salary/Yr. _____ ÷ 124,800 min./yr. = $ _____ /min.
PERSON 4° Cost/Min. = Salary/Yr. _____ ÷ 124,800 min./yr. = $ _____ /min.

PERSON 1° Cost/Min. = Salary/Yr. _____ × FCMLTPR
PERSON 2° Cost/Min. = Salary/Yr. _____ × FCMLTPR
PERSON 3° Cost/Min. = Salary/Yr. _____ × FCMLTPR
PERSON 4° Cost/Min. = Salary/Yr. _____ × FCMLTPR

STEPS: PRESENT — "Without Computer"

Step	Description	Quantity	Time in Minutes (A × B)	Cost/Min. (B)	Cost = A × B (C)
1.	IF ERROR, REPEAT STEPS ⑤ ⑳	9%	.089	.40	.36
2.	IF OK: PSS FILES PROFILE	1.5	.40	.60	
3.					
9.	TOTAL W/O "FAIL"	11.3	.40	4.52	
10.	TOTAL W/ "FAIL"				4.88

TOTAL Ⓐ PRESENT _____ 11.3
Ⓑ PROPOSED _____
= Ⓒ DIFFERENCE _____

STEPS: PROPOSED

NOTES:
ERRORS = 4.5/50/WK = 9%
COST FAIL = 9.8 MIN × .40 = $3.92

TOTAL Ⓐ PRESENT _____
Ⓑ PROPOSED _____
= Ⓒ DIFFERENCE _____

© 1985 McBer and Company, Boston, MA 02167

per minute. At best, they can write only 30 words per minute—and this is before word-processing, correction, and other paper-producing and paper-shuffling time is taken into account.

Cutting out paperwork can produce major savings. Firms that have mounted paperwork-reduction campaigns as simple as having managers identify the ten most useless pieces of paper they receive each week, and deleting same, have documented savings of 30% to 50%. For example, Intel found that it took 95 steps and 12 pieces of paper to order a mechanical pencil worth $2.79. At roughly .29 per minute per step, this paperwork cost $27.55, or ten times the cost of the pencil! Using work-simplification and paperwork-reduction techniques, Intel cut this process to eight steps and one piece of paper (Main, 1981).

EXAMPLE. *Benefits in the "we won't write" consulting firm:*

A Boston consulting firm is famous for its rule "We will not write." This firm reportedly has a ratio of professionals to support staff of 10 to 1. (By contrast, most professional service firms have a ratio of roughly one to one). A visitor invariably asks: "How do you get the work out? How do you write letters to clients? Proposals for work? Final reports? How do you communicate with each other?"

The answer: The most basic policy of this firm is: *we will not write anything under any circumstances to anybody*. We don't write letters to clients. We make oral proposals and final reports. If a client wants to tape record our presentation, have it transcribed by its word-processing department, and go through the rounds of producing drafts, correcting typos, reformatting, duplicating, and circulating a written document, we say they can go right ahead. Since most consultants are on the road and can't talk face to face, we talk with one another on the phone. You can call anyone anywhere in the world, and the time you'll spend even with international phone charges will be vastly less than the time it takes you to write a memo and your colleagues to read that memo.

Clients are sold on the cost benefits of this approach. For example, we can write you a final report, but it will cost you five days of time at $1500 per day = $7500, plus another five days of secretarial support at $250 per day, a total of $8750—and you'll get the written report two weeks after the project. Alternatively, we can make an oral report two days after the project ends. You'll save $8750 and get the results two weeks sooner. The client saves time and money, and the consultants transfer to the client (assuming the client wants it at all) the task of grinding out a report and paying the overhead costs. Both client and consultant get a higher level of service.

Optimize Levels of Service

Many internal service groups "overserve" because they do not have criteria for the optimum level of service. The strategy here is to define measurable criteria for when a service has accomplished its objective, then work to minimize input time and cost to meet these objective criteria.

> **EXAMPLE.** *Benefits of reducing training time for service representatives:*

A copying-machine firm had an eight-week course for training service people. Each week of training cost $1300 per trainee (school costs, trainee salaries, and per diem). The course included hands-on experience in fixing copiers and lots of nice-to-know theory (e.g., the physics of light reflection in fiber optics and the thermodynamics of fusing toner particulates) not directly related to fixing simple mechanical problems.

The firm knew that ten machine "bugs" accounted for 80% of all service calls. The cost of the service call had three parts:

1. *Call Duration*: the cost of the time it takes a service rep to fix a machine, including travel time.

2. *Call Frequency*: the number of times a service rep has to return to get the machine fixed right.

3. *Replacement Parts*: poorly trained fixers tend to replace too many parts (e.g., an entire $400 motor unit, as a result of not realizing the problem is a 50 cent solenoid on top of the motor).

To find the optimum level of training for service reps, the firm developed a criterion referenced instruction (CRI) test. It set up ten dead copiers, each with one of the ten most common bugs. On Friday afternoon of each week of training, each trainee was asked to fix as many of the bugs as he or she could. (Instructors stood by to "rebug" fixed machines as trainees rotated among the machines.)

Figure 6.11 shows the learning curve of trainees in terms of cost per simulated service call over the eight weeks of training. At the end of the first week, costs were very high. Trainees either could not fix the machines or could fix them only after a lot of time poring over manuals and figuring out the problem by themselves. By the end of the fourth week, however, trainees were about 80% efficient in fixing the machines. The additional four weeks of training provided very little "value added" in terms of reducing the cost per service call.

The firm decided that the training time for service reps could be cut in half. Whatever else they needed to learn about fixing copiers they

FIGURE 6.11
Optimum Training for Equipment
Service People

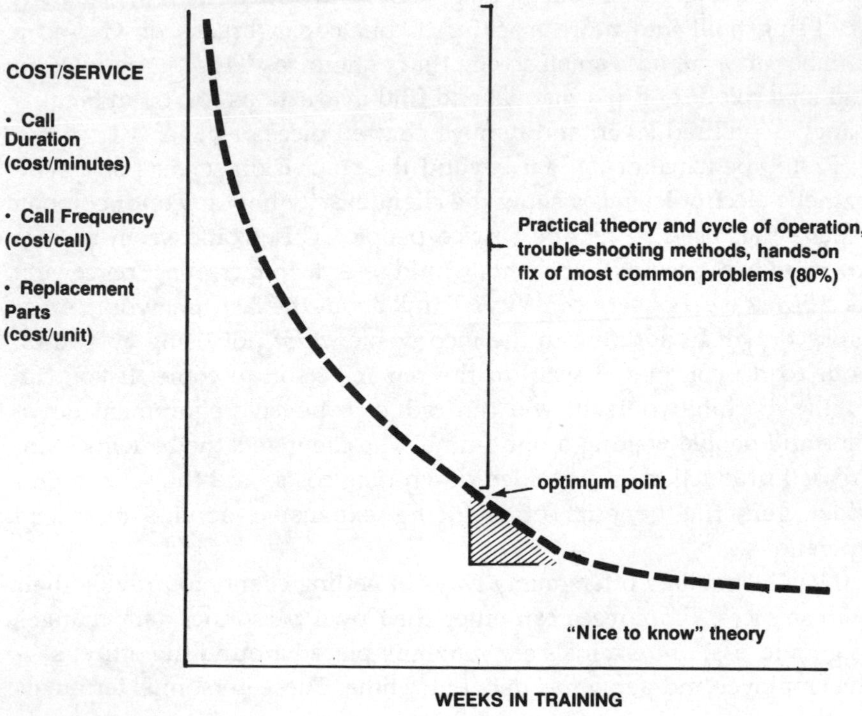

COST/SERVICE

• Call
Duration
(cost/minutes)

• Call Frequency
(cost/call)

• Replacement
Parts
(cost/unit)

Practical theory and cycle of operation, trouble-shooting methods, hands-on fix of most common problems (80%)

optimum point

"Nice to know" theory

WEEKS IN TRAINING

could learn on the job from experienced co-workers. (The firm also changed the course to emphasize practical theory and cycle of operation, hands-on troubleshooting, and fixing of the ten most common copier problems.) The firm trained 300 service reps a year. Cutting the training program from eight to four weeks saved 300 people × $1300 per week training cost × 4 weeks = $1,560,000.

Identifying the minimum level of service needed to accomplish an objective (i.e., the "point of diminishing returns") can save money by focusing, shortening, or simplifying many training and consulting services. However, optimum level of service analysis requires clearly defined results criteria for products and services (Sasser, Olsen, and Wychoff, 1978).

Delegate Service to the Client

One of the most cost-effective ways to increase level of service is to get the client to do it. For example, diagnostics and how-to-fix-it instructions are being built into more machines. Your copier breaks down and a number appears on a small screen that announces "16B." You look up 16B on a rolodex or in a manual and find instructions to "open breaker panel C, pull red lever, and remove charred piece of paper."

Prototype machines go far beyond this: television screens and sympathetic electronic voices show the client exactly how to conduct many repairs that used to require service people. This would seem to be a lower level of service that clients would resent. In fact, most perceive it as a *higher* level of service. Why? Think about the last time your copier broke down. In addition to the inconvenience of not being able to do your work, you had to wait for the repair person to come. If you can fix the machine yourself, you can reduce expensive equipment down time and people-waiting-around-time. The client gets the benefits of increased production and avoided down-time costs, and the service provider gets the benefits of reducing expensive service overhead operations.

New technology offers many ways of getting clients to provide their own services. Employees can enter their own personnel data changes (e.g., address) on terminals conveniently placed around the office, saving employee and personnel data-entry time. These personnel terminals can also provide a wide variety of information and referral services—for example, by explaining employees' medical benefits, describing available training courses and tuition-reimbursement policies, and scheduling appointments for employees to get services on the spot.

JOB-SHOP PRODUCTION METHODS

Increases in service delivery productivity can also be achieved by job-shop production management methods. These methods include work-flow scheduling and organization, and standardization of products.

Figure 6.12 summarizes the differences between job-shop and assembly-line production. Job shops have uneven demands for services and often deliver nonstandard custom products produced by individual contributors, who work independently in somewhat fragmented systems.

Job shops are made more productive by running them more like assembly lines, where work loads are balanced and standard products are delivered by teams coordinated to work on concurrent tasks. The great service-business success stories are firms that figured out how to turn job-shop service operations into assembly lines. The classic example is McDonalds' "technocratic hamburger," cooked not one at a time on demand but by the hundreds on assembly lines planned down to the centimeter a spatula moves (Levitt, 1972).

Scheduling

Service groups must work to balance work loads, avoiding swings from times of too little work (causing expensive unapplied, "sitting around waiting doing nothing" time) and too much work (causing expensive overtime, quality problems, sickness, absenteeism, and turnover from burnout). Flexible staffing from a pool of "rented" temporary workers off fixed overhead can minimize work-load fluctuation costs. Effective marketing can create an optimum backlog to ensure that people have a steady level of work.

Firms can create an "internal backlog" of high-priority unapplied activities like long-range marketing, professional development, R&D, and staff projects to occupy people who lack billable work. Have contin-

FIGURE 6.12
Job Shop Production Methods

Job Shops	Assembly Lines	Productivity Methods
• uneven demands for service	• level, predictable balanced work flows	• balance work loads - good planning and scheduling - flexible staffing: "rent" temporary workers - internal backlog: R&D, marketing, writing - market to increase backlog
• non-standard custom tailored "one off" products	• standard products	• modularize, "boiler-plate" products
• individual contributors, independent production	• team production	• use matrix teams to minimize interface losses
• fragmented production process	• linear production process	• plan concurrent work • stay small

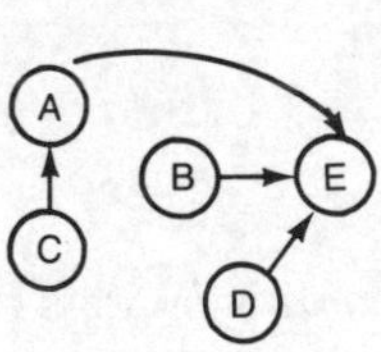

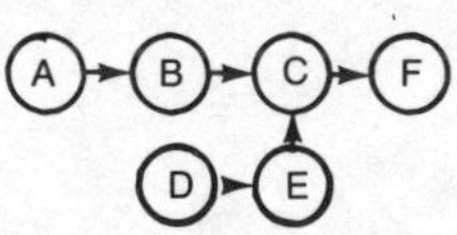

gency plans for use of personnel down time, at least for personnel you want to keep and not lay off.

Organization

In production systems inefficiencies occur (you lose time and money) at points of interface when one group of people has to "hand off" their part of a delivery effort to another group—for example, design engineers to manufacturing, or curriculum writers to trainers. Job-shop professionals tend to be independent, individual contributors who "do their own thing" without much attention to coordination or teamwork.

Interface losses are minimized by organizing work by matrix teams—groups of people representing all the skills needed to complete a project, who stay with the project from start to finish.

EXAMPLE. *Benefits of reducing learning-curve time in developing training programs:*

Many military and high-tech organizations use the "Instructional Systems Development" (ISD) method of producing training courses (Branson, Rayner, and Cox, 1975). The ISD system looks like a logical set of steps for producing a course: (1) task analysis/needs assessment; (2) course design; (3) course development (curriculum writing); (4) training; and (5) evaluation. In fact, ISD usually creates inefficient bureaucratic work flows because separate teams of specialists spring up to claim each step in the process. (In some military and civil service organizations task analysts and course designers actually have different job classifications.)

Interface losses in the ISD work flow are shown in Figure 6.13. When the analysis team starts, it knows nothing about the task. Over some period of time doing the necessary research, this team becomes fully productive but loses the learning-curve time indicated by the shaded area in Figure 6.13.

The analysis team "hands off" the project to the course design team, which also starts by knowing nothing about the task. The analysis team usually spends a fair amount of time at the end of its labor writing long memoranda and describing its findings to the design team. The design team must learn what the analysis team has learned and usually spends a lot of time meeting, briefing, orienting, arguing, and reading memos, while team members try to figure what the data really mean.

Over some period of time the design team also becomes fully productive, but it too suffers the learning-curve loss indicated by the shaded area. It writes a weighty memorandum describing and explaining its design, and hands this off to the development team—which also, as it starts out, knows nothing about the task.

The development team then spends much learning-curve time listening to briefings, and meeting and arguing with the design team until it

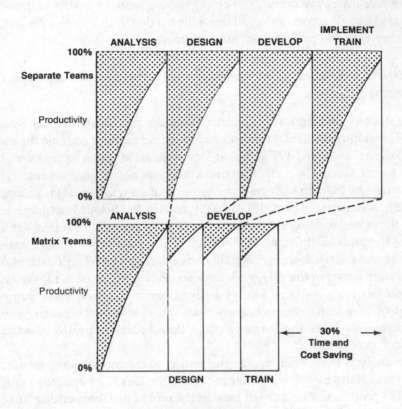

FIGURE 6.13
Interface Losses at Steps
in Producing a Training Program

ANALYSIS DESIGN DEVELOP IMPLEMENT TRAIN

Separate Teams

Productivity

100%

0%

ANALYSIS DEVELOP

Matrix Teams

Productivity

100%

0%

DESIGN TRAIN

30% Time and Cost Saving

TIME ON TASK ⟶

"learning curve" time lost writing memos, explaining findings, arguing about data each time "baton is handed off" from one specialized group to next

efficient work time

236

understands what it has to write. At the end of the development process the curriculum writers hand several large manuals to the trainers—who at this point, again, know nothing about the task. Professional trainers are notorious for their unwillingness to teach anything they have not "tailored" to reflect their own style. Invariably, the trainers spend much learning-curve time trying to understand why the designers designed the course the way they did, quarreling with the curriculum writers about how modules should be presented, and redesigning and rewriting what the previous two teams produced.

The trainers teach a pilot version of the course. ISD data indicate that most courses require 30% to 50% revision between the first and second pilot courses, and another 10% between the second pilot and the final version. After each pilot the trainers must go back to the curriculum writers—and sometimes to the designers and even the task analysts— to get more data, change the design, and rewrite parts of the course. Once again, analysts, designers, and curriculum writers have to learn what the trainers can tell them about what actually worked versus what didn't work in the classroom. Each time the task is handed off from one team to another, learning-curve time is wasted.

The solution is to use a matrix team consisting of a task analyst, a course designer, a curriculum writer, a trainer, and a "subject-matter expert" (a representative from the client system) to work together on each step of the process. Any inefficiencies that result when people are not performing their specialty (e.g., trainers doing needs assessment) are more than made up by the savings in learning-curve time. (In fact, cross-training in other specialties is often perceived as a development opportunity by the people involved.)

Matrix teams improve both quality and productivity. Curriculum writers who get firsthand experience interviewing clients in the field during the needs-assessment phase develop more realistic role plays, cases, and simulations. Trainers who participate in the design and development of a course have greater feelings of ownership about it and are in a position to revise it on the spot, greatly saving revision time between pilots.

My experience is that using matrix teams can cut overall course development time by one third. For example, the budget for a two-week course using the military standard of 100 days of development time to one day of delivery time was 1000 person-days. Use of a matrix team cut course development time from 1000 to 670 days; 330 days saved × the course developers' average cost per day of $346 = $114,180 benefits.

Other organization methods that can increase productivity include co-locating people, combining duplicated support systems, and planning to produce products in natural order.

Co-locate people who must work together on products and project, for example, in an open layout not more than 100 feet apart. Course writers are often located miles from engineering or marketing subject-matter experts and trainers. The time lost trying to communicate across such distances is substantial.

Combine duplicated support systems and services. For example, in developing technical training programs much time and money are saved if design engineers, task analysts, course designers, and curriculum writers all have access to the same word- and (even more important) image-processing computer. In one firm the engineering CAD/CAM system produced hundreds of accurate and beautiful mechanical drawings of various parts of machines. Curriculum writers developing a service rep training program had each of these drawings produced by hand by a graphic artist who cost $36 per hour and took six hours to produce each drawing: total cost was thus $216 per graphic illustration. Had the curriculum writers had access to the engineers' design computer, the firm could have saved $108,000 (500 drawings × $216 per drawing).

Whenever possible, work concurrently on tasks (i.e., do them in parallel rather than series, and in logical order). Increased coordination time is more than made up by reduction and overall project completion time, usually because people "downstream" in the production process spend much less unapplied time waiting for others "upstream" to complete their piece of the project before they can start. One caution: don't force products out of "natural" order. Wait for engineering to develop mechanical drawings and for the last engineering change order to go through before writing the technical manual or producing graphics. Tasks out of order invariably have to be redone at substantial expense.

Avoid or Minimize Customizing

The definition of a job shop is that it produces custom products. Despite this—and even if you can get paid for all custom-tailoring work you do—the more you can develop standard products and procedures to minimize custom-design time, the more efficient you will be. If you must customize, "modularize" products and services so that tailoring consists simply of pulling modules 1, 3, 5, 6, and 7, as opposed to 2, 4, 9, and 10, off a shelf. Put all modules on word-processing machines so that boiler plate can be quickly and easily tailored to specific clients' specifications. Make sure that all professionals know what is in the library, storeroom, or word-processing data bank so they do not reinvent or rewrite material that is already available.

Whenever possible, accept and urge clients to accept "temporary" products. It is often better to accept "on-time, rough, right, and cheap" materials than to insist on "late, pretty, wrong, and expensive" products. For example, a technical training group was famous for its beautiful full-color, expensively printed product support manuals. It invariably produced a lovely manual 18 months after the product had been introduced. During this period, service engineers relied on blurry design drawings, handwritten notes, and frantic calls to design engineers. In one case, a lovely manual was found to be 900 engineering change-orders out of date—and had to be rewritten from scratch at a cost of $300,000. Late, pretty, and wrong is no benefit.

TECHNOLOGY

Technology has deliberately been left for last in this discussion. Despite its obvious potential of increasing productivity, most students of white-collar productivity agree that most benefits in human-resource and knowledge-worker service delivery come from mundane savings in people's time (Bolte, 1982; Thor, 1981). For example, word-processing equipment greatly increases paperwork productivity, but word processing accounts for only 10% of office costs.

Computer and communications technologies that may offer larger productivity gains in the future include word, number, and image processing, shared information systems, telecommunications, and artificial intelligence.

Word processing offers the highest payoff in repetitive paper-factory operations like putting out mailing lists, editing complex documents that require many corrections, and producing documents (e.g., legal papers) in which much of the material is boiler plate, that is, standardized paragraphs or sections that simply need to be assembled. Spreadsheet programs offer number processors similar time savings in constructing and recalculating financial reports. Benefits of computerizing word and number processing are found in the usual way: documentation of the dollar value of time required to produce a given unit of work multiplied by the amount of time required before and after computerization.

Image processing and computer-assisted design/computer-assisted manufacturing methods (CAD/CAM) greatly reduce engineering and communication time. Printing out technical graphics (instead of drawing them by hand) and communicating designs directly to computer-driven numerical milling machines save human communication and machine set-up time, reducing engineering, R&D, and manufacturing interface losses.

Integrated human-resource management information systems enable many departments (e.g., equal opportunity, wage and compensation, and manpower planning) to use central personnel records. Shared information systems save duplication of information system hardware and personnel, and greatly speed report generation. Computerized legal, personnel, medical, and other data bases can significantly reduce professionals' research time.

"Communication substitutes for transportation"—teleconferencing, telemarketing, and telerepair procedures using telephone or computer links—can save time, travel, and expenses.

The most exciting opportunities for increasing productivity via technology in service work are illustrated by the automatic bank teller. This is a "service robot" that performs all the functions of a human teller—but it works 24 hours a day and with greater accuracy. It takes information, answers questions, and dispenses money. Automated machines have enabled California banks to eliminate 4000 tellers and many high-overhead branch banks. A full cost of $36,000 per year per teller multiplied by 4000 people means a savings of $144 million.

Diagnostics resident in machines provide detailed advice about how to fix them or, in some cases, actually fix themselves by switching to a backup component, thus savings customer and service rep time.

Computer-assisted instruction (CAI) is as much as 75% more efficient than human instruction for certain kinds of technical tasks, saving both trainer and trainee time, travel, and per diem expenses (Head, 1981).

Pribble (1985) and Kearsley (1984) report studies showing 25 to 40% faster learning (hence time savings) using CAI. And it is obviously less expensive to ''crash'' a computer simulator than a 747 jumbo jet or nuclear reactor: CAI is particularly cost effective in training people to use expensive and/or risky equipment.

Artificial-intelligence applications will continue to make more possible the automation of many professional services, including consultation and counseling. Inexpensive will-writing programs produce wills legal in 49 of the 50 United States. (Only Louisiana, with laws based on the Napoleonic code, is excepted—and only because appropriate software has not yet been written.) Computerized career-counseling and job-person matching is available in the military and at many universities.

The Army Research Institute found that junior officers entering the service from ROTC programs often wound up in military specialties they did not like and left the service. The Army developed an interactive video-disk career counseling module that lets ROTC graduates take an occupational preference test on a terminal that instantly analyzes officers' responses and tells them, for example: ''Your data indicate that the three specialties you'd be most interested in are intelligence, air defense, and mission control.'' Officers are then invited to play an alternative-scenarios ''adventure game'' by indicating which job specialty they would like to explore. They can see the schools they will attend at various points in their career and even attend samples of the classes (all on video disk). They can see the house they will live in in Germany, and what they will be doing in a war if one occurs. In short, they can ''play'' a 20- or 30-year career. If at any point officers decide the career they are exploring is not for them, they can easily extricate themselves from one ''life'' and go on to explore another.

Similar programs for college students let entering freshmen explore various majors by attending classes, seeing copies of typical final exams, and listening to professors they will study with for the next four years. Students even get Bureau of Labor statistics on the number of jobs and salaries anticipated for prospective majors four years hence and attend simulated job interviews in each field. Firms are developing career-counseling/internal-job-posting computer counselors that assess employee job preferences and competencies, and match them with available job openings in the company.

Artificial-intelligence programs able to provide sophisticated consulting services are increasing. For example, managers can be walked through wage and compensation plans and, simply by answering questions posed on the computer screen, get the information they need. Decision support system programs, given appropriate information about a prospect or an employee problem together with a salesperson's or manager's selling or managerial style, can advise salespeople on how to deal with a prospect's resistance, or a manager on how to deal with a disturbed employee.

The potential benefits of technology can be found by calculating the dollar value of the time saved per task or per individual and then multiplying by the total number of tasks or people the technology affects. But again the caution: whatever the hope of increasing productivity by technology, most savings will come from better management of people's time.

IMPLEMENTING PRODUCTIVITY PROJECTS

Estimates of productivity increases available from using these methods range from 9.5% (the average increase of American Productivity Center white-collar productivity projects; *Wall Street Journal*, 1982) to 30% to 50% (Main, 1981; Bolte, 1982).

Lessons of experience suggest the following steps in implementing a productivity project:

1. *Sensitize Management and Staff.* Charismatic speeches by top management, emphasizing the need for increased productivity if the firm is to survive and prosper, can get people's attention.

Teach people cost-benefit and productivity-improvement methods, and get their enthusiastic participation in studying their productivity and in working to improve it. (In other words, don't just "do it to them.") Training a "critical mass" of service-group people greatly increases the probability that cost-benefit and productivity methods will be adopted and used. Training just one person doesn't work: the person returns a lonely minority, advocating methods no one else understands. Training three to five people establishes a mutually reinforcing support group—people who speak the same language, know the same methods, and can help each other implement projects.

Reassure people that they will not be fired or laid off if they improve productivity. Few people will support an effort that is likely to cost them their jobs. Productivity increases *will* result in head-count savings, but these can usually be achieved by attrition.

2. *Define Productivity Measures.* Get baseline data on your current productivity per hour per unit applied rate and staff capacity metrics. Simply tracking and publicizing productivity data can change people's behavior.

3. *Pick an "Easy Win" for Your First Project.* Go after the easiest, biggest, fastest payoff, a "low-hanging fruit" (e.g., a particularly inefficient "dog" operation you know you can fix or kill). Pick something you can do on your own authority, something under your control. If you bite off too much—for example, a project requiring many higher levels of approval or capital equipment purchases—you risk having your effort delayed or blocked and losing your momentum. Focus: pick one project and do it well. Don't spread your resources thin.

4. *Publicize Your Savings.* A "win" builds credibility and makes the next project easier.

5. *Make Productivity Improvement a Continuous Process.* As soon as one low-hanging fruit has been plucked, go after the next easiest, biggest, fastest opportunity. As soon as one goal has been reached, set a more challenging goal. Demming, Juran, and others emphasize that productivity can *always* be improved, that you should never reach a goal and stop. Each person should constantly analyze his or her productivity and strive to improve it. The same goes for the firm as a whole.

CHAPTER **7**

Evaluation Design:

PROVING YOU MADE THE DIFFERENCE

Joe Smith, director of sales training, was feeling pretty good as he finished his report to the marketing VP's annual meeting: "So you see, in the year since I started my sales training program our sales have increased 25%!"

Then Ed, the product manager, spoke up: "Well, Joe, that's about when we replaced our old product with my new improved model. I'm sure increased product quality had something to do with increasing our sales." Next, Mike, the distribution manager, remarked: "Look, I and my staff put a real push on and got our products going through 10% more distribution outlets. I'd say that's accounted for about 10% of our increase in sales." Sharon, the advertising director, was next and said: "I put together a new ad campaign when Ed introduced our new improved product. The ad has just won an award for the best ad in our industry. I'd say my ad campaign probably increased our sales 15%."

Finally the economist spoke: "Hate to tell you folks, but last year was about the bottom of the recession. Now the economy is booming. *Everyone's* sales are up 25%."

This chapter shows you how to sort out the difference you and your program made from all the other influences having an effect.

Key Concepts.   Evaluation designs can be diagrammed using a few simple symbols.

Thinking through your design and isolating variables that may account for your results *before* you intervene can greatly increase your ability to argue that you made the difference.

Evaluation design uses five simple symbols (Campbell and Stanley, 1966; Cook and Campbell, 1979):

1. X = a "treatment" or intervention: your program, or whatever you do, for example, a training course or a consulting project. X_1, X_2, X_3 indicate successive programs in order of time. X is sometimes called an "independent variable" because you can manipulate it.

2. O = an observation or data collection point. O_1 = the first time you collect data, O_2 = the next time, O_3 = the third data collection point, etc.

A data collection O that precedes a program is called a pretest or baseline observation: $O \ X$. An O that follows the program is called a posttest observation: $X \ O$.

O measures are called "dependent" variables because changes in them "depend" on the X program.

3. R = a random sample (e.g., employees picked at random to fill out a survey or take a training course).

4. S = a stratified or "matched" sample. For example, if your firm employs 50% white males, 30% white females, 10% black males, and 10% black females, you could "stratify" your sample by race and sex by picking people to attend training in the same percentages as in the firm as a whole: 10 white males, six white females, two black males, and two black females in each class of 20 people.

5. SR = a stratified random sample, for example, picking employees to go to a course in the same ratio as employees in the firm, but randomly *within* a given category. You may decide that a class should be composed of 10% black males, but you will pick these black males at random.

Stratified, random, and stratified-random samples control for deliberate bias and outside influences that may affect program results. An example of deliberate bias is "stacking the deck" to prove a training program increases chances for promotion by picking only the most competent people to attend. Outside influences that can affect data include changes in management or the general economy, for example, a layoff announced just before giving a job satisfaction survey.

All evaluation designs can be expressed with these five symbols. You can use the symbols to identify a program's implicit evaluation design after the fact if you did not consciously choose an evaluation design for a program before launching it.

THE IDEAL DESIGN

The ideal design that all behavioral science textbooks say you should use in any evaluation effort is called an experimental control group.

Pretest, Posttest, Control-Group Design

Notation: $RO_1 \; X \; O_2$ Treatment group

$RO_1 \quad\quad O_2$ Control group

EXAMPLE:

Measurement of sales before (O_1) and after (O_2) a randomly selected group of salespeople attend a sales training program. The sales of the × "treatment group" are compared with the sales of a randomly selected "control" group of salespeople who did not attend the program.

Comment: This is the classic "true" experimental design. The trained treatment group's improvement in sales $(O_2 - O_1)$ can be compared with the control group's change in sales $(O_2 - O_1)$ during the same period of time. Any difference between the treatment group and the control group can be claimed to be the benefit of the training program.

This is how it works: the control-group salespeople, who did not get the training but sold the same product during the same period of time (from O_1 to O_2), "control" for all other factors in the environment that might have affected sales during that period. See how this solves our friend Joe's problem. Joe could compare the sales of the people he trained (his treatment group) with salespeople he did not train (his control group). Both groups of salespeople would be selling the same new product through the same expanded distribution system with the same advertising campaign in the same economy. If Joe's trained group did better than the control group and the only thing different between the two groups was Joe's training, Joe could claim that the benefit of training was his treatment group's sales $(O_2 - O_1)$ less the control group's sales $(O_2 - O_1)$.

Random selection of salespeople for both treatment (trained) and control (not trained) groups "controls" for other factors that may cause better or worse sales, for example, changes in personnel, good versus bad sales managers, booming versus lousy local economies, or (in either group) particularly competent versus incompetent salespeople.

Joe could cheat to prove his training works by selecting only the best salespeople to come to his course. These salespeople might sell more after training because they were better salespeople in the first place, not because they were trained.

If Joe is honest and thinks that salesperson differences (e.g., male versus female, white versus black, salespeople selling in booming Sun Belt versus depressed Snow Belt territories) might bias the effects of training, he can stratify both treatment and control groups to be sure each has equal numbers of each type of salesperson:

$$S \ O_1 \ X \ O_2$$
$$S \ O_1 \quad O_2$$

He can also randomly select people from each stratified type to be sure that individual biases don't affect results:

$$SR \ O_1 \ X \ O_2$$
$$SR \ O_1 \quad O_2$$

A random-control-group design is ideal because it controls for everything. If Joe selects his training and control groups randomly, he will automatically get an equal mix of high- and low-performing, white and black, male and female salespeople from good and bad sales districts, in proportion to these groups' representation in the entire sales force.

As you will see, the elements of this ideal design suggest how to fix any less-than-ideal design.

In the real world, experimental-control-group designs with random samples are often politically or ethically unacceptable, too difficult or too expensive. For example, it is usually ethically and politically impossible to give people negative treatments or deny them positive treatments. If you are trying to show that smoking or some industrial pollutant causes cancer, it is hardly ethical to encourage a treatment group to smoke or to expose them to the carcinogen to prove your point. Similarly, you cannot create poor organizational climate or bad supervision to show that these factors result in lower sales, higher absenteeism, or more grievances.

It is also very difficult to deny positive treatments once you have them. It is not ethical to withhold a life-saving drug from one group of children and let them die to prove that another group given the drug will live. Neither is it ethical to show that safety training works by withholding safety training from one group of employees in order to create a control group that gets hurt. Denying training that increases people's chances for promotion to create a control group is likely to get you a discrimination or reverse-discrimination suit. If Joe really has a sales training program that works, there is no way he can withhold it from part of the sales force just to create a control group and prove his point.

Evaluators deal with this problem by finding what are called "quasi-experimental designs" using "naturally occurring" treatment and control groups. A naturally occurring treatment group is one that is receiving the treatment naturally, for example, people who smoke, workers who have been exposed to an industrial pollutant for many years, salespeople working for a bad supervisor, or a plant with a historical record of many accidents or grievances. The evaluator does not create the X treatment by giving the ethically or politically impossible negative treatment. He or she simply finds a treatment group that has exposed itself or has been exposed to the treatment.

Similarly, evaluators can look for naturally occurring control groups—people or groups who for whatever reason did not get a treatment. By far the best way to create natural control groups is simply to go to a firm's files or historical records. A natural control group for such factors as sales, turnover, accidents, grievances, performance, appraisal ratings, and job satisfaction is simply the average of people or groups who did not get a treatment designed to affect these variables.

If you did not think of or have the resources to create an ideal experimental-control-group design, you need to look for data to create quasi-experimental designs—people and places where the treatment or lack of treatment occurred or did not occur naturally. "Grafting on" O observation data points and natural control groups is the secret to after-the-fact fixing of poor designs.

Another strategy is to use what is called a "wave" design.

"Wave" Designs

	Jan.	Feb.	Mar.	
Notation: Group One	O_1 X O_2	O_3	O_4
Group Two	O_1	O_2 X O_3	O_4
Group Three	O_1	O_2	O_3 X O_4

EXAMPLE:

Safety training conducted in Plant One in January, Plant Two in February, and Plant Three in March.

Comment: The idea of a wave design is that even the best-intentioned program with unlimited resources cannot get to everybody at once. If you start a sales or safety training program, you will train some people from some organizations one month, some more the next month, some more the third month (successive "waves" of treatment), and so on until you've trained everybody. The beauty of this design is that groups trained later serve as natural control groups for groups trained earlier. Groups Two and Three act as a control group for Group One during the period O_1 to O_2. Group Three acts as a control group for Group Two during the period O_2 to O_3. No one is denied the positive treatment, yet control groups are available for comparison with the treatment group. (Plants One, Two, and Three must be stratified, or randomly selected, so as to be comparable on the basis of employee accident rates and other key variables.)

All human resource and other programs have an implicit evaluation design. This design can be identified, diagrammed, and often improved to strengthen the case that the program made the difference. Typical designs, examples of their use and their weaknesses, and ways to fix them include the following:

NONDESIGNS

Evaluation implies measuring whether or not something has made a difference. Two data points, for example, O_1 and O_2, are needed to measure a difference. Non-designs lack measures or data to measure a difference.

A Treatment Without Data Collection Observations

Notation: X

EXAMPLE: A *training course.*

Comment: This is not an evaluation design, because there are no data collected that could indicate whether the treatment—training course X—made a difference in anything.

Fix: You can salvage a non-design by "grafting on" the missing parts of the ideal experimental-control-group design. In this case you could go to organizational records to get unobtrusive O_1 pretest data on training course participants, for example, sales, performance appraisal ratings, absenteeism, productivity, or any other measure the training might affect.

You can get your posttest O_2 data observation by tracking trained participants on the same measures, again using organizational record data, for six months to a year after training.

To create an *ad hoc* control group you can identify a random or stratified sample, for example, a group of people with the same demographic characteristics as your trainees, who did not go to the training. By obtaining their sales, performance appraisal, absenteeism, and other data for six months to a year before the treatment group is trained, and by tracking treatment-group participants for the same period after training, you have created the ideal treatment-control-group design by "grafting on" the observations shown in brackets:

$$[O_1] \ X \ [O_2] \ \text{Treatment group}$$
$$[O_1] \quad [O_2] \ \text{Control group}$$

You can now compare changes in the treatment group's data with those in your quasi-experimental control group in the usual fashion: treatment group $(O_2 - O_1)$ − control group $(O_2 - O_1)$ = changes attributable to training program X.

Pretest Observation, Treatment

Notation: O X

EXAMPLE:

A survey followed by a survey feedback problem-solving session.

Comment: An OD "survey guided development" effort is not an evaluation design because no data are collected after the OD session, X, that could be compared with pretest data to provide a measure of the change "difference."

Again the strategy is to fill in the missing parts of the ideal design: first you would get treatment-group O_2 posttest data by readministering the survey sometime after the OD session and seeing if there were any improvements on key survey variables.

You would of course be advised to look for hard results measures in addition to soft survey reactions measures. One way to do this is to look at what problems were identified in the problem-solving session and by establishing baseline costs or values for these problems. These cost-benefit data results become an O_1 measure. You can then follow up and value the result after the program at time O_2 and see if there is any $O_2 - O_1$ change in dollar results measures.

To create a quasi-experimental control group you could try to find a similar work group with similar problems (i.e., a control group stratified by problem type) that did not receive the OD intervention, or you could go to the organizational records and get average performance data for all similar work groups (a stratified random quasi-experimental control group) over the same period of time O_1 to O_2.

"WEAK" DESIGNS

Intervention, Posttest: The "One-Shot Case Study."

Notation: X O

EXAMPLE:

A training course followed by a reaction questionnaire or (better) a problem-solving/goal-setting workshop with follow-up three months later to see whether the problems were solved or the goals achieved.

Comment: Technically this is a non-design because, with only a post-test O_2, you have no O_1 to compare with the O_2 to measure a difference. Practically, this is an evaluation design of a sort because if you follow up and find that people have done something, you can try to claim that it was due to your treatment. In effect, what you are doing is assuming that the pretest O_1 is zero, that is, that your participants would not have done anything if they had not gone through your program.

$$(O_1) \; X \; O_2$$

This design is very weak because you have no real O_1 data on how people were doing before your X and you cannot be sure your X, as opposed to all other factors that may have influenced people, made the difference observed at O_2.

Fix: Get O_1 "before/pretest" data from organizational records or by interviews. For example, ask people: "Did you have any goals?" "What problems did you have at the time you attended the intervention?" If you can, calculate the baseline value of problems in dollars.

A second approach is to document "causal links" that show that your X in fact caused the O_2 outcome. This is an extremely important strategy that will be discussed in greater detail below and in Chapter 8, Designing Projects and Programs to Get Results. If people have identified a problem, described in great detail how they are going to fix it, and then can show they have in fact fixed it with dollar-measurable benefits, your evidence should be persuasive to reasonable people even if you don't have a kosher evaluation design.

A third approach is to identify other factors that could have affected your O_2 outcomes and refute alternative explanations.

EXAMPLES OF TRUE EVALUATION DESIGNS

Static Group Comparison Design

> *Notation*: $X \; O_t$ treatment group
> O_c comparison group control

EXAMPLE:

Measurement of promotion rate of people who participated in a training course versus those who did not.

Comment: This is a true evaluation design because it permits measurement of the difference O_t versus O_c between the treated and control subjects. The design is weak, however, because this difference may be due to other factors. For example, supervisors may select only their best subordinates to go to the course. Alternatively, more-motivated employees may select themselves to go to the course, by signing up for a development opportunity. More-competent or more-motivated employees are more likely to get promoted anyway. In either case the real factor in getting promoted may be selection or self-selection of participants, not the training.

Fix: Check to be sure there are no important differences between the people in each group; for example, retrospectively stratify by performance appraisal ratings to be sure the people who went to the course did not differ from the control-group people with whom you are comparing them.

Better fix: Select both trainees and control group randomly.

Posttest-Only Control-Group Design

Notation: R X O
R   O

EXAMPLE:

Comparison of promotion rates of a randomly selected group of people who attend a training course versus promotion rates of a random sample of controls at the same point in time after the training.

Comment: This is a true experimental design. Note how random selection of sample subjects solves the problem with the "static group" comparison design above. If trainees are randomly selected, supervisor bias, motivated self-selection, or some other such factor cannot distort results. Measuring promotion rates of both trainees and controls at the same point in time after the training controls for extraneous factors. For example, a decision to increase promotion rates would affect both groups equally.

A good way to control for self-selection is to get more people to sign up for the course than you can train. For example, if 40 people sign up, you can select 20 participants at random and use the remaining 20 as your control group. Since all volunteered for training, the control group is just as motivated and self-selected as the training group.

This design can also be stratified to study the effects of training on specific groups, for example, high or low performers, minority participants, or women. The control group would be stratified on the same basis.

Pretest, Intervention, Posttest Design

Notation: $O_1 \; X \; O_2$

EXAMPLE:

A measure of turnover, followed by an OD intervention designed to increase job satisfaction, followed by a second measure of turnover six months after the OD effort.

Comment: This is a true evaluation design because the $O_2 - O_1$ change can be used to see if the intervention made a difference. This design is weak, however, because you cannot tell whether the change was really due to the OD program, X, or to some other factor in the environment. For example, the main influence on turnover is the unemployment rate: when jobs are easy to get, people leave; when jobs are hard to get, people stay. Decrease in turnover could be due to the economy, to the arrival of a new boss, to increased bonuses authorized by corporate headquarters, or to a host of other factors.

Fix: Identify other variables that could have affected the $O_2 - O_1$ difference and refute alternative explanations. For example, check to see if the unemployment rate did in fact change, or if there had been any manager or compensation changes. If you can show that alternative explanations did not affect your results, you are in a much stronger position to claim the credit.

Better fix: Create a natural control group by getting organizational data for a comparable group that did not get the OD intervention or use the firm's average turnover rate for the O_1 to O_2 period. If turnover for your treatment group was much less than that for a comparable group or for the firm as a whole, you are in a strong position to claim the credit. All other factors—good and bad bosses, the economy, job design changes, and the like—will have influenced equally both the treatment and control groups.

An expanded version of $O_1 \times O_2$ designs are time-series designs. In time-series designs you collect data at a number of points before and after your intervention.

Single Intervention Without Control

Notation: $O_1\ O_2\ X\ O_3\ O_4$

EXAMPLE:

A unit's sales are tracked for six months before and after a sales training program.

Comment: Time-series designs in effect "use subjects as their own control," assuming that trends in measures will continue in the absence of an intervention and that any change in the trend line is caused by the intervention.

The weakness in this assumption is, of course, that some external influence could be the real cause of change from O_1 and O_2 to O_3 and O_4 (e.g., an upturn in the economy at about the same time the sales training occurred.)

Fix: Get time-series data from organizational records at the same O_1, O_2, O_3, and O_4 points on a sales group that didn't get the training (i.e., create a natural control, see Figure 7.1b).

Multiple Intervention Time-Series Designs

Notation: $O_1\ O_2\ X\ O_3\ O_4\ X_2\ O_5\ O_6\ X_3\ O_7\ O_8$

EXAMPLE:

A unit's turnover and sales rates are tracked over time as the unit receives repeated training courses or team-building workshops (e.g., follow-up reinforcement meetings).

FIGURE 7.1
Time Series Designs

a) Single intervention without control

Notation:

−12 mos.	−6 mos.		+6 mos.	+12 mos.
O_1	O_2	X	O_3	O_4

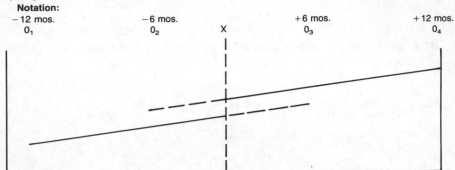

b) Single intervention

Notation:

SRO_1 O_2 O_3 O_4

SRO_1 O_2 X O_3 O_4

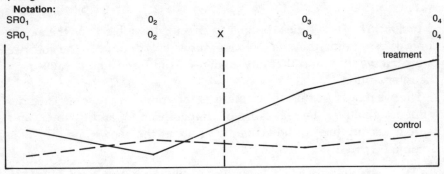

c) Multiple intervention with control

Notation:

O_1	O_2	X_1	O_3	O_4	X_2	O_5	O_6	X_3	O_7	O_8
O_1	O_2		O_3	O_4		O_5	O_6		O_7	O_8

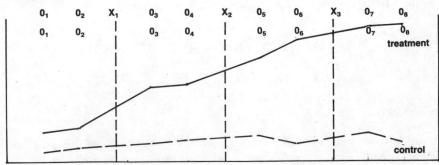

Comment: This design is helpful in determining when a treatment begins to have diminishing returns (i.e., when more investment in training is not going to increase performance any further). Its weakness is that, without a control, you cannot be sure what is causing the observed trend.

Fix: Get time-series data from organizational records on a group that didn't get the treatment (i.e., create a natural control group).

A useful special case of $O_1 \times O_2$ designs are systems throughput or input-process-output models. Systems models are useful when you know what output you want and have specific criteria for measuring for whether outputs meet quality standards.

EXAMPLE:

A training program for equipment service people.

Inputs are people (instructors, trainees, and administrators), learning materials, equipment, and facilities. The process is the training course itself and any OD intervention or counsulting efforts to improve it. Outputs are competent service people.

Outputs are usually evaluated on a pass/fail basis by a monitoring function. For example, the criterion for a good output might be fixing the ten most common machine bugs in a given period of time. Efficiency of the process is evaluated in terms of the percentage of probability "P" (on a scale of 0 to 1.0) of turning inputs (e.g., trainees) into good outputs. The proportion of bad outputs is given as $1.0 - P$.

For example, if you start with 100 trainees and your training is 80% effective ($P = .8$), for every 100 input trainees you will get $.8 \times 100$ input people $= 80$ competent service people. Likewise, $1.0 - .8 = .2 \times 100$ input people $= 20$ failures or dropouts.

System throughput models are useful for tracking productivity of recruiting, training, and other human resource programs because the productivity index—outputs divided by inputs—is easily calculated. A dollar value of productivity, cost/unit, is equally easy to get: the total cost of the program divided by number of good outputs equals cost per output.

Systems diagrams are also useful for documenting the steps and "causal flow" links between intervention outputs. Programs often in-

FIGURE 7.2

A Systems Analysis Model

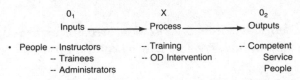

Training equipment service people

0_1 X 0_2

Inputs ⟶ Process ⟶ Outputs

- People -- Instructors   -- Training   -- Competent
  -- Trainees   -- OD Intervention   Service
  -- Administrators   People

- Learning materials

- Equipment
- Facilities

Outputs are evaluated on a pass/fail criterion by a monitoring function. ⓔ e.g., a score of 85% on a written exam, or 10 machines with major malfunctions fixed correctly.

The process is evaluated in terms of the percentage or probability, "P," (0 to 1.0) of turning inputs into "good" (passing) outputs; (1.0 - P) gives the percentage probability of "bad" outputs:

Good outputs = p × inputs
Bad outputs = 1 − p × inputs

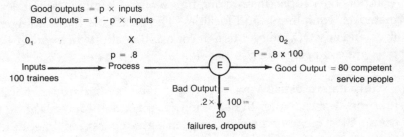

0_1 X 0_2

                                p = .8   P = .8 x 100
Inputs ⟶ Process ⟶ ⓔ ⟶ Good Output = 80 competent
100 trainees   service people
                              Bad Output =
                              .2 × ↓ 100 =
                                    20
                              failures, dropouts

volve many steps to produce an ultimate result. For example, most OD interventions end in a plan: a list of goals and action steps that one or more group members hope to accomplish. This plan becomes the input that drives the next step in the implementation process, producing outputs of completed action steps. These completed action steps become the inputs for a third step, influencing people or work processes to yield ultimate outputs (e.g., higher productivity or greater satisfaction).

EXAMPLE: *Organization development at an isolated military base near the Arctic Circle.*

The commanding officer of this facility was disturbed by very low morale, high desertion rates (anyone who got leave to go home to the

United States never came back), and disciplinary problems. He called in some OD consultants. The OD consultants gave a job satisfaction survey and confirmed that morale was very low. In the problem-solving/data-feedback meeting, one idea that emerged was to build a nice recreation center similar to those enjoyed by oil workers on the north slope of Alaska—including saunas, jacuzzis, athletic facilities, movies, arcade games—to give people something to do. The output of this session was a plan and action steps for convincing Pentagon budgeteers to put up the money for building this recreation center.

The plan was carried out, and over the next 18 months a recreation center was built, a tangible output of the implementation effort. Command personnel did in fact use the facility, and when the OD consultants came back and repeated the survey two years later, they found greater satisfaction, improved retention rates, and fewer disciplinary problems (see Figure 7.3).

The question is, what credit can the OD consultants claim for their original X intervention? This question is made harder by the fact that military two-year rotation policies meant that virtually all personnel at the base, from commanding officer to lowest enlisted person, were different at the O_2 point. The ideal test would be to find a control group—another isolated military base that did not have an OD intervention, did not think to build a recreational facility, and still had retention, morale, and disciplinary problems. A natural control group would control for changes in personnel and the civilian unemployment rate, military pay, good and bad commanding officers, changes in duty assignments, war versus peace, and other external factors.

Another approach would be to use the "identify and refute alternative hypotheses" strategy. If you can document that your intervention produced the plan, and that the plan was in fact followed and did produce the results predicted for it, then reasonable people would be hard pressed to deny you at least some of the credit. Your case is stronger if you can show that other variables that might have influenced the outcome (e.g., pay, the economy, duty assignments) had not changed during the intervening period.)

Differences due to change in personnel could be checked by surveying similar military bases (i.e., a stratified control). If attitudes toward the military were similar to those in your treatment group and remained

FIGURE 7.3

OD Consulting at a Military Base:
A Systems Model Showing Steps, Intervening Outputs and Causal Links

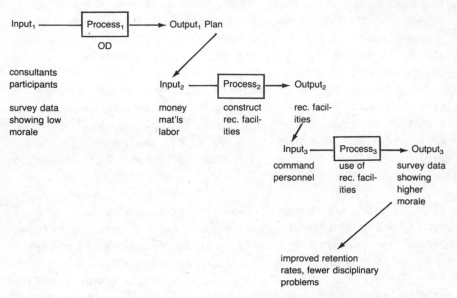

The outcome of a military OD intervention was a plan that included as a major action-step construction of a recreational facility. Inputs to this process included money, materials, construction workers, etc., which built the facility "output." The recreation building became an input into the lives of command personnel that led to the output of higher morale, improved retention rates, and fewer disciplinary actions.

stable during the intervention period, any change in the treatment group's morale could be claimed for the OD intervention.

Systems throughput models are useful in:

Distinguishing between inputs, processes, and outputs (intervening outputs and final outputs) in choosing what to measure in an evaluation design. Many training and OD evaluations cite only input and process measures—for example, "We delivered fifty communications workshops last year"—not outputs.

Documenting the link or causal flow from inputs and processes to outcomes. This can greatly strengthen the case that you made the difference, even if you did not use an ideal evaluation design.

Measuring the effectiveness and productivity of your process (i.e., your chances of making a difference, or your percentage yield of good outputs for your input costs).

EXOTIC DESIGNS FOR SPECIAL PROBLEMS

Solomon 4-Group Design

A problem in evaluation designs is that simply paying attention to or measuring people—for example, asking obtrusively, "Have you completed your affirmative action plan?"—can cause them to change. People may improve their performance simply because they feel singled out and special (the Hawthorne effect) or closely watched (the measurement effect). The Solomon 4-group design controls for Hawthorne and instrumentation influences.

$$\textit{Notation:} \quad (1) \; R \; O_1 \; X \; O_2$$
$$(2) \; R \; O_1 \quad O_2$$
$$(3) \quad\quad P \; O_2$$
$$(4) \; R \quad\quad O_2$$

EXAMPLE:

Some groups (1) are given an affirmative action workshop: the treatment, X. Some (2) are simply surveyed as to their existing affirmative action practices, O_1. Some (3) are given a "placebo" treatment, P (e.g., a short videotape on race relations). Some groups (4) receive nothing.

All groups are followed up after a certain period of time on some results measure (e.g., number of women or minorities hired or promoted). Comparing the X treatment group (1) O_2 with the P placebo group (3) O_2 tests for the Hawthorne effect: whether the full affirmative action workshop was more effective in causing change than just paying attention to this issue by showing people the videotape. Comparison of the $R \; O_1 \; O_2$ control group (2) with the posttest-only control group (4) O_2 tests how much the O_1 survey was itself a treatment: did just being measured or "getting wise" to the survey cause group (2)'s $O_2 - O_1$ difference? If a placebo, or just measuring people obtrusively with a sur-

vey, causes as much change as an expensive treatment, paying attention
to or surveying may be more cost effective.

Multitreatment Regression Designs

Sometimes when you have a number of interventions, you want to sort
out which makes how much of a difference in the result. This is the
problem faced by Joe or the marketing VP in the sales training case: how
much should the firm invest in training versus advertising versus product improvement versus distribution? Multitreatment regression designs can answer this question.

Notation:	O_1	X_1	O_2	treatment 1
	O_1	X_2	O_2	treatment 2
	O_1	$X_1 X_2$	O_2	treatments 1 and 2 together
	O_1		O_2	control

EXAMPLE:

The U.S. Navy invested heavily in both management training and organization development. It wanted to know which was most effective
in increasing personnel retention and ship operational readiness rates.
A multitreatment study was conducted on a stratified random sample
of ships. One group of ships received training for all supervisors. A
second group of ships received OD consulting. A third group received
both training and consulting on the assumption that OD interventions
would reinforce the training. A control group received neither training
nor consulting.

Training was found to make most of the difference. OD efforts did
not significantly change either retention or operational readiness. The
combination of training and OD appeared to be slightly but not significantly better than training alone. This led the Navy to reprogram its
human resources funds from OD consulting into training.

Statistical methods called regression or analysis of variance can tell
you how much each X and combinations of X's affect an outcome variable, hence where you should put your resources for maximum payoff.
Multi-treatment studies require large samples and are relatively difficult
and expensive to set up. If you feel you need to use this design, your

best advice is to contact your firm's industrial psychologist or faculty at a local university. Graduate students often are willing to conduct studies in order to collect data for their dissertations.

"THREATS TO VALIDITY": PITFALLS TO WATCH OUT FOR

Social scientists have cataloged the various "threats to validity," or reasons to be skeptical about whether or not a program has really made a significant difference. These threats may sound technical but are really just common sense. Most threats can be dealt with by using or creating, after the fact, an appropriate evaluation design.

Internal Validity

Internal validity threats are reasons for doubting that your treatment X really caused the difference in your outcome measure. Validity-threat questions and ways of answering them include:

1. *History.*   Did an external influence occur during the O_1 to O_2 period that may have influenced your outcome (e.g., a change in the unemployment rate that affected turnover)?

Fix: Create or find a control group subject to the same history influences during the same O_1 to O_2 period, or refute alternative explanations by identifying each history variable that could have affected your outcome and showing it did not change during the $O_1 - O_2$ period, or that it could not have affected your outcome variable.

2. *Maturation.*   Did the people or organization change simply as a result of time? Maturation was first identified in nutrition studies with children. Researchers wanted to know which foods made children grow. Unfortunately for the researchers, as children get older they grow anyway. Growth can be the result of maturation—natural change over time—rather than a given nutrition program X.

In organization research, maturation is the learning curve. People and work groups perform better and have higher morale simply as a result of being on the job or working together for longer periods of time. (Consultants know this and often choose to work with new groups. These groups will improve their performance anyway, but the consultants claim the credit for the natural maturation.)

Fix: Stratify by using control groups starting at the same maturation stage. Compare the O_1 to O_2 gain in productivity of a start-up group that received OD consulting help with that of a start-up group that did not. Even though both treatment and control groups will improve (see Figure 7.4), the new group receiving help should learn faster, mature more quickly, and have a greater gain in productivity if OD actually makes a difference.

FIGURE 7.4
Maturation

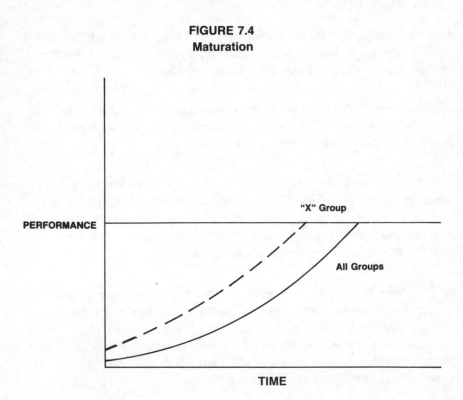

3. *Testing*. Did the observation method itself affect the outcome (e.g., did participants get angry at or "get wise to" an obtrusive survey)?

Fix: Use the Solomon 4-group design, which includes an $O_1 O_2$ control group that tests the power of the O_1 pretest to influence the O_2 posttest measure by comparing this O_2 group's results with a group that gets just one posttest O_2 measure.

4. *Instrumentation*.   Did the measure itself change? Was the posttest survey different from the pretest survey?

Fix: Check to be sure pretest and posttest measures are the same. You may need to transform the O_1 or O_2 measure to make it comparable to whichever measure it is being compared to.

5. *Regression Toward the Mean*.   This is a natural law that says that all extremes tend to move toward the average (e.g., two seven-foot parents tend to have a six-foot child; two three-foot parents tend to have a four-foot child). In organizations, this means that all high-performing groups will natrually tend to get worse, and all poorly performing groups will tend to get better. Astute fast-track managers and consultants know this and volunteer to take on turn-around situations, i.e., intervene with firms that literally "can't get any worse and have to get better." These low-performing groups will improve naturally, but the managers and the OD consultants will claim the credit. It follows that smart consultants do not intervene with high-performing groups: anything you do is likely to make them worse. If you're in perfect health, a good doctor will not prescribe any medicine, just bless you and send you on your way.

Fix: Stratify by performance (i.e., use a control group starting at the same performance level). If your treatment X is effective, treated high-performance groups will not get bad as fast as high-performing controls, and low-performing groups will get better faster than low-performing controls (see Figure 7.5).

An elegant use of controlling for regression toward the mean and maturation effects in a cost benefit evaluation of transition workshops

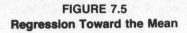

FIGURE 7.5
Regression Toward the Mean

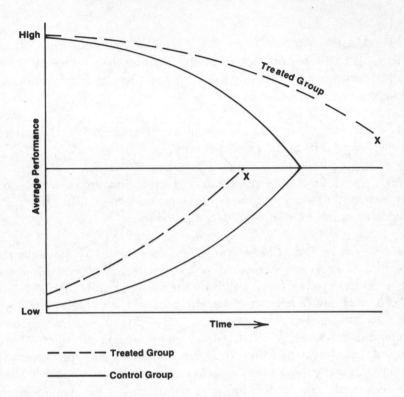

is shown in Figure 7.6. Transition workshops are problem-solving meetings used to reduce work groups' usual dip in performance when one boss leaves and a new boss takes over. The transition workshop gives the new boss a chance to hear all about workgroup problems from key subordinates and develop action plans to address these problems. The new boss need not be defensive, because any problems presumably are due to the old boss. A transition workshop can help a new boss get on board much faster; many claim that it saves them three or four months in learning-curve time.

Stewart (1980) tracked Army command performance indicators before and after commanding officer transitions for battalions receiving tran-

FIGURE 7.6
Transition Workshop Treatment and Control Groups

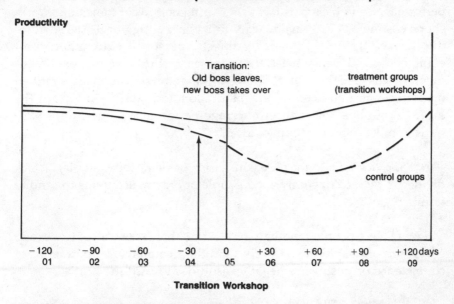

Transition Workshop

Significant differences were found for five Command Performance Indicators:

1. <u>AWOL</u> (Absent Without Leave): Units with transition workshops had half the AWOL rates of control groups in 120 days following change of command, a saving of 432.4 man-days at $29.33/man-day (direct cost!) = <u>$12,682 savings</u>

2. <u>Operational Readiness</u>: Units with transition workshops had 5% higher operational readiness rates than control groups. Savings in avoided capital equipment losses (tanks in armor units) = <u>$172,650</u>

3. <u>Personal Equipment Losses</u>: Average losses for transition workshop units were $27,905, 27% lower than for controls, with losses of $34,282 (a saving of <u>$6,377</u>)

4. <u>Unit Equipment Losses</u>: Average losses for transition units were $781, 88% lower than control groups' losses, $6391, a saving of <u>$5610</u>.

5. <u>Personnel Slotting</u>: Transition units saved <u>$5070</u> over control groups in better utilization of personnel.

Total savings for transition groups vs. control groups: $202,119
Total cost of transition workshops   11,750
Total benefit $190,369

$$\text{Return on investment} = \frac{190,369}{11,750} = 1620\%$$

sition workshops and control-group units that did not receive the workshops. His data show that transition workshops both reduce decline in performance and hasten its recovery during periods of transition. Workshops costing $11,750 saved Army units an average of $202,119 in reduced AWOL, operational readiness, personal equipment, unit equipment, and personnel slotting losses, a 1620% return on investment. In this case the control groups undergoing transition are stratified by performance and control for maturation and regression toward the mean: all groups will return to average performance, but groups with transition workshops improve faster.

6. *Selection*. Did you pick your cases or data, for example, "stack the deck" by selecting only good people or only malcontents to send to training?

Fix: Select people randomly or stratify, that is, use a control group composed of people similar to those in the treatment group in terms of competence or positive or negative attitudes toward the firm.

7. *Mortality*. Did your treatment of control groups' members change between the O_1 and O_2 data collection points, as did the military base in which 100% of the people turned over during a two-year period? Mortality is often a problem in firms that have high turnover.

Fix: Use a control group with the same mortality, and see if mortality makes a difference; or show that the different group of people you are collecting data from at the O_2 point is similar to the group that you measured at time O_1 (e.g., in attitude, demographics, and level of performance).

8. *"Compensatory Effects."* Did your control groups get angry and decide to get some X of their own or to beat out the "favored" treatment groups—a bias called "compensatory rivalry" or the "John Henry effect?" Alternatively, control-group members may feel disappointed at not getting the treatment and give up, a "resentful demoralization" effect. In either case, the difference in the outcome measure would not be caused by the treatment itself but by the control group's knowledge that they were not getting the treatment.

Fix: Isolate the treatment group from the control group. Use unobtrusive measures so that people don't know they are being measured or intervened with, or use a Solomon 4-group design to compare the effects of the full treatment versus a placebo treatment and no treatment.

Statistical Conclusion Validity

This means simply that there are all kinds of ways to cook the data. "Figures don't lie but liars figure." Any good evaluator can torture the data until they confess. You will without doubt get questions about how you have manipulated your data. The best advice is: when in doubt, get several cost or benefit figures. Average these figures and see how much they vary. Document your assumptions and be prepared to defend them. Anticipate people's questions and show how you have checked and refuted alternative hypotheses.

Take care to avoid double-counting costs or benefits. For example, managers of different levels may have set the same goal (e.g., to increase productivity or reduce turnover). If everybody claims the same result, you will wind up having more benefits than total revenues. This is absurd and will damage your credibility. When more than one person has set the same goal, divide by the number of people who claim a piece of the benefit.

Be prepared to deal with questions about opportunity "funny money." Distinguish honestly between opportunity benefits and real outlay dollar benefits. But point out that opportunity benefits are potentially real: they are the best indication of savings the organization can achieve if it makes hard managerial decisions.

External Validity

Internal validity threats ask whether your X in fact made a difference in the setting in which you tried it. External validity threats ask whether you can get the same benefits if you use a program with different people in a different setting.

1. *Selection of Treatment.* Does the treatment work only with certain groups of people? Programs are often pilot-tested on unrealistically

"good audiences," select participants not representative of the people who will actually use the program. For example, if a training program works with college-educated mid-level managers, will it work with non-college-educated first-level supervisors?

Fix: Stratify by type of person, that is, validate the program with subjects as close as possible to those with whom you will be conducting the program.

2. *Setting and Treatment.* If the X works in one place, will it work in another? Helicopters fly just fine at Fort Bragg in peacetime, but they don't fly in the Iranian desert. Training and OD programs may not "travel" very well. New programs are often piloted at corporate headquarters with lavish resources, nice training rooms, good equipment—settings very different from those in which they will actually be used.

Fix: Validate your programs in actual settings, with the instructors and resources that will be available in these settings.

3. *Construct Validity.* Just what is the X? Is a training program conducted by high-priced external consultants the same course when conducted by lower-paid and less-expert internal staff?

Fix: Be sure the X treatment is standardized and quality controlled. Validate programs by using average instructors or consultants working with typical participants in realistic settings.

SUMMARY

You are best advised to think about your evaluation design before you intervene. First, consider in advance the threats to your outcomes and alternative reasons for them. Identify the questions and doubts that may lead people to reject your findings. If possible, control for extraneous influences by creating or finding natural control groups. Second, get baseline data and document the links between your program outputs and final results benefits (e.g., goal-setting forms, action plans, and projected benefits) that show how people used your X to obtain those benefits. Third, identify alternative explanations for results and refute them one by one.

This is the strategy Joe used in documenting the impact of his sales training program. He first asked: "Did the new product formulation really make a difference in sales?" A survey of customers indicated it did not. He then asked: "Did salespeople in areas that had more distribution outlets sell more than areas without these distribution outlets?" The answer was no. Then: "Did advertising really make a difference?" Customer surveys showed little change in awareness of the product. Joe was also able to find natural control groups in parts of the country where the advertising campaign was not run. He compared data from these places with data obtained from places where it was run. Sales did not differ.

"Did the economy really make a difference?" The national economy had turned up significantly, but Joe was able to find natural control groups, sales areas in the Midwest where the economy had not improved. He compared these with sales areas in the Southwest where the economy was booming. Once again, sales of the product were found to be only slightly influenced by the external economy.

Finally Joe asked: "What *did* cause the 25% increase in sales, and where did it occur?" Most of it came from one salesperson landing a major industrial account. This salesperson had been trying to sell this account for ten years without success. Midway through the year, the salesperson attended Joe's training course. An important part of the training course was developing a very specific action plan to deal with one's most difficult prospect. Twice before in that year, the same salesperson had approached the client with the new product but without Joe's sales strategy. Now the salesperson developed this strategy, implemented it, and sold the difficult client. Joe was able to document so persuasively the link between the sales training and the actual sale that reasonable people had to accept that his training program had produced the lion's share of benefit from increased sales.

This strategy is described in more detail in Chapter 8, "Designing Projects and Programs to Get Results."

CHAPTER 8

Designing Projects and Programs to Get Results

"The way to win a Nobel Prize is to have an instinct for the jugular problem"

SIR PETER MEDAWAR

275

Key concept. The best way to show results is to nail down as specifically as possible the result you want to show *before* you intervene. No human resources person who wants results should *ever* intervene without first calculating the dollar value of the problem.

Adding three simple steps to every human resource task or program you undertake can ensure that you will always be able to evaluate your efforts in hard cost benefit terms. The steps are:

1. *Identify baseline performance on results measures* BEFORE you intervene: determine how an individual or organization is doing now in dollar terms ("value the problem") using the methods shown in Chapters 3 and 4.
2. *Set goals* to improve performance against the baseline value and calculate the potential benefit ("value the solution").
3. *Get follow-up data on the baseline measures and goals set* and calculate the actual saving or benefit resulting from your intervention ("value the result").

Figure 8.1 shows the addition of these cost-benefit steps to a typical problem-solving sequence used in consulting or training program development.

STEP 1. "VALUING THE PROBLEM"

Get baseline data on results measures. The most important step is to "value the problem," that is, to calculate the baseline costs of the way things are at the beginning of the program, before you intervene. This step helps you identify the *right* problem—that with the greatest dollar value to the organization—and to help you design *focused* interventions that will have the best chance of impact on the problem to show dollar benefits.

Japanese workers are taught a problem-finding technique called "five 'whys'": always ask "Why?" (or "*What* problem is that causing?" or "Can you give me a *specific example?*") at least five times when presented with a problem. The first two or three "whys" are likely to get you

FIGURE 8.1
Adding Cost-Benefit Calculation Steps
to Problem-Solving Consulting

• **PROBLEM IDENTIFICATION:** Setting priorities, selection

   *1. **"Value The Problem":** State in dollar terms what it <u>costs</u> you/organization <u>now</u>.

   *2. **"Value the Solution":** State in dollar terms what solution/program <u>could save</u> you/organization
   Do a "sensitivity analysis:" how much (what %) would you need
   to reduce the cost of the problem to pay for your program?

• **ANALYSIS:** Diagnosis, data collection, "root cause," etc.

• **ALTERNATIVES:** Generate solution options

• **DECISION MAKING:** Selection of best solution alternative

• **IMPLEMENTATION PLANNING/GOAL SETTING**

• **IMPLEMENTATION**

• **FOLLOW-UP** -technical assistance, trouble shooting
           - reinforcement
           - monitoring/evaluation

   *3. **"Value the Result":** State in dollar terms in "Final Report" what solution/program <u>actually saved</u>
   client/organization.

   *COST-BENEFIT STEPS ADDED: KEY MARKETING OPPORTUNITIES!

superficial answers, for example, "People don't communicate too good around here" in response to the question "*Why* do you want more supervisory training?" Following the advice to "value the problem" before intervening, the conversation could continue like this:

Consultant: Really? What communication problems have you seen?

Plant Manager: Well, I see them sitting around wasting a hell of a lot of time in meetings.

As soon as you hear the magic words "time" (wasted), "materials" (wasted), "equipment" (down) or other opportunity to value a problem, shift to asking the costing inquiry questions shown in Figure 3.1.

Consultant: How many supervisors do you see sitting around wasting time in how many meetings?

Plant Manager: Well, all four of them have a three-hour coordination meeting every week, and I don't see any coordination going on because they don't really have an agenda, a clear reason for being there.

Consultant: How much do the four supervisors make a year, on average?

Plant Manager: Thirty-five thousand dollars a year.

Consultant: You know, fully loaded, that means their time costs about $40 an hour each. That meeting for three hours is costing 4 people x $40/hour x three hours = $480/meeting. Over a year, 50 weeks, that means those meetings are costing you 50 weeks x $480/week = $24,000 a year.

Plant Manager: [Expletive deleted.]

At this point the HR consultant has established a baseline cost for a problem that he might affect by consulting or training: time wasted in meetings. More important, he knows how to focus his efforts to affect this problem: time management, or more specifically, meeting management.

Valuing the problem can lead you to jugular problems—and help you avoid wasting time and resources on trivial requests. Finnegan and McCampbell (1982) recommend that HR consultants ask clients straight out for "$100,000+ large dollar value problems . . . every manager has one, and you stand a good chance of getting one," and then prioritizing requests for service by the dollar value of the underlying problem "to take advantage of Pareto's law: 80% of the money trees are in 20% of the forest."

Some HR consultants are reluctant to probe clients' problems out of a belief that "one should take the client where he or she is" and "not take responsibility for the problem for him or her." This nondirective approach, usually a holdover from counseling training, is not good professional practice. Physicians who fail to probe patients' embarrassing symptoms and so miss a treatable cancer are guilty of gross malpractice. Human resource consultants *owe* their clients probing diagnostic questioning to avoid wasting their own, clients', and the firms' time and resources. Similarly, consultants who uncritically *"buy into"* vague or trivial problems to sell expensive services are kin to unscrupulous physicians who prescribe unneeded palliatives to healthy patients to sell drugs. No HR person should ever intervene without first identifying a problem valuable enough to be worth the cost of fixing it.

STEP 2. "VALUE THE SOLUTION"

Valuing the solution or "sensitivity analysis" means calculating how much an outcome changes if you change one of its input variables—or how big an outcome benefit would need to be to justify an input cost.

The training director can easily estimate how much savings in time lost in meetings would be needed to justify the training program. For example, if meeting management training for the four managers costs $2000, reduction in meeting time of just 50%—a saving of 4 people × $40/hour × 1½ hours × 50 weeks = $12,000/year—would more than pay for the training. Appraised in these terms, a $2000 training effort should be an easy sell to the plant manager.

STEP 3. "VALUE THE RESULT"

Having established the baseline data for meeting and turnover costs, cost-benefit evaluation of training results is very easy because you know exactly what to look for. The training director can get managers or their bosses to estimate how much time was spent in meetings after the training, and calculate the dollar value of any before-after changes. Savings in before-versus-after costs of time spent in meetings can be claimed by the training department.

Human resource people should always document and circulate simple one-page "final reports" of results they achieve. Such reports quickly change the perceived value of human resource groups.

These three cost benefit steps—valuing the problem, valuing the solution, and valuing the result—are key marketing opportunities for internal staff people. Stating the dollar value of people problems at the beginning has great power to get managers' attention. Being able to show a level of results needed to justify the costs of the program in terms of potential return or benefit is a very potent way to sell a program. Documenting the dollar benefits of interventions proclaims to all the worth of human resource or other knowledge workers' services.

Figure 8.2 shows a strategy for building cost-benefit baselines, goal setting, and results follow-up into training programs.

In preparing for an intervention, get trainees to identify as part of their prework the most important indices by which their performance is measured and any problems they are having in achieving desired performance in these measures (see Figure 8.3).

For example, in one manufacturing firm, management and participants in first-level supervisor training courses agreed on five performance measures for supervisors: employee suggestions received and implemented, days absent, grievances, quality problems, and credit hours earned (applied direct labor versus "sitting around waiting" time). The value of each of these results measures was calculated using the methods described in this book. For example, implemented suggestions were found to save the firm an average of $211.20. Approximately 50% of suggestions were implemented, so each suggestion had an expected value of $50\% \times \$211.20 = \$105.60$.

Figure 8.4 shows the results measures for first-level supervisors in an aerospace firm: employee suggestions, days absent, grievances, quality discrepancies and credit-hours earned (applied to specific fabrication tasks). Each result has a productivity index and dollar value. Supervisors can prioritize results measures by dividing the dollar value of a result by the total dollar value of the five results.

Trainees should discuss these performance measures and problems with their boss and get the boss's sign-off. The boss and the training department should keep a copy of performance measures and problems. This process (1) gets the boss's attention, letting him or her know that training will be related to bottom-line business results; (2) helps participants reality test performance measures and problems to ensure that they are focusing on the right aspects of their jobs; and (3) sets the boss up to support and reinforce trainees' learning and improvement efforts.

Bosses can also be asked to rate trainees' estimated productivity (see Table 4.2) and to complete other assessment instruments on the trainee at this time.

FIGURE 8.2
Baseline/Goal/Follow-Up Evaluation Strategy

Before Course	During Course	After Course Reinforcement
Trainees identify:	**Trainees use learning to:**	**Trainees:**
• Key performance indices (e.g., productivity measures) for their jobs and/or their work groups, with baseline data on these indices*	• Solve one or more specific problems and	• Discuss goals and action plans with their bosses*
• Major performance problems* they or their work groups are having that could be affected by management actions	• Set goals* and identify action steps to improve on one or more performance indices	• Attend "goal progress review meetings" • Additional training: time management, competency review, career planning, etc.

Managers:		**Evaluation**
• Discuss with trainees: - performance measures - problems		Trainees are followed up on: • Goals and action steps accomplished
• Fill out Assessment Instruments, e.g., rate participants' estimated productivity		• Improvement in performance indices
		*Managers:
		• Reality test goals and plans
		• Reinforce, encourage new behaviors
		• Fill out posttest assessment instruments, e.g., trainees' estimated productivity

* Carbon copies of performance baseline data, problems, goals, and action plans are kept by (1) participants, (2) their managers and (3) the trainers.

FIGURE 8.3
Performance Measures Form

Name: _____   Date: _____

Address: _____   Course: _____

        _____

        _____

Telephone: _____

To make your management training as relevant to "bottom line" business results as possible, please answer the following questions:

1. What are the five most important "hard" measures of your (or your group's) performance (e.g., sales, productivity, quality [reject rate], scrappage rates, etc.)?

    1.1 _____

    1.2 _____

    1.3 _____

    1.4 _____

    1.5 _____

If you have the information, please fill out Figure (8.4) which asks you to give "baseline" cost and production data for your measures.

2. What critical problems do you (or your work group) have that could be most affected by management or motivation of employees (e.g., turnover, grievances, absenteeism)?

    2.1 _____

    2.2 _____

    2.3 _____

Can you translate these problems into results measures, e.g., turnover, absenteeism? If you can, try to express these problems in measures that can be given a dollar cost or value, using Figure (8.4)

282

FIGURE 8.4
Worksheet for Identifying Productivity Measures, Baseline Index and Baseline $ Value

BASELINE MEASURE	PRODUCTIVITY INDEX			$ VALUE				PRIORITY WEIGHT
	# Baseline Units/Mo.	Base	Index	# Units/Mo.	x $ Value/Unit	= $ Value		$ Value ÷ Total Value (6)
1. Employee Suggestions								
a. # submitted		÷ person days/mo.	=		× $105.60	=	(1)	
b. # accepted								
2. Days Absent		÷ person days/mo.	=		× $207.48	=	(2)	
3. Grievances		÷ person days/mo.	=		× $979.00	=	(3)	
4. Quality Discrepancies - scrap - rework - HFM: "held for materials"		÷ person days/mo.	=		× $95.00	=	(4)	

FIGURE 8.4 continued

BASELINE MEASURE	PRODUCTIVITY INDEX			$ VALUE			PRIORITY WEIGHT
	# Baseline Units/Mo.	Base	Index	# Units/Mo. x $ Value/Unit = $ Value			$ Value ÷ Total Value (6)

5. Credit Hours Earned

$$\overline{} \div \overline{} = \overline{}$$
person days/mo.

Person hours available

− Hours Earned
= Hours Lost

x . $28.15 = ____ (5)

Total $ Value of opportunities for productivity improvement

____ (6)

284

If participants' performance measures are not already stated in terms of efficiency, effectiveness, or productivity metrics, teach trainees the measure development strategy described in Chapters 2 "Developing Measures," and 6 "Increasing Productivity," to identify results measures and calculate baseline cost data for the measure or problem. This training in productivity measure development is itself a valuable addition to any training program.

During the intervention, be it a training program or consulting session, get trainees to use what they have learned to solve key problems, and set specific goals with action steps to increase efficiency, effectiveness, or productivity. Numerous studies show that simply setting goals increases the probability of goal attainment to between 60% and 70% (Kolb and Boyatzis, 1970), and results in productivity increases averaging 19% (Latham and Locke, 1979). Including goals set in training and consulting all but guarantees that the majority of participants will show outcomes that can be stated in dollar terms. Use copies of the goal-setting form (see Figure 8.5) so that trainees, their bosses, and the training department know what goals are set and where trainees can be reached for follow-up.

After the intervention, trainees should discuss their performance improvement goals and action steps with their boss. Again, this process lets the boss reality test trainee goals and plans, and enlists his or her support and reinforcement in helping the trainee learn, change behavior, and improve performance. The training department can hold "goal progress review meetings" (e.g., get trainees back together at monthly intervals to discuss goals and problems), and to get new ideas and "a new head of steam" to use learning to improve performance. Trainers can also provide technical assistance and additional training to participants. Follow-up reinforcement meetings and technical assistance significantly increase trainees' performance improvement (McClelland and Winter, 1969).

Evaluation of training is easy if you have baseline performance data and specific improvement goals. The goal setting form (Figure 8.5) enables you, with a simple phone call, to get at least behavioral outcome data at the follow-up point. Ask (1) whether or not the person has accomplished the goals and action steps set in the program, and (2) how the person is doing on the performance measures established at the baseline point.

If trainees' results measures are not stated in dollar terms, use the standard benefit inquiry strategy to "value the result" of trainees' measure changes or problems solved in terms of time and outlay costs saved. Figure 8.6 shows this inquiry strategy in the baseline/goal follow-up format for a meeting management course.

FIGURE 8.5
Goal Setting Form (Carbon Triplicate)

Name: _____

Title: _____

Address
(for follow-up): _____

_____

_____

Telephone number
(for follow-up): _____

Goal: How will you use what you have learned in this course? What will you do?

_____

_____

_____

2. **Action Steps**   3. **Due Dates**

What (observable!) action steps   **By When?**

will you take?

a) _____   _____

_____   _____

_____   _____

b) _____   _____

_____   _____

_____   _____

c) _____   _____

_____   _____

_____   _____

Figure 8.5 continued

4. <u>Results</u>

What results or benefits will your goal and action steps have for your organization? Please be as specific as possible, e.g., "My HRD staff applied rates should increase 10% reducing costs per applied person-day from $500 to $450. Program X costs, now 100 person days @ $50/day = $50,000, will be reduced 10% to $45,000."

_____

_____

_____

_____

_____

_____

_____

A very effective use of this strategy was used by Davies and Browning (1984) in the HR program judged by the Instructional Systems Association and *Training Magazine* the best in U.S. industry in 1984. Davies and Browning showed that $160,000, 8.3% of their bank's total profits for 1983, were produced by a single training program for 12 bank operations managers costing $4200 (a cost-benefit ratio of 1:26). Managers were trained in basic productivity improvement techniques and then asked to plan and commit to implementing two productivity improvement projects with their two largest dollar value problem/opportunities. The clincher: at the end of the course, trainees had to present their projects to a senior management committee consisting of the bank's chairperson, president, and six senior vice presidents *and* make an appointment to present the *results* of their projects to the same senior management committee six to eight weeks later. Not suprisingly, most managers completed and documented dollar benefits from their projects.

Two points about Davies and Browning's design should be emphasized:

1. The training course was specifically designed to be more than "just training" in which participants *learned* productivity methods. It was designed to be an *intervention* which emphasized identification of real problems with large dollar value and specific *application* of learning to achieve dollar *results*.

2. The program included the powerful follow-up and reinforcement mechanism of presenting goals and results to top management.

FIGURE 8.6
Cost-Benefit Inquiry Strategy in Baseline/Goal/Follow-Up Evaluation Format

Identify/Objectives or Problems	Define Cost–Benefit Measures	Get Baseline Data
Ask: What are the measures, problems, tasks to which you will apply learning or consulting help?	Inquiry Strategy: To get dollar cost or value of key measures, problems, tasks	Ask/calculate: How are you doing on measure, problem, task now?
• What are the five most important measures of your job performance?	−steps? −who's involved? −making how much? −how long? −outlay costs?	
• What are the most important problems you have in improving performance on these measures?		
E.g., "We don't communicate well."	E.g., full cost/ dollar value of time wasted in meetings	E.g., 50 meetings, 500 hours @ $50/hour = $25,000

FIGURE 8.6 continued

Set Goals	Get Behavior Outcomes Data	Get/Calculate Cost-Benefit Results
Ask: How will you use learning, consulting, to --improve performance on this measure --solve this problem	Ask: What did you do (behavior) on action steps to solve problems? How are you doing on goal (results) performance measure?	Ask/calculate: Dollar value of action step behaviors taken, goals achieved, compared with baseline value of problem or performance measure
E.g., "I want to achieve goal (reduce meetings 20% by Dec. 31 due date)"	E.g., reduced meetings 15%	E.g., 15% x 500 hours = 75 hours saved x $50/hr. = $3750 saved
"Action Steps I will take": 1. Keep timesheets by next Mon. 2. Etc. by 3. Etc. by		

You may not always be able to include these elements in your designs, but the more you can include, the better will be your chances of showing results.

A benefit identification inquiry strategy can even be used to evaluate programs that have not asked participants to identify baseline measures or problems and set goals. This approach is harder and the benefit yield lower, but it can be sufficient to justify a program.

An after-the-fact benefit identification approach has the following steps:

1. Identify a random sample of projects or people.

2. Ask key client participants—the boss, trainees, or people most likely to have been affected by the program—to describe anything they did differently or that happened differently in the firm as a result of the program.

    a. Listen carefully for benefit calculation opportunities and pounce on time savings, increased productivity, outlay cost savings—any and all of the examples described in this book.

    b. Ask if the organization keeps any data on potential benefits, that is, if there are historical records that could be used to establish pretest baseline (or time-series) measures before the intervention. If you can find baseline values for benefit opportunity measures, you have created an $O_1 X O_2$ evaluation design by establishing the O_1. If you can't establish O_1 values, you have an $X O$ "case study" design in which you assume the O_1 condition is whatever people were doing before the intervention and "changed from" doing as a result of it.

3. Use the cost-benefit inquiry strategy (see Figure 3.1) to value any change or potential benefit, keeping track of your assumptions.

4. Ask how long the problem or baseline situation had existed and how likely it is that it would have been fixed or that performance would have improved anyway (i.e., without the program you are evaluating). Ask if any other factor could have caused or influenced the change, i.e., cover yourself on evaluation design questions by being prepared to refute alternate explanations for benefits found.

5. Find the average value and standard deviation of benefits from your random sample of projects or people studied. Many will not show any benefits; a few will show small benefits; fewer still will show major benefits.

6. Multiply the average value per project or person by the total number of projects or people, and claim this as the estimated value for the program.

    For example, Mitchell (1980) used this approach to evaluate a sample of 3743 OD consulting projects in the the U.S. Army. Most of these projects were very "soft" process consultation workshops.

Figure 8.7 shows the distribution of project results. Most projects, 86.6%, showed no dollar benefits. "Qualitative" successes were defined by reactions data that showed clients' feelings about programs, and "failures" by negative reactions data. The great majority of projects, 77%, had no data at all. Lest the Army be unfairly singled out, this distribution of benefits—or lack of same—is typical for most human resource efforts, largely because no attempt is made to evaluate them in cost-benefit terms.

Of the 13.4% of projects that produced dollar benefits, 9.3% showed "minor" benefits averaging $84,630, and 4.1% showed "major" benefits averaging $736,696. Despite the low yield, the 13.4% of projects that did show dollar results produced $142,515,196 in benefits, more than enough to justify their $56,790,539 cost. The Army's OE program had a one-year cost-benefit ratio of 1:2.5 ($142,515,196 benefits ÷ $56,790,539 cost) and a return on investment of 151% ($85,724,659 net benefits ÷ $56,790,539 invested).

Mitchell (1980) scrupulously tested all alternative hypotheses for benefits produced by successful projects and assumptions used in estimating total benefits. For example, the worst case estimate of benefits (at a 95% confidence interval below the average value) was $77,900,000—still more than sufficient to cost-justify the program.

This example shows that after-the-fact evaluations of even relatively soft programs can document significant dollar benefits from a few successful projects, using the inquiry strategies described in Chapters 3 and 4. If programs are set up using the baseline-goal-follow-up strategy, yields should be much higher: 60% to 70% of projects should show productivity improvement benefits averaging 19%.

A consistent finding about effective human resource consultants and their clients is: *those who think in outcome terms get outcome results*. The converse is also true: those who don't, don't. Spencer and Cullen (1978) found that consultants and clients who state objectives in vague reac-

FIGURE 8.7
Distribution of Cost-Benefit Outcomes
of Army Organization Effectiveness (OE)
Consulting Interventions

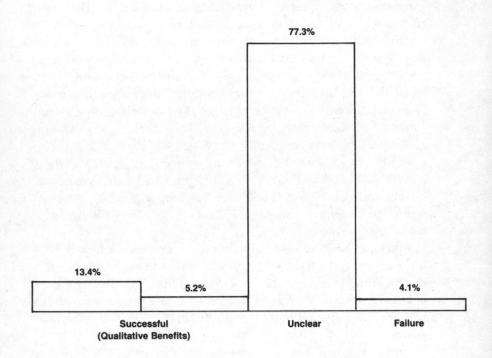

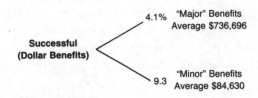

Cost-benefit analysis of 3743 organization development projects conducted by 349 consultants in the US Army during the period March 1979 to March 1980:

$ Benefits = $142,515,196 (actual and opportunity cost savings in dollars, time, personnel)

$ Cost = $ 56,790,539 (dollars, time, personnel)

$ Returns = $ 85,724,657

292

tions terms (e.g., "I want to improve team spirit, leave the troops feeling good"), when questioned six months later as to the effects of their program, reported only: "Well, I guess we felt better for a while, but there isn't anything really that I can show that happened as a result of the effort."

Consultants who stated problems precisely (e.g., "The client group's turnover was 10% worse than the rest of the company, and I wanted at minimum to get it back in line and planned to do 10% better") had clients who reported six months later: "We reduced turnover of critical skills people to the point that we now have retention 5% higher than average" (Spencer and Cullen, 1979; Cullen, Klemp, and Rossini, 1980).

In summary, developing cost benefit (efficiency, effectiveness, and productivity) measures has great power to improve human resource practice. It leads to precise problem diagnosis and diagnosis of the right problems—those with the greatest dollar value to the organization. It leads intervention designers to focus programs to deal with valuable problems, that is, to concentrate time and attention on the 20% of content and activities that will make 80% of the dollar difference and reduce time on content and activities that have much lower probability of pay-off.

People count what they care about and want to control, and they become what they measure. If you develop good measures, figure out how well you're doing now, and set goals to improve, follow-up evaluation is very likely to show that you *have* improved.

Cost-Benefit Analysis

SCIENCE OR POLITICAL SCIENCE?

What is a cynic? A man who knows the price of everything and the value of nothing.

OSCAR WILDE

Is cost-benefit analysis a science, or merely "political science"—a way of twisting data to get any answer you want? Clearly it can be both. The important question is its practical and moral utility. Does it make a difference? And is this difference beneficial or harmful to people and firms that use it?

Politically, numbers almost always increase human resource people's power. Since few personnel people have numbers, just coming to the table with costs and benefit analyses "seizes the high ground." It transmits the message that you care about bottom-line results, and it puts opponents in the position of having to respond to your analysis. If the logic of your approach is accepted, you have already won. You have created the dominant definition of the situation, the context of debate. Others will simply be arguing about whether your numbers are right.

TACTICAL ADVICE

To be of maximum use, CBA must be presented in a way that persuades others. The following are some "political science" tactics which work in most cases.

1. *Offer Analyses with Some Humility.* Introduce your findings with a low key admission of difficulty: "these things are hard to measure . . . we did our best. Here is how we did it (i.e., here are our assumptions) . . . ."Being open about the difficulty of attaching dollars to human activities often disarms opponents. Pointing out problems in your approach before others do preempts their attack. Frequently it has the paradoxical effect of changing their attitude from hostility to one of friendly interest and willingness to help.

2. *Avoid Emotional and Ideological Debates and Approach "Sacred Cows" with Care.* Sacred cows tend to be two types: unmeasurable, and politically untouchable.

Unmeasurable cows moo highly emotional appeals: "we do it because it's right!" or "we are talking about *human lives, a child's tears* (fill in your own favorite here)— you can't (be such a scrooge-hearted, fascist . . . as to) put a dollar value on that!"

You can, of course. I have never seen anything that couldn't be costed because I have never seen anything that didn't in some way involve human time or valued resources. Politically, however, it is suicidal to debate on these terms; from a personal cost benefit standpoint it is rarely worth your while.

Cows may be politically untouchable because to do so would publically embarrass or "call the question" on someone with more organizational power than you have.

If you start to price an untouchable cow, you may be told, "we don't want to know." In these cases you want to use CBA to better a given situation rather than challenging it.

For example, one firm supported an inner city training project which produced not very good clerical personnel at a staggering cost of $30,000 per hire. The pet project of the CEO or "Chairperson of the Board," this was really a public relations rather than human resources effort (and perhaps cost justifiable as such.) The human resources manager knew the rule that if you are going to shoot the king (or the king's cow), you had better get him (or her) on the first shot. (If you do not, you know who will be shot instead). In this case she tactfully noted just how much the sacred cow cost, suggested how it might be watered and fed for less, and finally got it moved off her budget onto community relations' overhead.

Occasionally, the sacred cow will be your own pet project. You may hesitate to evaluate it for fear of finding it doesn't work or isn't cost justifiable. Earlier I half facetiously suggested that CBA can be a no-lose game: if your program works, claim the credit. If it doesn't work, kill it and claim the savings. Honesty about your program results *is* usually the best policy. You beat others to the punch, appear sincerely concerned with what is best for the organization—and often can keep or even increase your budget to come up with "a new improved program which *will* work."

3. *"Frame," but Avoid Overkill.* "Framing" refers to the fact that people tend to react to or ignore costs by comparing them in size to costs they are used to dealing with. Sometimes they are skillfully led by someone trying to influence them. For example, auto salespeople are very skillful in using framing to get customers to buy seemingly small extras—"small" meaning costing relatively little compared with the purchase price of the car. Someone who has just spent $10,000 for a car is likely to perceive "just $135 more for racing stripes" as insignificant. For a training program, $50,000 seems—or can be made to seem—very

small in comparison with the potential benefit of saving $480,000 in turnover of critical skills engineers.

Use CBA to present your case in compelling terms by framing: show that benefits your audience cares about are large in comparison with the costs or resources you are requesting. Be careful to avoid promising or claiming benefits so large as to appear ridiculous—even if you think they are accurate. When in doubt use your most conservative data and assumptions. Promising or claiming 12,000% return on investment invites skepticism and attack from managers and accounting types used to very different orders of magnitude. Offer or claim benefits large enough to persuade your audience, but not so large as to provoke them.

EXAMPLE:

Army course developers wanted to sell an Armored Vehicle Recognition Course to NATO Generals. Armored Vehicle Recognition is a critical skill for forward observers, soldiers who sit on West German hillsides peering into the mist, looking for enemy activity. Observers make three recognition decisions: (1) Is anything there? If yes, (2) is it a cow or a tank? And (3) if it's a tank, is it one of ours or one of theirs? The third decision is critical because if it's one of theirs, you shoot it. Shooting a "friendly" is highly undesirable: it costs you a tank and the tank's crew, and it is very bad for morale.

The Army trainers found that observers, on average, were not very reliable in distinguishing friendly from enemy tanks and that their course could dramatically increase recognition accuracy. At the end of their presentation, the chief trainer concluded: ". . . And gentlemen, the entire training program will cost less than one-half of *one* . . ."—and up on the screen went a slide of half of a "friendly" Chieftain tank. Is there any way the Generals could have refused funding for this program?

The trainers resisted overkill. They were tempted to point out that the real cost of shooting a friendly tank was not the tank but the survivor benefits for the five men inside, and illustrate this by showing a slide of five grieving widows with 2.3 grieving children receiving survivor benefits well into the next century. They resisted the temptation. "Half a tank" was more than enough to cost-justify the program.

4. *Ask for Help: Use Others' Numbers and Assumptions*—especially to those you will be presenting findings to. Use this tactic in establishing baseline cost data and in responding "on your feet" if challenged when presenting results. For example, if you are using subjective estimates of employees' pretraining productivity, get these estimates from the managers who will be your audience. Note in your presentation that you used "the figures *you* (the managers) gave me." If managers themselves indicated that employees are only 60% productive, they are less likely to question benefits based on changes in productivity values.

Assume, but be honest about your assumptions. Making the best case for yourself is perfectly fair. You can make any assumptions you like, but others have a right to question your assumptions, so you must be prepared to defend them. The best way to handle skeptics is to explain the logic and data behind your assumptions, then acknowledge the skeptic's concern, and do an on-the-spot "sensitivity analysis." For example, say: "OK, let's see how much the result would change if we used your assumption." Redo the analysis on the spot, using the skeptic's assumption. Rarely will this analysis alter the point you are trying to make. Usually, you will co-opt and convince your skeptic, using his or her own data.

5. *Teach Others CBA Methods.* Simply circulating brief cost benefit analyses whenever you have the opportunity will educate colleagues and clients. Potential consumers of your work will realize CBA is possible, relevant, and practically applicable to human resource decisions. Often your boss, after he or she has seen a few, will come to expect them. Your peers, seeing the impact your analyses have, will pick up the technique, usually by asking you to show them how to do it. Your clients, benefiting from your "consumer education," will be more likely to ask your help in identifying and valuing problems. Over time, people will begin using the technique to further their own objectives.

6. *Persist!* It often takes time for CBA to influence decisions. Your initial attempts may be met with skepticism or outright rejection. This reaction does not mean you are wrong or even that your efforts have been in vain.

Given time, your analysis will often prevail as your numbers "sink in" to others thinking. You will often hear your numbers cited by others (usually without attribution or credit to you) to support the decision you first proposed. I have frequently heard the following story:

> I went back after the cost-benefit course and costed out our department's "dog" project. I found out it was costing us more than $500,000—about 10 times what we thought—because no one was taking into account how much of our time it was taking. My boss dismissed my analysis out of hand—just plain scoffed at my figures as "funny money." But over the next few months I heard lots of other people say "you know, someone figured out that (expletive deleted) program is costing us $500,000!" Finally, I even heard my *boss* use my numbers—without mentioning me, of course. And funny thing—the "dog" did get zapped in the next budget cycle.

The objective of CBA is to get people to think rigorously about the costs and effects of what they are doing. This goal may be accomplished even if your numbers are rejected or you are not allowed to get numbers at all.

For example, in a very secretive, closely held manufacturing firm, the training director saw quality problems which could be addressed by operator training. Her attempts to value the problem and solution were abruptly halted when management realized her inquiry would reveal top secret financial data about the firm's real costs and profits. Just her raising the question, however, alerted top management to the costs of poor quality. After a face-saving interval, the training director was given substantial resources to "do something about the problem." In one month, operator training saved the firm the cost of developing and implementing the training. She estimated (privately) annual benefits at more than $1 million.

To promote use of CBA, managers can teach, request, reward, mandate, and, as a last resort, punish. Show your staff how to do it, or get someone to train them. As noted in Chapter 6, "Improving Productivity," the best way to get a new technique used is to create a "critical mass" of people who share the same concepts, language, and methods—and reinforce one another in their use of them. Ask your staff to calculate the costs and expected benefits of existing and proposed projects. Reward those who submit good CBA's: let others see that speedy budget approval is more likely when a project proposal includes convincing return on investment data. If all else fails, mandate the inclusion of CBA data in proposals and reports: "you won't get your project funded unless you show management its benefits justify its cost. "Sanction those who resist the message by turning down or asking staff to do over analyses which do not meet your standards.

This book has argued the benefits of CBA itself: its power to focus decision makers' attention on the value of people, on their most important problems (those of highest cost to the firm), and hence on the firm's highest value services and people programs.

Cost-benefit analysis can provide better information for budgeting and planning: more accurate estimates of costs, optimum use of people's time. Make-versus-buy analyses can help managers acquire resources and deliver services at least cost.

Measures signal what an organization considers important. Because measures provide the basis for rewards, feedback, and punishment, they shape managerial behavior. Valuing the dollar consequences of personnel actions can help managers set goals, get feedback, and control outcomes. Firms can monitor whether they are increasing, maintaining, or liquidating their human assets.

An example is the impact of human resources accounting in the U.S. Navy. The Navy has always valued physical assets. Captains who run their ships aground know their naval careers are at an end. But before human resource accounting, captains who met all performance requirements while burning out their crews—so that half of their officers and sailors resigned from the Navy upon the ship's return to port—were still regarded as superior performers. Personnel were "someone else's business," not really a tangible value to be taken into account. Only when it was pointed out that a pilot costs $1,500,000 to acquire, a junior officer $300,000, and a technically qualified seaman $30,000 did the dollar value of retention begin to be considered in the evaluation of Navy leaders.

In summary, cost-benefit analysis provides a fair and objective approach to making decisions about people and programs. It provides a common language—dollars—into which everything can be translated and presented for honest debate. It obliges people to state their figures explicitly and come clean about their assumptions.

The strength of the scientific and democratic process is that truth emerges from honest debate. CBA cannot guarantee that politics will not intrude or sway decisions, but it increases the odds of deciding an issue on its merits.

Bibliography

Aft, L. S. *Productivity Measurement and Improvement*. Reston, Va.: Reston, 1983.

Allport, G. W. *The Nature of Prejudice*. Cambridge, Mass.: Addison-Wesley, 1954.

Amacom, N. N. Originally published under the title "Tapping the Human Resource." 1975.

Avner, B. "Integrated Personnel Systems." Columbus, Ohio: Nationwide Insurance Company, 1983.

Berry, C. A. *Good Health for Employers and Reduced Health Care Costs for Industry*. Washington, D.C.: Health Insurance Associations of America, 1981.

Biancardi, M. "The Cost-Benefit Factor in Safety Decisions," *Professional Safety*, November, 1978.

Bierman, H., Jr., and Seymour Smidt. *The Capital Budgeting Decision*. New York: Macmillan, 1966.

Bodily, S. E. "Why Should You Go to Court?," *Harvard Business Review, 59*(3), (May-June 1981).

Bolte, K. A. "Conquering the Administrative Marshmallow: Intel Corporation's War on White Collar Productivity." Santa Clara, Calif.: Intel, February 1981.

Bowers, D. G., "OD Techniques and their Results in 23 Organizations. The Michigan ICL Study." *Journal of Applied Behavioral Science*, 1973, *g*(1), 21–43.

Boyatzis, R. E. *The Competent Manager*. New York: John Wiley & Sons, 1982.

Branson, R. K., Gail T. Rayner, and J. Lamarr Cox. "Inter-Service Procedures for Instructional Systems Development: Executive Summary and Model." Tallahassee, Fla.: Center for Educational Technology, Florida State University, 1975.

Brooks, F. P., Jr. *The Mythical Man-Mouth: Essays on Software Engineering*. New York: Addison-Wesley, 1982.

Buffa, E. S. *Modern Production Management*. New York: John Wiley & Sons, 1968.

Business Week, "Casting Executives as Consultants." New York: McGraw-Hill, August 30, 1982.

Business Week, "Office Automation Restructures Business." New York: McGraw-Hill, October 8, 1984, pp. 124–125.

Business Week, "Sending the Staff Out to Solve Other Companies' Problems." New York: McGraw-Hill, January 16, 1984, pp. 54–55.

Calabresi, G., *The Cost of Accidents: A Legal and Economic Analysis*. New Haven, Conn., Yale University Press, 1970.

Campbell, D. T., and J. C. Stanley. *Experimental and Quasi-Experimental Designs for Research*. Chicago: Rand McNally, 1966.

Carroll, S., and S. H. Tosi, *Management by Objectives: Applications and Research*. New York: Macmillan, 1973.

Cascio, W. F. *Costing Human Resources: The Financial Impact of Behavior in Organizations*. Boston: Kent, 1982.

Charon, K. A., and J. D. Schlumpf, "IBM's Common Staffing System: How to Measure Productivity of the Indirect Workforce," *Management Review 70(8)*, (August 1981), pp. 8–14.

Cheek, L. M. "Cost Effectiveness Comes to the Personnel Function," *Harvard Business Review* (May–June 1973), 104.

Cohen, A. R. *Attitude Change and Social Influence*. New York: Basic Books, 1964.

Conley, B. C., "The Value of Human Life in the Demand for Safety," *The American Economic Review*, March 1976.

Cronbach, L. J., and G. C. Gleser. *Psychological Tests and Personnel Decisions*. Urbana: University of Illinois Press, 1965.

Cook, T. D., and D. T. Campbell. *Quasi-Experimentation Design and Analysis Issues for Field Settings*. Boston: Houghton Mifflin, 1979.

Cullen, B. J., G. O. Klemp, and L. A. Rossini. *Competencies of Organizational Effectiveness Consultants in the U.S. Army*, Final Report, Army Research Institute, Contract XX MOA 903-79-C-0427, Boston: McBer and Company, 1980.

Cullen, J. G., S. A. Sawzin, G. R. Sisson, and R. A. Swanson. "Training: What's it Worth?" *Training and Development Journal, 30(8)*, 12–20, 1976.

Cummings, N. A. "The Anatomy of Psychotherapy Under National Health Insurance," *American Psychologist 32(9)*, 711–718, September 1977.

Cummings, N. A., and W. T. Follette. "Psychiatric Services and Medical Utilization in a Prepaid Health Plan Setting," *Medical Care, 6*, 31–41, 1968.

Davis, H. *Productivity Accounting*. Philadelphia, Penn.: University of Pennsylvania Press, 1955.

Davies, B., and J. S. Browning. "First Interstate Bank: A Winning Program," *Training Magazine*, December 1984, pp. 53–59.

Dewhurst, R. F. J. *Business Cost-Benefit Analysis*. London: McGraw-Hill, 1972.

Driessnack, C. H. "Financial Impact of Effective Human Resources Management." *The Personnel Administrator* (December 1979), 62–66.

Droms, W. G. *Instructional Systems Association 1985 Financial Survey*. Washington, D.C.: Georgetown Univ. School of Business Administration, 1985.

Ferebee, J. S. "Are Your Managers Really Managing?" *Management Review* (January 1981), 18–22.

Fever, D. "Wellness Programs: How Well Do They Shape Up?" *Training Magazine*, April 1985, pp. 25–34.

Finnegan, G. T., and J. F. M. Campbell, "Role of Value Analysis," *Performance and Instruction XXI*, 5, June 1982, pp. 16–18.

Fitz-Enz, J. *How to Measure Human Resources Management*. New York: McGraw-Hill, 1984.

Flamholtz, E. *Human Resource Accounting*. Encino, Calif.: Dickerson, 1974.

Follman, J. F., Jr. *Alcoholism and Business*. New York: AMACOM, 1976.

Freeman, R. L., and J. L. Medoff, "The Two Faces of Unionism," *Public Interest*, Fall 1979, pp. 69–93.

French, K. E., and H. Meyer. "A Study of the Performance Appraisal Interview, Management Development and Employee Relations Services." New York: General Electric Co., 1964.

Fultz, J. F. *Overhead*. Cambridge, Mass: Abt, 1980.

Gelman, S. E., and R. Sandza. "The Boom in Worker Leasing," *Newsweek*, May 14, 1984 pp. 54–55.

Ghiselli, E. E. *The Validity of Occupational Aptitude Tests*. New York: John Wiley & Sons, 1966.

Goleman, D. "The New Competency Tests: Matching the Right People to the Right Jobs," *Psychology Today*, January 1981.

Gregerman, I. B. *Knowledge Worker Productivity*. New York: AMACOM, 1981.

Gross, P. H. "Valuation of Intangible Assets," In P. M. Kelley, ed., *The Economic Recovery Tax Act of 1981*. New York: AMA/AMACOM, 1982.

Hall, T. E. "How to Estimate Employee Turnover Costs," *Personnel* (July-August 1981), 43–52.

Harper, G. N. *1984 Operating Statistics for Professional Firms*. Cambridge, Mass.: Harper and Shuman, 1984.

Hart, R. A. *The Economics of Non-Wage Labor Costs*. Boston, Mass.: George Allen & Unwin, 1984.

Head, G. E. "A Cost Benefit Analysis of Individualized Criterion-Referenced Computer-Based Training." Dallas, Tex.: Instructional Communications, Inc., 1981.

Henderson, M. "The Value of Human Life," *Search*, January-February, 1975.

Holt, C. C., F. Modigliani, J. F. Muth, and H. A. Simon. *Planning Production, Inventories and Work Force*. Englewood Cliffs, N.J.: Prentice Hall, 1960.

Holoviak, S. J. *Costing Labor Contracts and Judging Their Financial Impact*. New York: Praeger, 1984.

Jones, R. L., and H. G. Trentin. *Management Controls for Professional Firms*, American Management Association, 1968.

Jones-Lee, M. W., *The Value of Life: An Economic Analysis*. Chicago, Ill., The University of Chicago Press, 1976.

Kane, J. and E. Lawler. "Methods of Peer Assessment," *Psychological Bulletin* (1979).

Kearsley, G. *Costs, Benefits and Productivity in Training Systems*. Boston: Addison-Wesley, 1982.

Kearsley, G. *Training and Technology*. Reading, Mass.: Addison Wesley, 1984.

Kendrick, J. W. *Measuring and Promoting Company Productivity*. Baltimore: Johns Hopkins Press, 1982.

Kiefhaben, A. K., and W. B. Goldbeck. "Worksite Wellness." District of Columbia, Washington Business Group on Health, 1983.

Kirkpatrick, D. C. *Evaluating Training Programs*. Madison: American Society for Training and Development, 1975.

Kochan, T. *Collective Bargaining and Industrial Relations*, Homewood, Ill.: Irwin, 1980.

Kolb, D. A. and A. L. Frohman. "An Organization Development Approach to Consulting," *Sloan Management Review 12*, 1970, 51–65.

Kolb, D. A., and R. E. Boyatzis. "Goal Setting and Self-Directed Behavior Change," *Human Relations* 23(5) (1970), 439–457.

Kuzmits, F. E. "How Much Is Absenteeism Costing Your Organization?" *The Personnel Administrator* (June 1979), 29–33.

Latham, G., and E. Locke. "Goal Setting: A Motivational Technique Which Works," *Organizational Dynamics* (Autumn 1979).

Layard, R. (ed.) *Cost Benefit Analysis: Selected Readings*. Baltimore, Md.: Penguin, 1972.

Lehrer, R. N., P. E., Ph.D. *White Collar Productivity*. New York: McGraw Hill, 1983.

Levitt, T. "Production Line Approach to Service," *Harvard Business Review* (September-October 1972), 41–52.

Lewin, A. V., and A. Zwaney. *Peer Nominations: A Model, Literature Critique, and a Paradigm for Research*. Springfield, Va.: National Technical Information Service, 1976.

Likert, R. *The Human Organization: Its Management and Value*. New York: McGraw-Hill, 1967.

Likert, R. "Human Resource Accounting: Building and Assessing Productive Organizations," *Personnel* (May/June 1973).

Locke, E., L. Saari, K. Shaw, and G. Latham. "Goal Setting and Task Performance: 1969–1980," *Psychological Bulletin, 90*(1) (1981), pp. 125–152.

MacKinnon, D. W. "An Overview of Assessment Center Methods," Technical Report No. 1. Greensboro, N.C.: Center for Creative Leadership, 1975.

Main, J. "How to Battle Your Own Bureaucracy," *Fortune*, June 29, 1981.

Main, J. "The Recovery Skips Middle Managers," *Fortune*, February 6, 1984.

McAfee, B., and W. Pottenberger. *Productivity Strategies*. Englewood Cliffs, N.J.: Prentice-Hall, 1982.

McClelland, D. C., and D. G. Winter. *Motivating Economic Achievement*. New York: Macmillan, 1969.

Meyer, H., E. Kay, and J. French. "Split Roles in Performance Appraisal," *Harvard Business Review*, 43 (1965), 123–129.

Midas, M. T. *The Productivity-Quality Connection*. Houston, Tex.: American Productivity Center, 1981.

Mischel, W. *Personality and Assessment*. New York: John Wiley & Sons, 1968.

Mishan, E. J., *Cost-Benefit Analysis: An Informal Introduction*. New York, N.Y., Praeger Press, 1975.

Mitchell, E., et al. "Organizational Effectiveness Cost Benefit Analysis Report - 1980." Fort Ord, Calif.: U.S. Army Organizational Effectiveness Center and School, 1980.

Mundel, M. E. *Improving Productivity and Effectiveness*. Englewood Cliffs, N.J.: Prentice Hall, 1983.

Myers, M. S., and V. S. Flowers. "A Framework for Measuring Human Assets," *California Management Review*, 16(45), 1974, pp. 5–16.

Naylor, J. C., and L. C. Shine. "A Table for Determining the Increase in Mean Criterion Score Obtained by Using a Selection Device," *Journal of Industrial Psychology*, 1965, pp. 33–42.

Neuman, J. L. "Make Overhead Cuts that Cost," *Harvard Business Review*, 1975.

Niehaus, R. J. *Computer Assisted Human Resource Planning*. New York: Wiley Interscience, 1979.

Niehaus, R. J. "Human Resource Planning Flow Models," *Human Resource Planning*, 3(4), 1980.

Odiorne, G. S. *Strategic Management of Human Resources*. San Francisco, Calif.: Jossey-Bass, 1984.

O'Neill, B. and A. B. Kelley, "Costs, Benefits, Effectiveness and Safety: Setting the Record Straight," *Professional Safety*, August 1975.

Ornati, O. A.; Edward J. Giblin; and Richard R. Floersch. *The Personnel Department: Its Staffing and Budgeting*. New York: AMACOM, 1982.

Oswald, R. "Unions and Productivity," in J. Rosow *Productivity: Prospects for Growth*. New York: Van Nostrand, 1981, pp. 98–99.

Phillips, J. *Handbook of Training Evaluation and Measurement Methods*. Houston, Tex.: Gulf Publishing Co., 1984.

Pribble, R. "Enter the Videodisc," *Training Magazine*, March 1985, pp. 91–99.

Rais, A. *Managing by Objectives*. Glenview, Ill.: Scott, Foreman and Co., 1974.

Recht, J. L. "How to Do a Cost-Benefit Analysis of Motor Vehicle Accident Countermeasures." Chicago, Ill., National Safety Council, 1966.

Rinefort, F. C. "Cost-effective requirements: A New Direction for OSHA?" *Professional Safety*, November 1978, pp. 27–29.

"A cost-benefit analysis of selected Texas industries: A New Look at Occupational Safety." *The Personal Administrator*, November 1977, pp. 29–36.

The Economics of Safety: How much risk is acceptable, if any?" *Professional Safety*, July 1979, pp. 44–47.

Rice, D. and B. C., "The Economic Value of Human Life," *American Journal of Public Health*, November 1967.

Sasser, W. E., R. P. Olsen, and D. D. Wyckoff. *Management of Service Operations*, Boston: Allyn and Bacon, 1978.

Schmidt, F. L., J. E. Hunter, R. C. McKenzie, and T. W. Muldrow. "Impact of Valid Selection Procedures on Work-Force Productivity," *Journal of Applied Psychology*, 64, 1979, pp. 609–626.

Spencer, L. M., Jr. "Calculating Human Resource Program Costs and Benefits." W. R. Tracey, ed., *Human Resource Management and Development Handbook*. New York: AMACOM, 1985.

Spencer, L. M., Jr. "Calculating the Costs and Benefits of Human Resource Interventions," *Training Magazine*, July 1984.

Spencer, L. M., Jr. *Cost-Benefit Workshop*. Boston, McBer and Company, 1985.

Spencer, L. M., Jr. *Soft Skill Competencies*. Edinburgh: Lindsay & Co. (The Scottish Council for Research in Education), 1983.

Spencer, L. M., Jr., and B. J. Cullen. *Evaluation of Army Organizational Development Interventions*. Alexandria, Va.: Army Research Institute (DAH78-C-0003)a, 1979.

Spencer, L. M., Jr., and B. J. Cullen. "Taxonomies of Organizational Change: Literature Review and Analysis." Arlington, Va.: Army Research Institute ARI Technical Report TR-78-A23, September 1978.

Stewart, CPT W. L. "Fort Carson Evaluation of Organizational Effectiveness (OE) Operations," *OE Communique*. Fort Ord, Calif.: U.S. Army Organizational Effectiveness Center and School, April 1979.

Swanson, R. A., and G. D. Geroy. "Forecasting the Economic Benefits of Training." St. Paul, Minn.: University of Minnesota Center for Employee Training and Development, 1984.

Taylor, J. C., and D. G. Bowers. *The Survey of Organizations*. Ann Arbor: Institute for Social Research, 1972.

Thaler, R. and S. Rosen, "The Value of Saving a Life: Evidence from the Labor Market" from Household Production and Consumption, N.E. Terleckyj (ed.), New York Columbia University Press, 1976.

Thompson, M. *Benefit-Cost Analysis for Program Evaluation*. Beverly Hills, Calif.: Sage, 1980.

Thor, C. G. "You Too Will Study Collar Productivity." Houston, Tex.: American Productivity Center, 1981.

Tung, R. L. "Selection and Training Procedures of U.S., European and Japanese Multinationals." *California Management Review* 23(1), Fall 1982, pp. 57–71.

U.S. Chamber of Commerce *Employee Benefits 1983*. Washington, D.C., 1984.

U.S. Department of Labor Bureau of Labor Statistics *Employee Benefits in Medium and Large Firms, 1984*. Washington, D.C.: U.S. Government Printing Office, 1984.

Vougn, C. F. and B. Asbell. "Productivity: A Practical Program for Improving Productivity. New York: AMACOM, 1979.

Wall Street Journal "Office Productivity Efforts Yield 9.5% Gain, Business Study Shows," Wednesday, October 13, 1982, p. 42.

Webb, E. J., D. T. Campbell, R. D. Schwartz, and L. Sechrest. *Unobtrusive Measures*. Chicago, Ill.: Rand McNally, 1966.

Webb, E. J., D. T. Campbell, R. D. Schwartz, L. Sechrest, and J. B. Grove, *Non-Reactive Measures in the Social Sciences*. Boston, Mass.: Houghton Mifflin, 1981.

White, J. R., and H. F. Froeb. "Small Airways Dysfunction in Nonsmokers Chronically Exposed to Tobacco Smoke," *New England Journal of Medicine*. March 1980, pp. 270–273.

Writer, F.W., and K.M. Rowland. "Personnel Decisions: A Bayesian Approach," *California Management Review, 22(3)*, Spring 1980.

Zeckhauser, R. "Procedures for Valuing Lives," *Public Policy*, 1975, p. 419.

APPENDIX

This appendix provides Lotus (or other) spreadsheet templates and BASIC programs for the most important worksheets in the book[1]:

1. Calculating the full cost of your time and applied person day rate (Tables 3.5 and 3.7) and
2. Costing worksheet (Table 3.8 and Figure 3.3)

Both the spreadsheet templates and BASIC program have advantages and disadvantages.

The advantages of *spreadsheet* templates include: fewer lines of code to enter (hence fewer chances to make mistakes and create bugs), greater flexibility (easier to modify or "tailor" to your unique needs), and ability to handle much larger analyses: steps are limited in number only by your computer's memory or your spreadsheet's range limit (e.g., for Lotus, 2048 rows). Spreadsheets have the *disadvantages* of requiring more

---

[1]IBM-compatible PC DOS/MS DOS 5 1/4 floppy discs containing templates and a BASIC program for these and other tables in the book are available from McBer and Company, 137 Newbury Street, Boston, MA USA 02116, (617) 437–7080.

work to use: You must enter commands to add steps and step options and change formats to enter longer variable names.

The *BASIC* program has the *advantage* of doing more of the formating and totaling for you. Its *disadvantages* include many more lines of code to enter (hence more mistakes and bugs), lack of flexibility (BASIC programs are hard to edit, modify, or tailor), and inability to handle large analyses (BASIC can use only 64K of computer memory, limiting you to about 20 analysis steps).

If you have access to Lotus or a spreadsheet program, some familiarity with using templates, and/or will be doing large analyses, use the spreadsheets. If you are not familiar with computers, want to see what computer analysis can do for you, and/or will be doing small analyses, use the BASIC program.

SPREADSHEET TEMPLATES

Entering the Templates

Boot Lotus (or other spreadsheet program) and enter Appendix A.1 and A.2 labels and formulas in the cells indicated. Save your templates using the File Save command (/FS) and the names "FULLCOST" and "CBA-COSTS." (If you are using a spreadsheet other than Lotus, modify cell formulas to your program's conventions.)

Calculating the Full Cost of a Person's Time and Billing Rate

Appendix A.1 provides the cell formulas for the "Your Data" columns of Tables 3.5 and 3.7. Calculating the full cost of a person's time and billing rate.

You can choose the method of calculating labor cost by the data you enter. If you want to use:

1. *Salary cost per time paid*, enter "260" (or the number of days in your firm's pay year) on line (2); "0" on lines (4) Paid days off, (11) Total Fringe %, (14) Overhead %, (17) Profit %, and "1.00" for (25) 'Gross applied rate.'

2. *Direct labor cost per time worked*, enter as above plus your Paid days off on line (3).

3. *Direct labor cost plus total fringe costs*, enter as above plus your Total fringe % on line (11).

4. *Full labor cost* (total fringe plus overhead), enter as above plus your Overhead % on line (14).

5. *Full labor cost plus profit*, enter as above plus your desired Profit % on line (17).

6. *Full labor cost per applied person day or billing rate*, enter as above and enter your "gross" applied rate on line (25). If you are not in a profit center, enter "O" on line (17) profit %.

Enter your data in the input fields shown as "_____." Note that "260" has been entered for (2) Days paid/standard year. You can override this entry if you are paid on a different number of days per year basis.

The template will calculate your Full Labor cost per *(20) Day, (22) Hour* [given your entry of (21) *Hours* paid/day], and *(23) Minute* worked; your *(24) Full Cost Multiplier; (26) "Net" applied rate* [given your entry of your (25) "Gross" applied rate]; full cost per applied unit of time or billing rate (the amount you need to charge to cover all your costs and make your desired profit) per *(28) Day, (30) Hour* and *(32) Minute*; and lastly, your *(33) Billing rate multiplier* (the number you multiply your salary cost/days, hours, or minutes in a standard year by to find your billing rate or full cost per applied unit of time).

Note that several of the calculated fields will show "0" or "ERR" (division by zero errors) until you enter data.

To *print* your analysis, enter {Alt} {p}. These entries call a Lotus "macro" in cell I3 which prints the worksheet.

To *erase* the contents of a cell, enter {Alt} {e}. These entries call a macro in cell I5 which uses the Lotus Range Erase (/RE~) command.

```
A1:  'Appendix A.1 Template for Calculating the Full Cost of a Person's Time
D2:  'YOUR DATA
A4:  '1) Salary/Year
G4:  (C2) \_
A5:  '   divided by
A6:  '2) Days paid/standard year
E6:  260
A7:  '   equals
A8:  '3) Labor cost/day paid
G8:  (C2) +G4/E6
A9:  '  (2) Days paid minus
A10: '4) Paid Days off
E10: \_
A11: '   equals
A12: '5) Direct Labor Days Worked/Year
E12: +E6+E10
A13: '   x (3) labor cost/day equals
A14: '6) Direct Labor Cost/Year
G14: (C2) +E12*G8
A16: 'FRINGE
A17: '   (4) Days off/(2) Days paid equals
A18: '7) Paid days off fringe %
E18: (F3) -E10/E6
A19: '   x (1) Salary/year equals
A20: '8) Paid days off fringe cost
F20: (C2) +G4*E18
A21: '9) Out of pocket fringe %
E21: (F3) \_
A22: '   x (1) Salary/year equals
A23: '10) Out-of-pocket fringe cost
F23: (C2) +G4*E21
A24: '11) Total fringe %
E24: (F3) \_
A25: '   x (1) Salary/year equals
A26: '12) Total Fringe cost
G26: (C2) +G4*E24
A27: '   (6) Direct labor + (12) Total fringe =
A28: '13) SUBTOTAL: Direct Labor + Fringe Cost
G28: (C2) +G14+G26
A30: 'OVERHEAD
A31: '14) Overhead %
E31: \_
A32: '   x (13) Direct Labor + Fringe equals
A33: '15) Overhead Cost
G33: (C2) +G28*E31
A34: '   plus (13) Direct Labor + Fringe equals
A35: '16) SUBTOTAL: Drct Lbr+Frng+Ohd
G35: (C2) +G28+G33
A37: 'PROFIT
A38: '17) Profit %
E38: \_
A39: '   x (16) Lbr+Frng+Ohd equals
A40: '18) Profit
G40: (C2) +G35*E38
A41: '   plus (16) Lbr+Frng+Ohd equals
```

```
A42:  '19) TOTAL: Full labor cost/year
G42:  (C2) +G35+G40
A44:  'FULL LABOR COSTS
A45:  '   (19) Full cost divided by Time Unit worked/year
A46:  '20) Full Labor cost/day
D46:  +E12
E46:  'days/year=
G46:  (C2) +G42/E12
A47:  '21) Hours paid/day
D47:  8
A48:  '22) Full labor cost/hour
D48:  +D46*D47
E48:  'hours/year=
G48:  (C2) +G42/D48
A49:  '23) Full labor cost/minute
D49:  +D48*60
E49:  'min./year=
G49:  (C2) +G42/D49
A51:  'FULL COST MULTIPLIER
A52:  '   (20) Full cost/(3) Sal. cost/day paid equals
A53:  '24) Full cost multiplier
G53:  (F2) +G46/G8
A55:  'APPLIED (DIRECT "BILLABLE") COSTS
A57:  '25) "Gross" applied rate %
D57:  (F2) \_
E57:  'x days paid/year
A58:  '   x (2) Days paid/(5) Days worked=
A59:  '26) "Net" applied rate %
D59:  (F2) +D57*E6/E12
E59:  'x days worked/year
A60:  '   x (5) Days worked=
A61:  '27) Applied/billable days
D61:  +E6*D57
E61:  '/year
A62:  '   (19) Full cost/(27) Applied days=
A63:  '28) Full cost/applied day
G63:  (C2) +G42/D61
A64:  '   (19) Full cost divided by
A65:  '29) Applied/billable hours
D65:  +D61*D47
E65:  '/year
A66:  '   equals
A67:  '30) Full cost/applied hour
G67:  (C2) +G42/D65
A68:  '   (19) Full cost divided by
A69:  '31) Applied/billable min.s
D69:  +D65*60
E69:  '/year
A70:  '   equals
A71:  '32) Full cost/applied min.
G71:  (C2) +G42/D69
A73:  'BILLING RATE MULTIPLIER
A74:  '   (28) Full cost/applied day/(3) Sal.cost/day=
A75:  '33) Billing rate multiplier
G75:  (F2) +G63/G8
```

APPENDIX A.2

Costing Worksheet

Appendix A.2 provides cell formulas for the Costing Worksheet (Table 3.8 and Figure 3.3). The template starts by requesting firm labor time and cost data and continues with an expandable cost worksheet limited only by your computer's memory. The following abbreviations are used in the template shown in Table A.2.1:

    * = Instruction or note

    > = Data entry: days worked and paid days off; fringe, overhead and profit rates; peoples names, salaries and applied rates; project and step names; labor time and expense units and unit costs.

    ! = Calculated figures: full costs, labor and expense cost totals, and step and option totals

Labor time and cost data. On the first eight lines (rows 4–11), enter your firm's standard time paid and cost data. US industry average data are shown as an example: 260 days paid in a standard year, 30 paid days off, a total fringe benefit rate of 35%, overhead rate of 115%, and profit rate of 0% (assuming an internal cost center). You can override these example figures by entering your own data. The template will calculate your cumulative full cost multiplier opposite each data entry line. (Try a range of fringe and overhead rates and see the effects on your full cost). You can choose the method of calculating labor costs following directions one to five (ignoring line numbers) on page 312 in Appendix A.1.

Given these data, the worksheet will calculate your full cost multiplier (FCM) for time paid in a standard year (usually 260 days, 2080 hours, or 124, 800 minutes) in cell F13. You can override this calculation by entering any other multiplier you want to use in cell F13, e.g., "3." To retrieve the calculated multiplier enter {*Alt*} {*f*}. These entries call a Lotus "macro" in cell AA16 which replaces the FCM calculation equation in cell F13.

To calculate full costs per applied person-day and billing rates, enter up to five persons' salaries in cells B17–B21 and net applied rates in cells E17–E21. Net applied rates are shown as 1.00 in the example. Each per-

TABLE A.2.1 COSTING WORKSHEET

Human Resource Cost/Benefit Analysis Template

*Enter your firm's standard time and cost data:
>Days paid/year: 260 Days
>Fringe paid days off/year: 30 Days
!Direct Labor Days/Year 230 Days

		Full Cost Multiplier
!Direct labor cost/year		0.88 X Salary/Year
>Fringe rate (.xx):	0.35	1.23 X Salary/Year
>Overhead rate(x.xx):	1.15	2.65 X Salary/Year
>Profit rate (.xx):	0.00	2.65 X Salary/Year
! Your full cost multiplier (DL Time Worked)=		2.65 X Salary/Year
FCM for Standard year (Time paid)=		3.00 X Salary/Time paid

*Billing rates for Professional Staff: Net

>Person	>Salary/yr	!Full Cost/ Day	>Applied Rate	!Billing Rate
Smith	$25,000	$288.52	1.00	$288.52
Jones	$40,000	$461.64	0.75	$615.52
Managers	$35,000	$403.93	1.00	$403.93
		$0.00	1.00	$0.00
		$0.00	1.00	$0.00

PROJECT:
>Time unit (1=days,8=hours,480=minutes): 1 Days
Step.....I. Plan Training Program

>Person	>*	>Salary/Yr	!Cost/Time	>Time	!Total --Labor--	>Expense	>Cost/Unit	>*Units	!Total --Expense	!Step Total I	!Step Total II
Smith	1	$25,000	$288.52	5	$1,443	Materials	$260.00	1	$260		
TOTAL					$1,443				$260	$1,703	

| PROGRAM TOTALS | | | | | | | | | | $1,703 | $0 |

son's full cost per day will be shown in cell C17–C21 and billing rates in cells F17–F21. If you need to calculate additional persons' billing rates, enter {Alt} {b}. These entries call a macro in cell AA19 which inserts a row and copies the format for calculating a billing rate.

Save your worksheet using your program's File Save command (in Lotus:/FS name ~) and a name of your choice. This creates a template "tailored" to your firm's financial data which you can use for subsequent analyses.

Costing Worksheet. Enter the following data:

1. *Project Name.* Enter the analysis or project name in cell B22.

2. *Time Unit.* Indicate the unit of time you will use in cell E23 by entering "1" for days, "8" (or the number of hours you are paid per day if other than "8"), and "480" for minutes. (If you are paid on a basis of other than 8 hours per day, enter the number of hours you are paid a day times 60; for example, for a 7.5 hour day, enter 7.5 × 60 = 450 minutes.)

3. *Step Calculations.* Enter name of the first step in your analysis, beginning with a roman numeral "I." opposite the word "Step": (Use roman numerals for step numbers because the program treats arabic numbers as values. Alternatively, begin name lines with an apostrophe " ' "; the program treats following characters as a label or comment.)

    3a. *Labor costs.* Enter the *name* or title (up to 15 characters) of the person(s) involved in the step, the *number* of persons, their (average) salary per year, and amount of *time* each spent on the step in the columns indicated. The program will calculate each person's labor cost per unit of time using the firm's data, and the total labor cost per person for the step. Labor names or titles more than 15 characters long will be stored by the program and shown in the cell entry window, but truncated on the screen or printout. If you need to display a longer labor name or title, you can either insert a row (using the Row Insert command "/WIR") above the calculation line and use it for your name or title, or continue the name in the cell beneath the first cell. Note that "Salary/ Year" and "Labor Total" cells are formated to round to whole dollar values ("CO:"currency-0 decimal place). You can change this format by using the Range Format Currency (/RFC.n decimal places) command. For example, if you are using minutes as your time unit, you will probably want to use dollars and cents (/RFC.2).

    3b. *Expense costs.* Enter the *name* (up to 9 characters) of direct outlay expenses, *number* of units, and *cost* per unit of the expense. The template will calculate the total expense cost.

Expense names longer than 9 characters can be displayed in the same way as extended labor names.

Additional lines: Note that first step format has room for only 1 line of labor or expense data. To add a line within a step, move the cursor *ONTO the dashed line-----in Column A above the word "TOTAL" and enter {Alt} {L}*. These entries call a Lotus "macro" in cell AA7 which inserts a row and copies the labor and expense calculation formulas from N4–W4. (If you are using a spreadsheet program which does not support "macro" commands, insert and/or copy a row which includes the labor and expense calculation formulas.)

Step totals. The template will automatically calculate labor, expense, and step cost totals.

Step options. To compare the costs of one or more options or alternative ways of performing a step, *move the cursor to the Column A cell BELOW the double dashed line = = = = = below the word "TOTAL"* of the preceding step and enter *{Alt} {0}*. These entries call a "macro" in cell AA5 which inserts rows and copies a step calculation format from cells N10-Y15 into your worksheet directly below your "baseline" step cost calculation. This takes about 5 seconds. The only difference in the step option format is the "Option" title and placement of the step option total in column L to the right of the "baseline" step cost total in column K for easier comparison. Name the step option following "Option:" Insert additional lines, if needed, in the same way as for the baseline step. (If you are using a spreadsheet which lacks "macro" commands, insert rows and/or copy the step calculation format from another part of your worksheet.)

4. *Additional steps*. To add a step, enter *{Alt S}*. These entries call a Lotus "macro" in cell AA3 which inserts rows and copies the step cost calculation format in cells N1-X7. Follow instructions 3a–3b.

NOTE: When entering additional lines, step options, or steps, *be sure* you have the cursor in Column A and on the right row: *on* the dashed line ---- above TOTAL for lines within a step and *below* the double dashed line = = = = below the previous step or step option "TOTAL" (but *above* "PROGRAM TOTALS") for step options and steps. Failure to position the cursor in the right cell may result in loss of data overwritten by the next calculation format.

5. *Analysis and option totals.* When you have entered all step and option data, the template will automatically total all step and step option costs and calculate the savings of the option versus the baseline program.

NOTE: The cost comparison format has many uses, including budgeting; tracking projects by comparing actual costs with budgeted amounts; choosing between alternatives; conducting "make versus buy" analyses; and calculating "before" (baseline) versus "after" benefits from cost savings.

Line Printing. Enter {*Alt*} {*P*}. These entries call a "macro" which prints our entire cost worksheet analysis in *compressed* (132 characters per line) print. The macro stops and asks you to enter the number of the last row in your analysis (usually the "PROGRAM TOTALS" row). If you are using a spreadsheet other than Lotus and/or your printer does not support compressed print, use your program's print command to print the entire range of your worksheet.

Macros are placed in cells Z1-AA18. An additional macro in cell AA13 called by entering {Alt} {e} erases the contents of a cell using the Lotus Range Erase (/RE~) command.

```
A1:  'Human Resource Cost/Benefit Analysis Template
N1:  'Step......
O1:  \.
Z1:  'macros
N2:  '>Person
O2:  ">#
P2:  ">Salary/Yr
Q2:  '!Cost/Time
R2:  ">Time
S2:  "!Total
T2:  ">Expense
U2:  ">#  Units
V2:  ">Cost/Unit
W2:  "!Total
A3:  '*Enter your firm's standard time and cost data:
N3:  '----------
O3:  '-----------
P3:  '-------------
Q3:  \-
R3:  \-
S3:  "----Labor
```

```
T3:  '----------
U3:  '----------
V3:  '-----------
W3:  '----Expense
Z3:  'step
AA3: '/wir~/wir~/wir~/wir~/wir~/wir~/wir~/cn1.x7~~
A4:  '>Days paid/year:
E4:  260
F4:  'Days
Q4:  (F2) +P4*$F$13/($E$4*$E$23)
S4:  (C0) +O4*Q4*R4
W4:  (C0) +U4*V4
A5:  '>Fringe paid days off/year:
E5:  30
F5:  'Days
N5:  \-
O5:  \-
P5:  \-
Q5:  \-
R5:  \-
S5:  \-
T5:  \-
U5:  \-
V5:  \-
W5:  \-
Z5:  'option
AA5: '/wir~/wir~/wir~/wir~/wir~/cn10.y15~~
A6:  '!Direct Labor Days/Year
E6:  +E4-E5
F6:  'Days
N6:  "TOTAL
S6:  (C0) @SUM(S4..S5)
W6:  (C0) @SUM(W4..W5)
X6:  (C0) +S6+W6
F7:  '     Full Cost Multiplier
N7:  \=
O7:  \=
P7:  \=
Q7:  \=
R7:  \=
S7:  \=
T7:  \=
U7:  \=
V7:  \=
W7:  \=
X7:  \=
Z7:  'line
AA7: '/wir~/cn4.w4~~
A8:  '!Direct labor cost/year
F8:  (F2) +E6/E4
G8:  'X Salary/Year
A9:  '>Fringe rate (.xx):
E9:  (F2) 0.35
F9:  (F2) +F8+E9
G9:  'X Salary/Year
Z9:  'print
AA9: '/ppral.L(?)~
A10: '>Overhead rate(x.xx):
E10: (F2) 1.15
F10: (F2) +F9+(E10*F9)
G10: 'X Salary/Year
N10: ' Option:
O10: \.
AA10: 'oml~mrl36~p100~s\027\015~
A11: '>Profit rate (.xx):
```

```
E11:  (F2) 0
F11:  (F2) +F10+(F10*E11)
G11:  'X Salary/Year
N11:  '---------
O11:  '-----------
P11:  '------------
Q11:  \-
R11:  \-
S11:  "----Labor
T11:  '---------
U11:  '---------
V11:  '-----------
W11:  '----Expense
AA11: 'ouqgq(home)
A12:  '! Your full cost multiplier (DL Time Worked)=
F12:  (F2) +F11+(E11*F11)
G12:  'X Salary/Year
Q12:  (C2) +P12*$F$13/($E$4*$E$23)
S12:  (C0) +O12*Q12*R12
W12:  (C0) +U12*V12
A13:  '      FCM for Standard year (Time paid)=
F13:  (F2) +$F$12*($E$4/$E$6)
G13:  'X Salary/Time paid
N13:  \-
O13:  \-
P13:  \-
Q13:  \-
R13:  \-
S13:  \-
T13:  \-
U13:  \-
V13:  \-
W13:  \-
Z13:  'erase
AA13: '/re~
A14:  '*Billing rates for Professional Staff:
E14:  "Net
N14:  "TOTAL
S14:  (C0) @SUM(S12..S13)
W14:  (C0) @SUM(W12..W13)
Y14:  (C0) +S14+W14
A15:  '>Person
B15:  '>Salary/yr
C15:  ' !Full Cost/
E15:  ">Applied
F15:  "!Billing
N15:  \=
O15:  \=
P15:  \=
Q15:  \=
R15:  \=
S15:  \=
T15:  \=
U15:  \=
V15:  \=
W15:  \=
X15:  \=
Y15:  \=
C16:  '     Day
E16:  "Rate
F16:  "Rate
Z16:  'fcmltplr
AA16: '/cab16~f13~
AB16: (F2) +$F$12*($E$4/$E$6)
C17:  (C2) +B17*$F$13/$E$4
```

```
E17:  (F2) 1
F17:  (C2) +C17/E17/$E$23
C18:  (C2) +B18*$F$13/$E$4
E18:  (F2) 1
F18:  (C2) +C18/E18/$E$23
Z18:  'billrate
AA18: '/wir~/ca21.f21~~
C19:  (C2) +B19*$F$13/$E$4
E19:  (F2) 1
F19:  (C2) +C19/E19/$E$23
C20:  (C2) +B20*$F$13/$E$4
E20:  (F2) 1
F20:  (C2) +C20/E20/$E$23
C21:  (C2) +B21*$F$13/$E$4
E21:  (F2) 1
F21:  (C2) +C21/E21/$E$23
A22:  'PROJECT:
A23:  '>Time unit (1=days,8=hours,480=minutes):
E23:  480
A24:  'Step......
B24:  \.
A25:  '>Person
B25:  ">#
C25:  ">Salary/Yr
D25:  '!Cost/Time
E25:  ">Time
F25:  "!Total
G25:  ">Expense
H25:  ">#  Units
I25:  ">Cost/Unit
J25:  "!Total
K25:  "!Step
L25:  "!Step
M25:  "!Saving
A26:  '---------
B26:  '-----------
C26:  '------------
D26:  \-
E26:  \-
F26:  "----Labor
G26:  '---------
H26:  '---------
I26:  '-----------
J26:  '----Expense
K26:  "Total I
L26:  "Total II
M26:  "I-II
D27:  (F2) +C27*$F$13/($E$4*$E$23)
F27:  (C0) +B27*D27*E27
J27:  (C0) +H27*I27
A28:  \-
B28:  \-
C28:  \-
D28:  \-
E28:  \-
F28:  \-
G28:  \-
H28:  \-
I28:  \-
J28:  \-
A29:  "TOTAL
F29:  (C0) @SUM(F27..F28)
J29:  (C0) @SUM(J27..J28)
K29:  (C0) +F29+J29
A30:  \=
```

```
B30:  \=
C30:  \=
D30:  \=
E30:  \=
F30:  \=
G30:  \=
H30:  \=
I30:  \=
J30:  \=
K30:  \=
A33:  \=
B33:  \=
C33:  \=
D33:  \=
E33:  \=
F33:  \=
G33:  \=
H33:  \=
I33:  \=
J33:  \=
K33:  \=
L33:  \=
M33:  \=
A34:  '    PROGRAM TOTALS
K34:  (C0) @SUM(K27..K33)
L34:  (C0) @SUM(L27..L33)
M34:  (C0) +K34-L34
```

APPENDIX A.3

with Kim Welch

BASIC Program

Entering the BASIC Program. Boot BASIC (or BASICA) from your DOS and enter the program code provided in Appendix A.3. If you are using a BASIC other than PCDOS or MSDOS BASIC, you may need to modify code to be compatible with your system. Save your program using the SAVE command and the name "d:CBA."

We have tried to make the BASIC program act as much like a spreadsheet as possible, using defined input "cells" and cursor controls to move among cells (a method suggested by Ford (1984.) To move the cursor use the following keys:

[^] Up Arrow moves the cursor to the first input cell of the line above the current input cell.

[v] Down Arrow moves the cursor to the first input cell of the line below the current input cell.

[<] Left Arrow moves the cursor one space to the left within a cell and if at the far left margin of a cell, to the preceding input cell.

[>] Right Arrow moves the cursor one space to the right within an input cell.

[Back Space] moves the cursor one space to the left within an input cell.

[Home] moves the cursor to the beginning of an input cell.

[End] moves the cursor to the space past the last character in an input cell.

[Crtl] [End] erases the contents of a cell.

[RETURN] enters data in a cell and moves the cursor to the next input cell. [RETURN] with no data entered in the first input cell of a new Step or Labor or Expense field moves the cursor to the next input field (i.e., entering a null'''' indicates to the program that you have finished entering data).

MENU. When you run the BASIC program, you first see the program menu:

TABLE A.3.1 PROGRAM "MAIN MENU"

COST CALCULATION PROGRAM

Lyle Spencer, Kim Welch
McBer and Company
137 Newbury Street
BOSTON, MA 02116
(617) 437-7080

                        MAIN MENU

          1. ENTER ORGANIZATION COST DATA
          2. ENTER NAMES AND APPLIED RATES
          3. CALCULATE PROGRAM COSTS
          4. CALCULATE BENEFITS: BEFORE VS AFTER
          5. SAVE DATA TO DISK
          6. GET DATA FROM DISK
          7. OUTPUT TO LINE PRINTER
          8. EXIT PROGRAM

             SELECT

           (C) copyright McBer & Co., 1985

1. *Enter organization cost data.* Enter "1" to provide your firm's
labor time and cost figures:

TABLE A.3.2. "YOUR FIRM'S ORGANIZATION COST DATA"

ENTER YOUR FIRM'S ORGANIZATION COST DATA

1.STANDARD DAYS PAID PER YEAR: 260

2.STANDARD HOURS WORKED PER DAY: 8.00

3.FRINGE BENEFIT RATE (%):   35

4.FRINGE DAYS PAID (HOLIDAYS,VACATION,ETC):   30

   INCLUDE IN FRINGE RATE? (Y/N) Y

5.OVERHEAD RATE (%): 115

6.PROFIT RATE (%):   0

7.YOUR ENTERED FULL COST MULTIPLIER IS: 3.00

             PRESS [Esc] TO RETURN TO MAIN MENU

As with the spreadsheet template, you can choose the method of
calculating labor costs by the data you enter for lines (1)–(6). The

"default" entries you see are the United States industry averages.

Salary cost per time paid: Enter "260" (or the number of days in your firm's pay year) on Line (2); "8" or the number of hours you are paid a day on Line (2); "0" on Lines (3) Total Fringe Benefit Rate (%), (4) Fringe Days Paid off (and "Y" to the question "Included in Fringe Rate?"), (5) Overhead Rate (%), and (6) Profit %.

Direct labor cost per time worked: Enter as above plus your Fringe Days Paid off on Line (3) and "Y" to the question "Included in Fringe Rate?"

Direct labor cost plus total fringe costs: Enter as above plus your total Fringe Benefit Rate (%) on Line (3) and "Y" on "N" for Yes or No to the question "Included in Fringe Rate?" depending on whether your entered fringe benefit rate includes paid days off.

Full labor cost (total fringe plus overhead): Enter as above plus your Overhead Rate (%) on Line (5).

Full labor cost plus profit: Enter as above plus your desired profit rate (%) on line (6).

The program will calculate your full cost multiplier and display it on Line (7). You can choose to use this calculated value by pressing [RETURN] and returning to the Main Menu, or override the calculated value by entering the multiplier you want to use in your analysis (e.g., "3") and then pressing [RETURN]. Once you have entered a value, it will be used in all worksheet calculations to determine labor costs. Select Menu option (5) to save your data. This will create a cost analysis program "tailored" with your firm's data for use in subsequent analyses.

2. ***Enter names and applied rates.*** Select "2" on the Main Menu to enter the names (or initials), number, salaries, applied rates (and whether applied rates are "gross" (G) percentage of days paid, or "net" (N) percentage of days worked per year) of people involved in the program you want to cost. The program will recognize the name or initials entered and calculate the full cost per applied person unit of time in the costing worksheet. If you do

not want to adjust labor costs for time or billable percentage, enter
"1.00" and "N" for applied rate and gross or net basis of calculation. This date entry screen is especially useful if you do want
to adjust for the applied or billable time of several professionals
involved in a program. Table A.3.3 shows the billing rates for people in the Table 3.9 Costing a Training Program example.

3. *Calculate program costs.* To calculate the costs of a program, select
    "3" on the Main Menu. If data have been entered in the program,
    "Data from a previous analysis will be overwritten" will appear on
    the screen and you will be asked to respond "Y" (yes) or "N" (no)
    to the question "Do you wish to use these data?" If you answer
    "Y", analysis data entered will be displayed. Answering "N" will
    cause previous data to be erased and give a blank worksheet.
    The program will next ask you to "Enter the name of the project to
    be costed_____" and to "Enter the unit of labor: day, hour or min-
    ute." "HOUR" will be shown as the default time value. Change
    this by typing in the unit you want to use in your analysis. Your
    project name (limited in length by the input cell) and unit of time
    will be used and noted when your analysis is printed out.

TABLE A.3.3   ENTER NAMES AND APPLIED RATES

INITIALS, SALARY/YEAR, AND APPLIED RATES FOR UP TO 9 PEOPLE

PERSON'S NAME	#	SALARY/YEAR	APPLIED RATE	G / N	FULL COST/DAY
1 Smith	1	$ 30000	1.00	N	$ 391.30
2 Supers	8	$ 25000	1.00	G	$ 288.46
3 Foremen	80	$ 20000	1.00	G	$ 230.77
4					
5					
6					
7					
8					
9					

PRESS [Esc] TO RETURN TO MAIN MENU

Table A.3.4 Step 2: STEP NAME TRAINER TRAINING

```
STEP 2    STEP NAME  Trainer Training

LABOR COSTS:
N °   PERSON        °  # °SALARY/YEAR° COST/DAY ° DAYS  °LABOR TOTAL ° STEP TOTA
1 ° Smith           °  1 ° $  30000  °$  350.76 °    5  °$  1753.80 °
2 ° Supers          °  8 ° $  25000  °$  292.30 °    5  °$ 11692.00 °
3 °                 °    °           °          °       °           °
4 °                 °    °           °          °       °           °
5 °                 °    °           °          °       °           °
6 °                 °    °           °          °       °           °
      TOTAL                                             $ 13445.80 °

EXPENSE COSTS:
N °    EXPENSE           °     COST/UNIT   °  # UNITS  °EXPENSE TOTAL°
1 ° Smith per diem       ° $      20.00    °    5.00   °$    100.00 °
2 ° materials            ° $      50.00    °    8.00   °$    400.00 °
3 ° travel to site       ° $     350.00    °    8.00   °$   2800.00 °
4 ° Supers per diem      ° $      75.00    °   40.00   °$   3000.00 °
5 ° training room        ° $     150.00    °    5.00   °$    750.00 °
6 °                      °                 °           °            °
      TOTAL                                            $   7050.00 °
      STEP TOTAL                                                   °$    20495.
```

When you press [RETURN] to enter your unit of time, you will see the Table 3.8 and Figure 3.3 costing worksheet format, with Labor costs above Expense costs. Table A.3.4. shows Step 2 of Table 3.9 Costing & Training Program calculated using the BASIC program.

First enter the name of the step (limited in length by input cell). If you press [RETURN] without entering anything, the program will assume you are done and display totals for all program steps. Next, enter the name or title of person(s) involved in the step. The program will prompt you for data to be entered by displaying the "inquiry strategy" question to be answered and highlighting the input cell in which to put data. If you have previously entered person(s) names or titles under Menu option "2", number and labor cost per time unit will be displayed. If you have not previously entered these data, enter the number, salary per year and labor time spent by persons involved in the program, and the program will calculate labor cost totals. You can enter up to 6 persons or titles per step. If you need to enter additional persons, use the next step, naming it "Step X-continued." If you press [RETURN] without entering anything in the "person" column, the program will jump to the first line of the expense cost worksheet.

Enter the name, cost per unit and number of each expense as

prompted by the question and highlighted cell displayed. The program will calculate expense cost totals and step labor plus expense total costs. If you enter [RETURN] without entering anything in the "Expense" column, the program will jump to the next step, asking you for the name of the step.

Enter step names, as well as labor expense cost data for additional steps (to a limit of 20) in the same way. After you have entered data for the last step of your analysis, press [RETURN] without entering anything when asked for a new step name. The program will total and display the cost of all steps in your analysis. Pressing any key will return you to the Main Menu. Table A.3.5 shows the total cost of the example shown inTable 3.9 Costing a Training Program.

Table A.3.5 Project costs for: Training Program

```
PROJECT COSTS FOR: TRAINING COURSE


STEP 1 Development of Course     $      3767.60
STEP 2 Trainer Training          $     20495.80
STEP 3 Delivery of Training      $     48429.60
STEP 4 Evaluation                $      1152.28

TOTAL COST:                      $     73845.28
```

```
              PRESS ANY KEY TO CONTINUE
```

4. *Calculate benefits: Before vs. After.*   Select "4" on the Main Menu to compare the costs of two ways of doing a porject, for example, "before versus after," "centralized versus decentralized,;; or "budget versus actual."

Enter data in the same way as for costing a project. The only difference in the "comparison" program is that each step has two options. For example, the name of step one will show "STEP 1 OPTION 1 STEP NAME__." After you have entered data for this step option or [RETURN] to indicate that the option has no costs (e.g., an unnecessary step deleted in a work simplification effort), you will see "STEP 1 OPTION 2 STEP NAME__." When you have entered data for all steps and options, enter [RETURN] without entering anything for the next step options one and two and the program will total the costs of both options for each step and display the step total program costs and cost differences.

5. *Save data to disk.*   Select "5" on the Main Menu to save an analysis to a floppy disk. The program will prompt you for a file name: "Enter name of file to write to _____." File names can be up to eight letters in length with an additional 3 letter extension, for example, "d:filename. ext," where "d" is the disk drive (e.g., "A" or "B") the file is saved to.

6. *Get data from disk.*   Select "6" on the Main Menu to get data from a floppy disk. The program will prompt you for a file name: "Enter name of file to read from:_____." Enter a file name in the form "d:filename. ext." The program will display "INITIALIZING DATA" while it is reading data from the disk, then return to the Main Menu.

7. *Output to line printer.*   Select "7" on the Main Menu to print out analysis data on your line printer. Data for all steps, options, and totals will be printed in "sparse format" (i.e., empty cells and blank lines are not printed).

8. *Exit program.*   Select "8" on the Main Menu to return to DOS.

REFERENCE

Ford, N., "Controlling input using INKEY$," *PC Tech Journal*, Vol. 2, No. 2, August 1984, pp. 32–39.


```
10 'Cost Benefit Analysis Program
20 'Version: 1.1     Date 10/17/85
30 'Target Machine: IBM PC and 100% compatibles
40 'Language:       IBM BASIC, 2.0
50 '
60 'Concept:        Dr. Lyle Spencer
70 'Programmer:     Kim Welch
80 '
90  GOTO 190
100 LOCATE  1,27: PRINT "COST CALCULATION PROGRAM"
```

```
110 LOCATE   3, 2: PRINT "Lyle Spencer, Kim Welch"
120 LOCATE   4, 2: PRINT "McBer and Company
130 LOCATE   5, 2: PRINT "137 Newbury Street"
140 LOCATE   6, 2: PRINT "BOSTON, MA  02116"
150 LOCATE   7, 2: PRINT "(617) 437-7080"
160 LOCATE 24,20: PRINT "(C) copyright McBer & Co., 1985";
170 RETURN
180 '
190 'default organizational data
200 TIME.UNIT$ = "HOUR": TIME.UNIT = 1
210 DAYS.PAID = 260: HOURS.WORKED = 8
220 FR.RATE = 35: FR.DAYS = 30: FR.INCL$ = "Y"
230 OH.RATE = 115: PROFIT.RATE = 0
240 FC.MULT = 3
250 '
260 YES = NOT NO: NO = NOT YES
270 'set up screen and color variables
280 'check for monitor type here
290 DEF SEG = 0
300 IF (PEEK(&H410) AND &H30) = &H30 THEN
        MONOCHROME = YES ELSE MONOCHROME = NO
310 DEF SEG
320 IF MONOCHROME THEN BG = 0: CURSOR.SIZE = 13
        ELSE BG = 1: CURSOR.SIZE = 7
330 SCREEN 0,0,0,0: WIDTH 80
340 FG = 7: COLOR FG, BG: KEY OFF: CLS
350 '
360 'global varibles and initial values
370 STEP.MAX = 20: N.MAX = 6
380 S = STEP.MAX: O = 2: N = N.MAX
390 OPTION BASE 1
400 DIM STEP.COUNT(S), STEP.NAME$(S,O), STEP.TOTAL(S,O)
410 DIM LAB.NAMES$(S,O,N), LAB.NUMBER(S,O,N), LAB.SALARY(S,O,N), LAB.COST(S,O,N),
        LAB.TIME(S,O,N), LAB.TOTAL(S,O,N), TOTAL.LAB(S,O)
420 DIM EXP.NAMES$(S,O,N), EXP.COST(S,O,N), EXP.NUMBER(S,O,N), EXP.TOTAL(S,O,N),
        TOTAL.EXP(S,O)
430 '
440 'various format strings
450 U5$ = "$#####.##": U6$="$######.##": U7$ = "$#######.##":
    U8$ = "$########.##"
460 B$ = CHR$(179)
470 E$ = CHR$(17) + CHR$ (196) + CHR$(217)
480 '
490 'edit keys used by inkey routine
500 ESC = 27: ESC$ = CHR$(ESC)
510 ENTR = 13: ENTR$ = CHR$(ENTR)
520 BACKSPACE = 8: BACKSPACE$ = CHR$(BACKSPACE)
530 CURSOR.LF = 75: CURSOR.RT = 77
540 END.KEY = 79: INS.KEY= 82: DEL.KEY = 83
550 HOME = 71: CTRL.END = 117
560 'other cursor keys
570 CURSOR.UP = 72: CURSOR.DN = 80
580 PAGE.UP = 73: PAGE.DN = 81
590 '
600 CLS   'display main menu and get selection
610 GOSUB 100 'McBer information
620 LOCATE  9,33: PRINT "MAIN MENU"
630 LOCATE 11,20: PRINT "1. ENTER ORGANIZATION COST DATA"
640 LOCATE 12,20: PRINT "2. ENTER NAMES AND APPLIED RATES"
650 LOCATE 13,20: PRINT "3. CALCULATE PROGRAM COSTS"
660 LOCATE 14,20: PRINT "4. CALCULATE BENEFITS: BEFORE VS AFTER"
670 LOCATE 15,20: PRINT "5. SAVE DATA TO DISK"
680 LOCATE 16,20: PRINT "6. GET DATA FROM DISK"
```

```
690 LOCATE 17,20: PRINT "7. OUTPUT TO LINE PRINTER"
700 LOCATE 18,20: PRINT "8. EXIT PROGRAM"
710 LOCATE 20,20: PRINT "   SELECT      "
720 '
730 'get selection
740 LOCATE 20, 20: FL = 101: GOSUB 1040
750 CHOICE = VAL(IN$)
760 IF CHOICE < 1 OR CHOICE > 8 THEN 740
770 IF CHOICE = 3 THEN OPT = NO: O = 1: GOTO 820
780 IF CHOICE = 4 THEN OPT = YES: O = 2: GOTO 820
790 ON CHOICE GOSUB 5010, 7010, 2005, 2005, 6000, 6000, 4000, 920
800 GOTO 600
810 '
820 IF STEP.COUNT(1) = 0 THEN 790
830 CLS: KASE = 1: GOSUB 8150: LOCATE 3
840 PRINT " Data from a previous analysis will be overwritten.": PRINT
850 PRINT " Do you wish to use this previous data? (Y/N)";
860 LOCATE ,48: FL = 301: GOSUB 1040
870 IF N$ = ESC$ THEN 600
880 IF IN$ = "Y" THEN 790
890 IF IN$ = "N" THEN GOSUB 8260: GOTO 790
900 GOTO 860
910 '
920 CLS: LOCATE 5,18: PRINT "HAVE YOU SAVED YOUR WORK FROM THIS SESSION?"
930 KASE = 1: GOSUB 8150 'esc to return
940 IN$ = INKEY$: IF IN$ = "" THEN 940
950 IF IN$ = ESC$ THEN GOTO 600
960 SYSTEM
970 '
980 '
1000 '''''interactive input routine'''''
1010 'From an algorithm by Nelson Ford, PC Tech Journal, Vol. 2, No. 2
1020 'FL is the field length passed at call
1030 '
1040 DEF SEG = 0: POKE 1050, PEEK(1052): DEF SEG 'clear keyboard buffer
1050 INS.LENGTH = 0: CURSOR.POS = 1
1060 MOVE.IT = NO: KY = 0
1070 CURSOR.START = POS(0)
1080 CHAR.CODE = FIX(FL / 100)
1090 FL = FL - CHAR.CODE * 100
1100 IF CHAR.CODE <> 1 THEN 1140
1110 'its a number, check its length, right justify in field
1120 IF CHAR.CODE = 1 THEN IF LEN(PROMPT$) > FL THEN PROMPT$ = LEFT(PROMPT$,F
1130 PROMPT$ = SPACE$(FL-LEN(PROMPT$))+PROMPT$
1140 IN$ = SPACE$(FL)
1150 IF IN$ <> "" THEN IN$ = LEFT$(PROMPT$ + SPACE$(FL), FL)
1160 INS.LENGTH = LEN (PROMPT$): PROMPT$ = ""
1170 COLOR BG, FG
1180 LOCATE, CURSOR.START, 1: PRINT IN$;
1190 LOCATE, CURSOR.START + CURSOR.POS - 1
1200 N$ = INKEY$: IF N$ = "" THEN 1200
1210 IF LEN (N$) = 1 THEN 1340
1220 'check for edit keys
1230 KY = ASC(RIGHT$(N$,1))
1240 IF KY = CURSOR.LF THEN
        IF CURSOR.POS > 1 THEN CURSOR.POS = CURSOR.POS - 1: GOTO 1190
        ELSE GOTO 1310
1250 IF KY = DEL.KEY THEN
        IN$ = LEFT$(IN$, CURSOR.POS - 1) + RIGHT$(IN$, FL - CURSOR.POS) + " "
        INS.LENGTH = INS.LENGTH - 1: GOTO 1180
1260 IF KY = INS.KEY THEN
        IF INSERT = NO THEN INSERT = YES: LOCATE,,,4,CURSOR.SIZE: GOTO 1180
        ELSE INSERT = NO: LOCATE,,,CURSOR.SIZE: GOTO 1200
1270 IF KY = HOME THEN
        CURSOR.POS = 1: GOTO 1190
```

```
1280 IF KY = CTRL.END THEN
         IN$ = LEFT$ (IN$,CURSOR.POS - 1) + SPACE$(FL - CURSOR.POS + 1):
         INS.LENGTH = CURSOR.POS - 1: GOTO 1180
1290 IF KY = CURSOR.RT THEN
         CURSOR.POS = CURSOR.POS - (CURSOR.POS < INS.LENGTH): GOTO 1190
1300 IF KY = END.KEY THEN
         CURSOR.POS = INS.LENGTH + 1: GOTO 1190
1310 MOVE.IT = YES
1320 GOTO 1590 'not an edit key but end input routine
1330 'check for appropriate input
1340 IF N$ = ESC$ THEN KY = ESC: GOTO 1310
1350 IF CURSOR.POS = 1 THEN
         IF N$ = "-" OR N$ = "+" THEN
             IN$ = N$: COLOR FG, BG: LOCATE ,,0: RETURN
1360 IF CURSOR.POS > FL THEN 1420
1370 IF CHAR.CODE = 0 AND N$ >= " " AND N$ <= "z" OR N$ = "." THEN 1490
1380 IF CHAR.CODE = 1 AND N$ >= "0" AND N$ <= "9" OR N$ = " " THEN 1490
1390 IF CHAR.CODE = 2 THEN
         IF N$ >= " " AND N$ < "a" THEN 1490
         ELSE IF N$ >= "a" AND N$ <= "z" THEN N$ = CHR$(ASC(N$) - 32): GOTO 1490
1400 IF CHAR.CODE = 3 THEN
         IF N$ = "Y" OR N$ = "N" THEN 1490
         ELSE IF N$ = "y" OR N$ = "n" THEN N$ = CHR$(ASC(N$) - 32): GOTO 1490
1410 IF CHAR.CODE = 4 THEN
         IF N$ = "G" OR N$ = "N" THEN 1490
         ELSE IF N$ = "g" OR N$ = "n" THEN N$ = CHR$(ASC(N$) - 32): GOTO 1490
1420 IF N$ = ENTR$ THEN 1590
1430 IF N$ <> BACKSPACE$ OR CURSOR.POS = 1 THEN 1200
1440 '
1450 IN$ = LEFT$(IN$, CURSOR.POS - 2) + RIGHT$(IN$, FL - CURSOR.POS + 1) + " "
1460 CURSOR.POS = CURSOR.POS - 1: INS.LENGTH = INS.LENGTH - 1
1470 GOTO 1180
1480 '
1490 IF NOT INSERT THEN
         MID$(IN$, CURSOR.POS, 1) = N$: GOTO 1540
1500 IF INS.LENGTH >= FL THEN 1200
1510 IN$ = LEFT$(LEFT$(IN$, CURSOR.POS - 1) + N$ +
         RIGHT$(IN$, FL - CURSOR.POS + 1), FL)
1520 CURSOR.POS = CURSOR.POS + 1: INS.LENGTH = INS.LENGTH + 1
1530 GOTO 1180
1540 IF CURSOR.POS = 1 THEN IN$ = N$ + SPACE$(FL - 1): PRINT IN$;:
         LOCATE, CURSOR.START: INS.LENGTH = 1
1550 PRINT N$;
1560 CURSOR.POS = CURSOR.POS + 1
1570 IF CURSOR.POS > INS.LENGTH THEN INS.LENGTH = CURSOR.POS - 1
1580 IF FL => 1 THEN 1180
1590 COLOR FG, BG: LOCATE,CURSOR.START,0,CURSOR.SIZE: PRINT IN$;
1600 IN$ = LEFT$(IN$, INS.LENGTH): INSERT = NO
1610 RETURN
1620 '
2000 'get project name and time unit
2005 CLS: R(1) = 4: CHANGED = NO: I = 0
2010 LOCATE R(1),1: PRINT "ENTER NAME OF PROJECT TO BE COSTED:   ";:
         GOSUB 5840: PRINT PROJ.NAME$
2015 PRINT: PRINT "ENTER UNIT OF LABOR TIME: DAY, HOUR, OR MINUTE:   ";:
         GOSUB 5840: PRINT TIME.UNIT$
2020 KASE = 1: GOSUB 8150 'esc to return
2025 '
2030 I = 1
2035 LOCATE R(I),C(I): FL = 20: PROMPT$ = PROJ.NAME$
2040 GOSUB 1040: IF MOVE.IT THEN 2140
2045 PROJ.NAME$ = IN$
2050 '
2055 I = I + 1
2060 LOCATE R(I),C(I): FL = 206: PROMPT$ = TIME.UNIT$
```

```
2065 GOSUB 1040: IF MOVE.IT THEN 2140
2070 TEST$ = "DAYS HOUR MINUTE"
2075 LOCATE R(I)+2,1
2080 IF INSTR(TEST$, IN$) = 0 THEN PRINT "INVALID TIME UNIT": GOTO 2060
     ELSE PRINT SPACE$(17)
2085 IN$ = LEFT$(IN$,1): IF IN$ <> LEFT$(TIME.UNIT$,1) THEN CHANGED = YES:
     GOSUB 2175 'get time conversion factor
2090 IF IN$ = "D" THEN TIME.UNIT$ = "DAY"
     ELSE IF IN$ = "H" THEN TIME.UNIT$ = "HOUR"
     ELSE TIME.UNIT$ = "MIN"
2095 IF IN$ = "D" THEN TIME.UNIT = HOURS.WORKED
     ELSE IF IN$ = "H" THEN TIME.UNIT = 1
     ELSE TIME.UNIT = 1/60
2100 IF CHANGED THEN GOSUB 2205   'do time conversion
2105 '
2110 KASE = 2: GOSUB 8150 'press enter
2115 N$ = INKEY$: IF N$ = "" THEN 2115
2120 IF N$ = ENTR$ THEN 2295
2125 IF N$ = ESC$ THEN RETURN ELSE 2115
2130 '
2135 'handle cursor keys
2140 KY = ASC(RIGHT$(N$,1))
2145 IF KY = ESC THEN RETURN
2150 IF KY = CURSOR.LF OR KY = CURSOR.UP OR KY = PAGE.UP THEN
        IF I <> 1 THEN 2030
2155 IF KY = CURSOR.DN OR KY = PAGE.DN THEN
        IF I = 1 THEN 2055
2160 ON I GOTO 2035, 2060
2165 '
2170 'time conversion
2175 IF TIME.UNIT$ = "DAY" THEN
        IF IN$ = "H" THEN TIME.FACTOR = HOURS.WORKED
        ELSE IF IN$ = "M" THEN TIME.FACTOR = HOURS.WORKED * 60
2180 IF TIME.UNIT$ = "HOUR" THEN
        IF IN$ = "D" THEN TIME.FACTOR = 1/HOURS.WORKED
        ELSE IF IN$ = "M" THEN TIME.FACTOR = 60
2185 IF TIME.UNIT$ = "MIN" THEN
        IF IN$ = "D" THEN TIME.FACTOR = 1/(HOURS.WORKED * 60)
        ELSE IF IN$ = "H" THEN TIME.FACTOR = 1/60
2190 RETURN
2195 '
2200 'recalculate full.cost
2205 FOR I = 1 TO 9: IF INITIALS$(I) <> "" THEN GOSUB 7680: NEXT I
2210 'recalculate steps
2215 IF STEP.COUNT(1) > STEP.COUNT(2) THEN MAX = STEP.COUNT(1)
     ELSE MAX = STEP.COUNT(2)
2220 QUIET = YES: SO = O 'save option
2225 IF MAX > 0 THEN KASE = 4: GOSUB 8150 'recalculating
2230 FOR S = 1 TO MAX
2235   FOR O = 1 TO 2
2240     IF STEP.NAME$(S,O) = "" THEN 2260
2245       FOR N = 1 TO N.MAX
2250         IF LAB.NAME$(S,O,N) <> "" THEN LAB.TIME(S,O,N) =
                LAB.TIME(S,O,N) * TIME.FACTOR: GOSUB 7870: GOSUB 3035:
                GOSUB 3060
2255       NEXT N
2260     NEXT O
2265 NEXT S
2270 QUIET = NO: O = SO 'restore option
2275 CHANGED = NO
2280 RETURN
2285 '
2290 'display step work sheet
2295 S = 0
2300 S = S + 1: IF NOT OPT THEN GOTO 2500
```

```
2305 IF O = 2 THEN O = 1 ELSE O = 2
2310 IF STEP.NAME$(S,2) = "" THEN STEP.NAME$(S,2) = STEP.NAME$(S,1)
2315 '
2500 CLS: PRINT: PRINT " STEP" S;: IF OPT THEN PRINT "  OPTION" O;
2505 PRINT  "  STEP NAME";: C = POS(0) + 2: PRINT "  " STEP.NAME$(S,O)
2510 PRINT: PRINT " LABOR COSTS:"
2515 PRINT " N" TAB(4) B$ "   PERSON" TAB(17) B$ "  #" TAB(23) B$ "SALARY/YEAR"
     TAB(35) B$ " COST/" TIME.UNIT$ TAB(46) B$ " " TIME.UNIT$ "S" TAB(55) B$
     "LABOR TOTAL" TAB(68) B$ " STEP TOTAL"
2520 '
2525 FOR N = 1 TO N.MAX 'fill in existing values
2530    PRINT N TAB(4) B$;
2535    IF LAB.NAME$(S,O,N) = "" THEN GOSUB 2600: GOTO 2560
2540    PRINT TAB(6) LAB.NAME$(S,O,N);
2545    GOSUB 2620 'print number, salary, and cost
2550    PRINT TAB(46) B$ USING "######"; LAB.TIME(S,O,N);
2555    PRINT TAB(55) B$ USING U6$; LAB.TOTAL(S,O,N);: PRINT TAB(68) B$
2560 NEXT N
2565 PRINT TAB(6) "TOTAL" ;
2570 IF TOTAL.LAB(S,O) <> 0 THEN
        PRINT TAB(56) USING U6$; TOTAL.LAB(S,O);
2575 PRINT TAB(68) B$
2580 GOTO 2645
2585 '
2590 'blank out a labor line
2595 LAB.NAME$(S,O,N) = "": LAB.NUMBER(S,O,N) = 0: LAB.SALARY(S,O,N) = 0:
     LAB.COST(S,O,N) = 0:  LAB.TIME(S,O,N) = 0:  LAB.TOTAL(S,O,N) = 0
2600 PRINT TAB(17) B$ TAB(23) B$ TAB(35) B$ TAB(46) B$ TAB(55) B$ TAB(68) B$
2605 RETURN
2610 '
2615 'print number, salary, cost
2620 PRINT TAB(17) B$ USING "####"; LAB.NUMBER(S,O,N);
2625 PRINT TAB(23) B$ " " USING "$#######"; LAB.SALARY(S,O,N);
2630 PRINT TAB(35) B$ USING U5$; LAB.COST(S,O,N);
2635 RETURN
2640 '
2645 PRINT: PRINT " EXPENSE COSTS:"
2650 PRINT " N" TAB(4) B$ "   EXPENSE" TAB(23) B$ "   COST/UNIT" TAB(40) B$
     TAB(44) "# UNITS" TAB(54) B$ "EXPENSE TOTAL" TAB(68) B$
2655 FOR N = 1 TO N.MAX
2660    PRINT N TAB(4) B$;
2665    IF EXP.NAME$(S,O,N) = "" THEN GOSUB 2740: GOTO 2690
2670    PRINT TAB( 6) EXP.NAME$(S,O,N);
2675    PRINT TAB(23) B$ " " USING U8$; EXP.COST(S,O,N);
2680    PRINT TAB(40) B$ TAB(44) USING "####.##"; EXP.NUMBER(S,O,N);
2685    PRINT TAB(54) B$ USING U8$; EXP.TOTAL(S,O,N);: PRINT TAB(68) B$
2690 NEXT N
2695 PRINT TAB(6) "TOTAL";
2700 IF TOTAL.EXP(S,O) <> 0 THEN
        PRINT TAB(55) USING U8$; TOTAL.EXP(S,O);
2705 PRINT TAB(68) B$
2710 PRINT TAB(6) "STEP TOTAL" TAB(68) B$;
2715 IF STEP.TOTAL(S,O) <> 0 THEN
        PRINT TAB(69) USING U8$; STEP.TOTAL(S,O);
2720 GOTO 2760
2725 '
2730 'blank out an expense line
2735 EXP.NAME$(S,O,N) = "": EXP.COST(S,O,N) = 0: EXP.NUMBER(S,O,N) = 0:
     EXP.TOTAL(S,O,N) = 0
2740 PRINT TAB(23) B$ TAB(40) B$ TAB(54) B$ TAB(68) B$
2745 RETURN
2750 '
2755 'get step name
2760 LOCATE 2,C: FL = 25: PROMPT$ = STEP.NAME$(S,O)
2765 IF O = 2 AND PROMPT$ = "" THEN PROMPT$ = STEP.NAME$(S,O)
```

```
2770 GOSUB 1040: IF MOVE.IT THEN 3565
2775 IF IN$ <> "" THEN STEP.NAME$ (S,O) = IN$
     ELSE GOTO 3430
2780 '
2785 'input labor data
2790 N = 0: Q$ = "": FOUND = NO
2795 'begin here
2800 N = N + 1: R = N + 5
2805 'name
2810 Q = 1: GOSUB 3765
2815 LOCATE R,6: FL = 10: PROMPT$ = LAB.NAME$(S,O,N)
2820 GOSUB 1040: IF MOVE.IT THEN 3610
2825 IF IN$ = "" OR IN$ = SPACE$(LEN(IN$)) THEN
         GOSUB 2595: GOSUB 3075: GOTO 3005 'we're done
2830 LAB.NAME$(S,O,N) = IN$
2835 GOSUB 7870 'look for initials, salary, applied rate
2840 IF FOUND THEN GOSUB 2620: GOTO 2965  'number, salary, cost, skip to time
2845 'how many
2850 Q = 2: GOSUB 3765
2855 LOCATE R,19:FL = 103:PROMPT$ = MID$(STR$(LAB.NUMBER(S,O,N)),2)
2860 GOSUB 1040: IF MOVE.IT THEN 3610
2865 LAB.NUMBER(S,O,N) = VAL(IN$): IF LAB.TOTAL(S,O,N) > 0 THEN GOSUB 3060
2870 LOCATE ,19: PRINT USING "###"; LAB.NUMBER(S,O,N)
2875 'salary
2880 Q = 3: GOSUB 3765
2885 LOCATE R,25: PRINT "$ ";
2890 FL = 106: PROMPT$ = MID$(STR$(LAB.SALARY(S,O,N)),2)
2895 GOSUB 1040 IF MOVE.IT THEN 3610
2900 IF VAL(IN$) <> LAB.SALARY(S,O,N) THEN LAB.SALARY(S,O,N) = VAL(IN$):
         GOSUB 3035 'calculate new lab.cost
2905 IF LAB.TOTAL(S,O,N) > 0 THEN GOSUB 3060
2910 LOCATE, 27: PRINT USING "######"; LAB.SALARY(S,O,N)
2915 IF MOVE.IT THEN 3610
2920 'cost
2925 Q = 4: GOSUB 3765
2930 LOCATE R,36: PRINT "$ ";
2935 X = LAB.COST(S,O,N): GOSUB 3125 'format prompt$
2940 FL = 107: PROMPT$ = X$
2945 GOSUB 1040: IF MOVE.IT THEN 3610
2950 LAB.COST(S,O,N) = VAL(IN$): LOCATE,36: PRINT USING U5$; LAB.COST(S,O,N);
2955 IF LAB.TOTAL(S,O,N) > 0 THEN GOSUB 3060
2960 'time
2965 Q = 5: GOSUB 3765
2970 LOCATE R,49: FL = 104: PROMPT$ = MID$(STR$(LAB.TIME(S,O,N)),2)
2975 GOSUB 1040: IF MOVE.IT THEN 3610
2980 LAB.TIME(S,O,N) = VAL(IN$):LOCATE,49: PRINT USING "####"; LAB.TIME(S,O,N)
2985 GOSUB 3060
2990 '
2995 IF N < 6 THEN 2800 'do it again
3000 'blank out question
3005 LOCATE 4,16: PRINT SPC(60)
3010 'done with labor part goto expense
3015 GOTO 3160
3020 '
3025 'labor calculations
3030 'cost
3035 LAB.COST(S,O,N) = TIME.UNIT * LAB.SALARY(S,O,N) * FC.MULT / (DAYS.PAID
     * HOURS.WORKED * APPL.RATE)
3040 IF LAB.COST(S,O,N) < .1 THEN LAB.COST(S,O,N) = 0
3045 IF NOT QUIET THEN LOCATE,36: PRINT USING U5$; LAB.COST(S,O,N);
3050 RETURN
3055 'line total
3060 LAB.TOTAL(S,O,N)= LAB.NUMBER(S,O,N) * LAB.COST(S,O,N) * LAB.TIME(S,O,N):
3065 IF NOT QUIET THEN LOCATE,56: PRINT USING U6$; LAB.TOTAL(S,O,N);:
         PRINT TAB(68) B$;
```

```
3070 'labor total
3075 TOTAL.LAB(S,O) = 0
3080 FOR NN = 1 TO N.MAX
3085     TOTAL.LAB(S,O) = TOTAL.LAB(S,O) + LAB.TOTAL(S,O,NN)
3090 NEXT NN
3095 IF NOT QUIET THEN LOCATE 12,56: PRINT USING U6$; TOTAL.LAB(S,O);:
        PRINT TAB(68) B$;
3100 GOSUB 3395 'step total
3105 LOCATE R 'restore current row
3110 RETURN
3115 '
3120 'format to 2 decimal places
3125 X = X + .005
3130 X$ = MID$(STR$(X),2)
3135 P = INSTR(X$, ".")
3140 X$ = LEFT$(X$, P + 2)
3145 RETURN
3150 '
3155 'input expense data
3160 N = 0
3165 'begin here
3170 N = N + 1: R = N + 15
3175 'name
3180 Q = 1: GOSUB 3830
3185 LOCATE R,6: FL = 15: PROMPT$ = EXP.NAME$(S,O,N)
3190 GOSUB 1040: IF MOVE.IT THEN 3660
3195 IF IN$ = "" OR IN$ = SPACE$(LEN(IN$)) THEN
        GOSUB 2735: GOSUB 3365: GOTO 3300 ' we're done
3200 EXP.NAME$(S,O,N) = IN$
3205 'cost per unit
3210 Q = 2: GOSUB 3830
3215 LOCATE R,25: PRINT "$     ";
3220 X = EXP.COST(S,O,N): GOSUB 3125 'format prompt$
3225 FL = 108: PROMPT$ = X$
3230 GOSUB 1040: IF MOVE.IT THEN 3660
3235 EXP.COST(S,O,N) = VAL(IN$): LOCATE,25: PRINT USING U8$; EXP.COST(S,O,N);
3240 IF EXP.TOTAL(S,O,N) > 0 THEN GOSUB 3350
3245 'how many
3250 Q = 3: GOSUB 3830
3255 LOCATE R,44: FL = 107: PROMPT$ = MID$(STR$(EXP.NUMBER(S,O,N)),2)
3260 X = EXP.NUMBER(S,O,N): GOSUB 3125 'format prompt$
3265 PROMPT$ = X$
3270 GOSUB 1040: IF MOVE.IT THEN 3660
3275 EXP.NUMBER(S,O,N) = VAL(IN$): LOCATE,44: PRINT USING "####.##";
        EXP.NUMBER(S,O,N);
3280 GOSUB 3350
3285 '
3290 IF N < 6 THEN 3170 'do it again
3295 'blank out question
3300 LOCATE 14,18: PRINT SPC(40)
3305 '
3310 'we are done with a step
3315 KASE = 2: GOSUB 8150 'enter
3320 N$ = INKEY$: IF N$ = "" THEN 3320
3325 IF N$ = ENTR$ THEN
        IF OPT AND O = 1 THEN 2305
        ELSE 2300
3330 GOTO 3425
3335 '
3340 'various expense calculations and step total
3345 'line total
3350 EXP.TOTAL(S,O,N) = EXP.COST(S,O,N) * EXP.NUMBER(S,O,N)
3355 LOCATE R,55: PRINT USING U8$; EXP.TOTAL(S,O,N);: PRINT TAB(68) B$;
3360 'expense total
3365 TOTAL.EXP(S,O) = 0
```

```
3370 FOR NN = 1 TO N.MAX
3375    TOTAL.EXP(S,O) = TOTAL.EXP(S,O) + EXP.TOTAL(S,O,NN)
3380 NEXT NN
3385 LOCATE 22,55: PRINT USING U8$; TOTAL.EXP(S,O);: PRINT TAB(68) B$;
3390 'step total
3395 IF S > STEP.COUNT(O) THEN STEP.COUNT(O) = S
3400 STEP.TOTAL(S,O) = TOTAL.LAB(S,O) + TOTAL.EXP(S,O)
3405 IF NOT QUIET THEN LOCATE 23,69: PRINT USING U8$; STEP.TOTAL(S,O);
3410 LOCATE R 'restore current row
3415 RETURN
3420 '
3425 'display project totals
3430 TOTAL1 = 0: TOTAL2 = 0
3435 CLS: PRINT: PRINT TAB(5) "PROJECT COSTS FOR: " PROJ.NAME$
3440 PRINT: PRINT
3445 IF OPT THEN 3480
3450 'show program cost (menu choice 3)
3455 FOR S = 1 TO STEP.COUNT(1)
3460    PRINT "STEP" S STEP.NAME$(S,1) TAB(36) USING U8$; STEP.TOTAL(S,1);:
       TOTAL1 = TOTAL1 + STEP.TOTAL(S,1): PRINT
3465 NEXT S
3470 GOTO 3530
3475 'show benefits (menu choice 4)
3480 PRINT TAB(39) "OPTION 1" TAB(53) "OPTION 2" TAB(66) "DIFFERENCE": PRINT
3485 IF STEP.COUNT(1) > STEP.COUNT(2) THEN MAX = STEP.COUNT(1)
       ELSE MAX = STEP.COUNT(2)
3490 FOR S = 1 TO MAX
3495    PRINT "STEP" S;: IF STEP.NAME$(S,1) <> "" THEN PRINT STEP.NAME$(S,1);
       ELSE PRINT STEP.NAME$(S,2);
3500    PRINT TAB(36) USING U8$; STEP.TOTAL(S,1);:
       PRINT TAB(50) USING U8$; STEP.TOTAL(S,2);
3505    TOTAL1 = TOTAL1 + STEP.TOTAL(S,1):
       TOTAL2 = TOTAL2 + STEP.TOTAL(S,2)
3510    PRINT TAB(64) USING U8$; STEP.TOTAL(S,1) - STEP.TOTAL(S,2);
3515    PRINT
3520 NEXT S
3525 '
3530 PRINT: PRINT "TOTAL COST:" TAB(36) USING U8$; TOTAL1;
3535 IF OPT THEN PRINT TAB(50) USING U8$; TOTAL2;:
       PRINT TAB(64) USING U8$; TOTAL1 - TOTAL2;
3540 '
3545 KASE = 3: GOSUB 8150 'any key
3550 N$ = INKEY$: IF N$ = "" THEN 3550
3555 RETURN
3560 '
3565 ' handle cursor keys for step name
3570 KY = ASC(RIGHT$(N$,1))
3575 IF KY = ESC THEN RETURN
3580 IF KY = PAGE.UP THEN GOTO 3710
3585 IF KY = PAGE.DN THEN 3740
3590 IF KY = CURSOR.DN AND STEP.NAME$(S,O) <> "" THEN GOTO 2785
3595 GOTO 2760
3600 '
3605 'handle cursor keys for labor data
3610 KY = ASC(RIGHT$(N$,1))
3615 IF KY = ESC THEN RETURN
3620 IF KY = PAGE.UP THEN GOTO 3710
3625 IF KY = PAGE.DN THEN 3740
3630 IF KY = CURSOR.LF THEN
       IF Q = 1 THEN KY = CURSOR.UP
       ELSE ON Q - 1 GOTO 2810, 2850, 2880, 2925
3635 IF KY = CURSOR.UP THEN
       IF N = 1 THEN LOCATE 4,16: PRINT SPC(60): GOTO 2760
       ELSE N = N - 2: GOTO 2800
```

```
3640 IF KY = CURSOR.DN THEN
        IF N < 6 THEN GOTO 2800 ELSE GOTO 3005
3645 ON Q GOTO 2815, 2855, 2885, 2930, 2970
3650 '
3655 'handle cursor keys for expense data
3660 KY = ASC(RIGHT$(N$,1))
3665 IF KY = ESC THEN RETURN
3670 IF KY = PAGE.UP THEN GOTO 3710
3675 IF KY = PAGE.DN THEN 3740
3680 IF KY = CURSOR.LF THEN
        IF Q = 1 THEN KY = CURSOR.UP
        ELSE ON Q - 1 GOTO 3180, 3210, 3250
3685 IF KY = CURSOR.UP THEN
        IF N = 1 THEN LOCATE 13,6: PRINT SPC(40): N = N - 1: GOTO 2800
        ELSE N = N - 2: GOTO 3170
3690 IF KY = CURSOR.DN THEN
        IF N < 6 THEN GOTO 3170 ELSE GOTO 3300
3695 ON Q GOTO 3185, 3215, 3255
3700 '
3705 'page up
3710 IF S = 1 THEN O = 1: GOTO 2500
3715 IF OPT THEN IF O = 2 THEN O = 1: GOTO 2500
3720 IF OPT THEN O = 2
3725 S = S - 1: GOTO 2500
3730 '
3735 'page down
3740 IF OPT AND O = 1 THEN O = 2: GOTO 2500
3745 IF S = 20 THEN 2500
3750 IF O = 2 THEN O = 1
3755 S = S + 1: GOTO 2500
3760 '
3765 'labor questions to answer
3770 LOCATE 4, 16: PRINT SPC(LEN(Q$)) 'blank out previous question
3775 ON Q GOTO 3780, 3785, 3790, 3795,3800, 3805
3780 Q$ = "WHO IS INVOLVED (NAME, INITIALS OR TITLE)?": GOTO 3810
3785 Q$ = "HOW MANY ARE INVOLVED?": GOTO 3810
3790 Q$ = "HOW MUCH DOES PERSON MAKE (SALARY/YEAR)?": GOTO 3810
3795 Q$ = "HOW MUCH IS THIS PERSON'S COST PER " + TIME.UNIT$ + "?": GOTO 3810
3800 Q$ = "HOW MUCH TIME DOES PERSON SPEND ON THIS STEP?": GOTO 3810
3805 Q$ = "SALARY CAN NOT BE ZERO (0)": GOTO 3810
3810 COLOR BG, FG: LOCATE, 16: PRINT Q$: COLOR FG, BG
3815 RETURN
3820 '
3825 'expense questions to answer
3830 LOCATE 14,18: PRINT SPC(LEN(Q$)) 'blank out previous question
3835 ON Q GOTO 3840, 3845, 3850
3840 Q$ = "EXPENSE NAME": GOTO 3855
3845 Q$ = "EXPENSE COST PER UNIT": GOTO 3855
3850 Q$ = "NUMBER OF EXPENSE ITEMS?": GOTO 3855
3855 COLOR BG, FG: LOCATE, 18: PRINT Q$: COLOR FG, BG
3860 RETURN
3865 '
4000 'printer output
4005 IF STEP.COUNT(1) <> 0 OR STEP.COUNT(2) <> 0 THEN 4035
4010 CLS: LOCATE 7,27: PRINT "NO DATA HAS BEEN ENTERED"
4015 KASE = 3: GOSUB 8150 'any key
4020 N$= INKEY$: IF N$ = "" THEN 4020
4025 RETURN
4030 '
4035 ON ERROR GOTO 8010
4040 CLS: KASE = 1: GOSUB 8150: LOCATE 3
4045 PRINT " This option prints your cost analysis worksheet";
4050 PRINT " in a sparse format.": PRINT
4055 PRINT " For a screen display, use either option 3 or 4 from the";
```

```
4060 PRINT " main menu.": PRINT
4065 PRINT " Make sure your printer is on, and the paper is aligned."
4070 PRINT " Press any key other than [Esc] to begin printing."
4075 N$ = INKEY$: IF N$ = ""  THEN 4075
4080 IF N$ = ESC$ THEN RETURN
4085 KASE = 0: GOSUB 8150 'blank line
4090 'organizational data
4095 LPRINT " YOUR FIRM'S ORGANIZATION COST DATA USED IN THIS ANALYSIS": LPRIN
4100 LPRINT " 1.STANDARD DAYS PAID PER YEAR:    " USING "###"; DAYS.PAID: LPRIN
4105 LPRINT " 2.STANDARD HOURS WORKED PER DAY:    " USING "##.#"; HOURS.WORKED:
     LPRINT
4110 LPRINT " 3.FRINGE BENEFIT RATE (%):    " USING "###"; FR.RATE: LPRINT
4115 LPRINT " 4.FRINGE DAYS PAID (HOLIDAYS,VACATION,ETC):    " USING "###";
          FR.DAYS: LPRINT
4120 LPRINT "    INCLUDED IN FRINGE RATE:    " FR.INCL: LPRINT
4125 LPRINT " 5.OVERHEAD RATE (%):    " USING "###"; OH.RATE: LPRINT
4130 LPRINT " 6.PROFIT RATE (%):    " USING "###"; PROF.RATE: LPRINT
4135 LPRINT " 7.YOUR ENTERED FULL COST MULTIPLIER IS:    " USING "##.##";
          FC.MULT: LPRINT
4140 '
4145 LPRINT: LPRINT: LPRINT: LPRINT: LPRINT
4150 '
4155 O = 1: IF STEP.COUNT(2) > 0 THEN OPT = YES
4160 IF STEP.COUNT(1) > STEP.COUNT(2) THEN MAX = STEP.COUNT(1)
     ELSE MAX = STEP.COUNT(2)
4165 FOR S = 1 TO MAX
4170     IF STEP.NAME$(S,O) = "" THEN 4185
4175     GOSUB 4225 'print the spreadsheet
4180     LPRINT: LPRINT: LPRINT
4185     IF OPT THEN
             IF O = 1 THEN O = 2: GOTO 4175
             ELSE O = 1
4190     LPRINT: LPRINT
4195 NEXT S
4200 '
4205 'now print the summary
4210 GOTO 4400
4215 '
4220 'subroutine to print a sparse worksheet
4225 LPRINT: LPRINT " STEP" S;: IF OPT THEN LPRINT "  OPTION" O;
4230 LPRINT "   STEP NAME";: C = POS(0) + 2: LPRINT "  " STEP.NAME$(S,O)
4235 LPRINT: LPRINT " LABOR COSTS:"
4240 LPRINT " N" TAB(4) B$ "    PERSON" TAB(17) B$ "  #" TAB(23) B$ "SALARY/YEA
     TAB(35) B$ " COST/" TIME.UNIT$ TAB(46) B$ " "  TIME.UNIT$ "S" TAB(55) B$
     "LABOR TOTAL" TAB(68) B$ " STEP TOTAL"
4245 '
4250 FOR N = 1 TO N.MAX 'fill in existing values
4255     IF LAB.NAME$(S,O,N) = "" THEN 4295
4260     LPRINT N TAB(4) B$;
4265     LPRINT TAB(6) LAB.NAME$(S,O,N);
4270     LPRINT TAB(17) B$ USING "####"; LAB.NUMBER(S,O,N);
4275     LPRINT TAB(23) B$ " " USING "$#######"; LAB.SALARY(S,O,N);
4280     LPRINT TAB(35) B$ USING U5$; LAB.COST(S,O,N);
4285     LPRINT TAB(46) B$ USING "######"; LAB.TIME(S,O,N);
4290     LPRINT TAB(55) B$ USING U6$; LAB.TOTAL(S,O,N);: LPRINT TAB(68) B$
4295 NEXT N
4300 LPRINT TAB(6) "TOTAL" TAB(56) USING U6$; TOTAL.LAB(S,O);
4305 LPRINT TAB(68) B$
4310 '
4315 LPRINT: LPRINT " EXPENSE COSTS:"
4320 LPRINT " N" TAB(4) B$ "    EXPENSE" TAB(23) B$ "    COST/UNIT" TAB(40) B$
     TAB(44) "# UNITS" TAB(54) B$ "EXPENSE TOTAL" TAB(68) B$
4325 FOR N = 1 TO N.MAX
4330     IF EXP.NAME$(S,O,N) = "" THEN 4360
4335     LPRINT N TAB(4) B$;
```

```
4340     LPRINT TAB(6) EXP.NAME$(S,O,N);
4345     LPRINT TAB(23) B$ " " USING U8$; EXP.COST(S,O,N);
4350     LPRINT TAB(40) B$ TAB(44) USING "####.##"; EXP.NUMBER(S,O,N);
4355     LPRINT TAB(54) B$ USING U8$; EXP.TOTAL(S,O,N);: LPRINT TAB(68) B$
4360 NEXT N
4365 LPRINT TAB(6) "TOTAL" TAB(55) USING U8$; TOTAL.EXP(S,O);
4370 LPRINT TAB(68) B$
4375 LPRINT TAB(6) "STEP TOTAL" TAB(68) B$ TAB(69) USING U8$; STEP.TOTAL(S,O);
4380 RETURN
4385 '
4390 '
4395 'display project totals
4400 TOTAL1 = 0: TOTAL2 = 0
4405 LPRINT: LPRINT TAB(2) "PROJECT COSTS FOR: " PROJ.NAME$
4410 LPRINT: LPRINT
4415 O = 1
4420 IF OPT THEN 4455
4425 'show program cost (menu choice 3)
4430 FOR S = 1 TO STEP.COUNT(1)
4435     LPRINT TAB(2) "STEP" S STEP.NAME$(S,1) TAB(36) USING U8$;
         STEP.TOTAL(S,1);: LPRINT
4440 TOTAL1 = TOTAL1 + STEP.TOTAL(S,1)
4445 NEXT S
4450 GOTO 4510
4455 'show benefits (menu choice 4)
4460 LPRINT TAB(39) "OPTION 1" TAB(53) "OPTION 2" TAB(66) "DIFFERENCE": LPRINT
4465 IF STEP.COUNT(1) > STEP.COUNT(2) THEN MAX = STEP.COUNT(1)
         ELSE MAX = STEP.COUNT(2)
4470 FOR S = 1 TO MAX
4475   LPRINT "STEP" S STEP.NAME$(S,1);
4480   LPRINT TAB(36) USING U8$; STEP.TOTAL(S,1);: LPRINT TAB(50) USING U8$;
         STEP.TOTAL(S,2);
4485   TOTAL1 = TOTAL1 + STEP.TOTAL(S,1):
         TOTAL2 = TOTAL2 + STEP.TOTAL(S,2)
4490   LPRINT TAB(64) USING U8$; STEP.TOTAL(S,1) - STEP.TOTAL(S,2);
4495   LPRINT
4500 NEXT S
4505 '
4510 LPRINT: LPRINT "TOTAL COST:" TAB(36) USING U8$; TOTAL1;
4515 IF OPT THEN LPRINT TAB(50) USING U8$; TOTAL2;: LPRINT TAB(64) USING U8$;
         TOTAL1 - TOTAL2;
4520 KASE = 3: GOSUB 8150 'any key
4525 LPRINT CHR$(12) 'page eject
4530 N$ = INKEY$: IF N$ = "" THEN 4530
4535 ON ERROR GOTO 0
4540 RETURN
4545 '
5000 'organization data
5010 FIRST.ROW = 5: LAST.ROW = 15: CHANGED = NO
5020 CLS: LOCATE 2,20: PRINT "ENTER YOUR FIRM'S ORGANIZATION COST DATA": PRINT
5030 'fill it in
5040 LOCATE FIRST.ROW,1: I = 0
5050 PRINT " 1.STANDARD DAYS PAID PER YEAR:    ";: GOSUB 5840:
         PRINT USING "###"; DAYS.PAID
5060 PRINT: PRINT " 2.STANDARD HOURS WORKED PER DAY:    ";: GOSUB 5840:
         PRINT USING "##.##"; HOURS.WORKED
5070 PRINT: PRINT " 3.FRINGE BENEFIT RATE (%):    ";: GOSUB 5840:
         PRINT USING "###"; FR.RATE
5080 PRINT: PRINT " 4.FRINGE DAYS PAID (HOLIDAYS,VACATION,ETC):    ";:
         GOSUB 5840: PRINT USING "###"; FR.DAYS
5090 PRINT: PRINT "    INCLUDE IN FRINGE RATE? (Y/N) ";: GOSUB 5840:
         PRINT FR.INCL$
5100 PRINT: PRINT " 5.OVERHEAD RATE (%):  ";: GOSUB 5840:
         PRINT USING "###"; OH.RATE
```

```
5110 PRINT: PRINT " 6.PROFIT RATE (%):   ";: GOSUB 5840:
     PRINT USING "###"; PROF.RATE
5120 PRINT: PRINT " 7.YOUR ENTERED FULL COST MULTIPLIER IS:   ";:
     GOSUB 5840: IF FC.MULT > 0 THEN GOSUB 5800 ELSE GOSUB 5760
5130 '
5140 KASE = 1: GOSUB 8150 'esc to return
5150 '
5160 'days paid per year
5170 I = 1
5180 FL = 103: PROMPT$ = MID$(STR$(DAYS.PAID), 2)
5190 LOCATE R(I),C(I): GOSUB 1040
5200 IF MOVE.IT THEN 5880
5210 IF DAYS.PAID <> VAL(IN$) THEN DAYS.PAID = VAL(IN$): CHANGED = YES:
         LOCATE R(I),C(I): PRINT USING "###"; DAYS.PAID;
5220 LOCATE,C(I): PRINT SPC(FL - LEN(IN$)) IN$
5230 'hours worked
5240 I = I + 1
5250 FL = 105: PROMPT$ = MID$(STR$(HOURS.WORKED),2)
5260 X = HOURS.WORKED: GOSUB 3125 'format prompt$
5270 PROMPT$ = X$
5280 LOCATE R(I),C(I): GOSUB 1040
5290 IF MOVE.IT THEN 5880
5300 IF HOURS.WORKED <> VAL(IN$) THEN HOURS.WORKED = VAL(IN$): CHANGED = YES:
         LOCATE R(I),C(I): PRINT USING "##.##"; HOURS.WORKED;
5310 'fringe rate
5320 I = I + 1
5330 FL = 103: PROMPT$ = MID$(STR$(FR.RATE),2)
5340 LOCATE R(I),C(I): GOSUB 1040
5350 IF MOVE.IT THEN 5880
5360 IF FR.RATE <> VAL(IN$) THEN FR.RATE = VAL(IN$): CHANGED = YES:
         LOCATE R(I),C(I): PRINT USING "###"; FR.RATE;: GOSUB 5760
5370 'fringe paid days off
5380 I = I + 1
5390 FL = 103: PROMPT$ = MID$(STR$(FR.DAYS),2)
5400 LOCATE R(I),C(I): GOSUB 1040
5410 IF MOVE.IT THEN 5880
5420 IF FR.DAYS <> VAL(IN$) THEN FR.DAYS = VAL(IN$): CHANGED = YES:
         LOCATE R(I),C(I): PRINT USING "###"; FR.DAYS;: GOSUB 5760
5430 'included in fringe rate
5440 I = I + 1
5450 FL = 301: PROMPT$ = FR.INCL$
5460 LOCATE R(I),C(I): GOSUB 1040
5470 IF MOVE.IT THEN 5880
5480 IF FR.INCL$ <> IN$ THEN FR.INCL$ = IN$: CHANGED = YES: LOCATE R(I),C(I):
     PRINT FR.INCL$;: GOSUB 5760
5490 'overhead rate
5500 I = I + 1
5510 FL = 103: PROMPT$ = MID$(STR$(OH.RATE),2)
5520 LOCATE R(I),C(I): GOSUB 1040
5530 IF MOVE.IT THEN 5880
5540 IF OH.RATE <> VAL(IN$) THEN OH.RATE = VAL(IN$): CHANGED = YES:
         LOCATE R(I),C(I): PRINT USING "###"; OH.RATE;: GOSUB 5760
5550 'profit rate
5560 I = I + 1
5570 FL = 103: PROMPT$ = MID$(STR$(PROF.RATE),2)
5580 LOCATE R(I),C(I): GOSUB 1040
5590 IF MOVE.IT THEN 5880
5600 IF PROF.RATE <> VAL(IN$) THEN PROF.RATE = VAL(IN$): CHANGED = YES:
         LOCATE R(I),C(I): PRINT USING "###"; PROF.RATE;: GOSUB 5760
5610 'entered full cost multiplier
5620 I = I + 1
5630 KASE = 2: GOSUB 8150 'enter to continue
5640 FL = 105: PROMPT$ = MID$(STR$(FC.MULT),2)
5650 X = FC.MULT: GOSUB 3125 'format
5660 PROMPT$ = X$
```

```
5670 LOCATE R(I),C(I): GOSUB 1040
5680 IF MOVE.IT THEN KASE = 1: GOSUB 8150: GOTO 5880
5690 IF VAL(IN$) > 10 THEN 5630
5700 IF FC.MULT <> VAL (IN$) THEN FC.MULT = VAL(IN$): CHANGED = YES:
     LOCATE R(I),C(I): PRINT USING "##.##"; FC.MULT
5710 '
5720 IF CHANGED THEN TIME.FACTOR = 1: GOSUB 2205 'time.unit stays the same
5730 RETURN ' we're done
5740 '
5750 'calculate multiplier
5760 ACTUAL.DAYS = DAYS.PAID - FR.DAYS
5770 IF FR.INCL$ = "Y" THEN FC = ACTUAL.DAYS / DAYS.PAID
     ELSE FC = 1
5780 FC = FC + FR.RATE / 100: FC = FC + (FC * OH.RATE / 100):
     FC = FC + (FC * PROF.RATE / 100): FC = FC * (DAYS.PAID / ACTUAL.DAYS)
5790 FC.MULT = CINT(FC * 100) / 100
5800 LOCATE R(8),C(8): PRINT USING "##.##"; FC.MULT
5810 RETURN
5820 '
5830 'keep track of row and col
5840 I = I + 1: R(I) = CSRLIN: C(I) = POS(0)
5850 RETURN
5860 '
5870 'handle cursor keys for org data
5880 KY = ASC(RIGHT$(N$,1))
5890 IF KY = ESC THEN 5720
5900 IF KY = CURSOR.LF OR KY = CURSOR.UP THEN I = I - 1 ELSE 5920
5910 IF I <= 7 THEN
         ON I + 1 GOTO 5170, 5180, 5250, 5330, 5390, 5450, 5510, 5570
5920 IF KY = CURSOR.DN THEN
         ON I GOTO 5240, 5320, 5380, 5440, 5500, 5560, 5620, 5630
5930 IF KY = PAGE.UP THEN 5140
5940 IF KY = PAGE.DN THEN I = 8: GOTO 5630
5950 ON I GOTO 5180, 5250, 5330, 5390, 5450, 5510, 5570, 5630
5960 '
5970 '
6000 'disk I/O routines
6010 'get file name
6020 CLS: LOCATE 5,1: PRINT "ENTER NAME OF FILE TO ";
6030 IF CHOICE = 5 THEN MODE$ = "O": PRINT "WRITE TO:"
     ELSE MODE$ = "I": PRINT "READ FROM:": LOCATE 7,1:
         PRINT "CAUTION: CURRENT DATA WILL BE CLEARED"
6040 KASE = 1: GOSUB 8150
6050 LOCATE 5,38: FL = 14: PROMPT$ = "": GOSUB 1040
6060 IF N$ = ESC$ THEN RETURN
6070 '
6080 ON ERROR GOTO 8070
6090 OPEN MODE$, 1, IN$
6100 ON ERROR GOTO 0
6110 IF CHOICE <> 5 THEN GOTO 6520
6120 '
6130 'write organizational data
6140 LOCATE 9,1: PRINT SPACE$(45) 'blank out any error messages
6150 KASE = 7: GOSUB 8150 'saving data
6160 WRITE #1, DAYS.PAID, HOURS.WORKED, FR.RATE, FR.DAYS, FR.INCL, OH.RATE,
     PROF.RATE, FC.MULT
6170 COUNT = 0 'how many names, etc
6180 FOR I = 1 TO 9:
6190   IF INITIALS$(I) <> "" THEN COUNT = COUNT + 1
6200 NEXT I
6210 WRITE #1, COUNT
6220 FOR I = 1 TO 9
6230     IF INITIALS$(I) <> "" THEN
             WRITE #1, INITIALS$(I), NUMBER(I), SALARY(I), APPLIED(I), AR$(I),
             FULL.COST(I)
```

```
6240 NEXT I
6250 'now project name and time unit
6260 WRITE #1, PROJ.NAME$, TIME.UNIT$, TIME.UNIT
6270 'write option and step data
6280 FOR O = 1 TO 2
6290    WRITE #1, STEP.COUNT (O)
6300    IF STEP.COUNT(O) = 0 THEN 6480
6310   FOR S = 1 TO STEP.COUNT(O)
6320       WRITE #1, STEP.NAME$(S,O)
6330       COUNT = 0 'how many labor entries
6340       FOR N = 1 TO N.MAX:
                IF LAB.TOTAL(S,O,N) > 0 THEN COUNT = COUNT + 1:
             NEXT N
6350       WRITE #1, COUNT
6360       FOR N = 1 TO N.MAX
6370           IF LAB.TOTAL(S,O,N) > 0 THEN WRITE #1, LAB.NAME$(S,O,N),
                LAB.NUMBER(S,O,N), LAB.SALARY(S,O,N), LAB.COST(S,O,N),
                LAB.TIME(S,O,N), LAB.TOTAL(S,O,N)
6380       NEXT N
6390       WRITE #1, TOTAL.LAB(S,O)
6400       COUNT = 0 'how many expense entries
6410       FOR N = 1 TO N.MAX:
                IF EXP.TOTAL(S,O,N) > 0 THEN COUNT = COUNT + 1:
             NEXT N
6420       WRITE #1, COUNT
6430       FOR N = 1 TO N.MAX
6440           IF EXP.TOTAL(S,O,N) > 0 THEN WRITE #1, EXP.NAME$(S,O,N),
                EXP.COST(S,O,N), EXP.NUMBER(S,O,N), EXP.TOTAL(S,O,N)
6450       NEXT N
6460       WRITE #1, TOTAL.EXP(S,O), STEP.TOTAL(S,O)
6470    NEXT S
6480 NEXT O
6490 CLOSE #1: RETURN
6500 '
6510 ' read from disk
6520 LOCATE 9,1: PRINT SPACE$(45) 'blank out any error messages
6530 GOSUB 8260 'initialize arrays
6540 KASE = 6: GOSUB 8150 'getting data
6550 'read organizational data
6560 INPUT #1, DAYS.PAID, HOURS.WORKED, FR.RATE, FR.DAYS, FR.INCL, OH.RATE,
     PROF.RATE, FC.MULT
6570 INPUT #1, COUNT
6580 FOR I = 1 TO COUNT: INPUT #1,
        INITIALS$(I), NUMBER(I), SALARY(I), APPLIED(I), AR$(I), FULL.COST(I):
     NEXT I
6590 INPUT #1, PROJ.NAME$, TIME.UNIT$, TIME.UNIT
6600 'read option and step data
6610 FOR O = 1 TO 2
6620 INPUT #1, STEP.COUNT (O)
6630    IF STEP.COUNT(O) = 0 THEN 6760
6640   FOR S = 1 TO STEP.COUNT(O)
6650       INPUT #1, STEP.NAME$(S,O)
6660       INPUT #1, COUNT
6670       FOR N = 1 TO COUNT
6680           INPUT #1, LAB.NAME$(S,O,N), LAB.NUMBER(S,O,N), LAB.SALARY(S,O,N)
                          LAB.COST(S,O,N), LAB.TIME(S,O,N), LAB.TOTAL(S,O,N)
6690       NEXT N
6700       INPUT #1, TOTAL.LAB(S,O), COUNT
6710       FOR N = 1 TO COUNT
6720           INPUT #1, EXP.NAME$(S,O,N), EXP.COST(S,O,N), EXP.NUMBER(S,O,N),
                EXP.TOTAL(S,O,N)
6730       NEXT N
6740       INPUT #1, TOTAL.EXP(S,O), STEP.TOTAL(S,O)
6750    NEXT S
6760 NEXT O
```

```
6770 CLOSE #1: RETURN
6780 '
6790 '
7000 'enter names and applied rates
7010 CLS: LOCATE 1,10:
     PRINT "INITIALS, SALARY/YEAR, AND APPLIED RATES FOR UP TO 9 PEOPLE"
7020 LOCATE 4,6
7030 PRINT " PERSON'S NAME " B$ "  #  " B$ " SALARY/YEAR " B$ " APPLIED RATE "
     B$ " G / N " B$ " FULL COST/" TIME.UNIT$
7040 '
7050 FOR I = 1 TO 9 'fill it in
7060    GOSUB 7230
7070    PRINT TAB(6) I;
7080    IF INITIALS$(I) = "" THEN GOSUB 7230: R = R + 1: GOTO 7170
7090    PRINT TAB(10) INITIALS$(I);
7100    PRINT TAB(21) B$ " "; USING "###"; NUMBER(I);
7110    PRINT TAB(27) B$ " "; USING "$#######"; SALARY(I);
7120    PRINT TAB(41) B$ "    "; USING "###"; APPLIED(I);
7130    PRINT TAB(56) B$ "    "; AR$(I);
7140    GOSUB 7680 'redo calculations
7150    PRINT TAB(64) B$ "    " USING U6$; FULL.COST(I)
7160    R = R + 1
7170 NEXT I
7180 KASE = 1: GOSUB 8150    'esc to return
7190 GOTO 7260
7200 '
7210 'blank out a line
7220 INITIALS$(I) = "": SALARY(I) = 0: APPLIED(I) = 0: AR$(I) = "":
     FULL.COST(I) = 0
7230 PRINT TAB(21) B$ TAB(27) B$ TAB(41) B$ TAB(56) B$ TAB(64) B$
7240 RETURN
7250 '
7260 I = 0: R = 4
7270 'start loop here
7280    I = I + 1: IF I > 9 THEN 7650 'no more entries allowed
7290    IF AR$(I) = "" THEN AR.BASE = 0
7300    'name
7310    R = R + 2
7320    Q = 1: LOCATE R,10: FL = 10: PROMPT$ = INITIALS$(I)
7330    GOSUB 1040: IF MOVE.IT THEN 7750
7340    IF IN$ = "" OR IN$ = SPACE$(LEN(IN$)) THEN GOSUB 7220: GOTO 7650
7350    INITIALS$(I) = IN$
7360    'how many
7370    Q = 2: LOCATE R,23: FL = 103: PROMPT$= MID$(STR$(NUMBER(I)),2)
7380    GOSUB 1040: IF MOVE.IT THEN 7750
7390    NUMBER(I) = VAL(IN$)
7400    LOCATE, 23: PRINT USING "###"; NUMBER(I)
7410    'salary
7420    Q = 3: LOCATE R,30: PRINT "$ ";: FL = 106:
        PROMPT$=MID$(STR$(SALARY(I)),2)
7430    GOSUB 1040: IF MOVE.IT THEN 7750
7440    IF VAL(IN$) <> SALARY(I) THEN SALARY(I) = VAL(IN$):
        LOCATE,30: PRINT USING "$#######"; SALARY(I);: GOSUB 7680:
        IF FULL.COST(I) > 0 THEN GOSUB 7730
7450    'applied rate
7460    Q = 4: LOCATE R,47
7470    X = APPLIED(I): GOSUB 3125 'format prompt$
7480    FL = 104: PROMPT$ = X$
7490    GOSUB 1040: IF MOVE.IT THEN 7750
7500    IF VAL(IN$) > 1 THEN 7460
7510    IF VAL(IN$) <> APPLIED(I) THEN APPLIED(I) = VAL(IN$):
        LOCATE, 47: PRINT USING "#.##"; APPLIED(I);: GOSUB 7680: GOSUB 7730
7520    'is the rate gross or net?
7530    Q = 5: LOCATE R,60: FL = 401: PROMPT$ = AR$(I)
7540    GOSUB 1040: IF MOVE.IT THEN 7750
```

```
7550    AR$(I) = IN$:  LOCATE ,60: PRINT AR$(I);
7560    GOSUB 7680: GOSUB 7730
7570    'full cost
7580    Q = 6: LOCATE R,67: PRINT "$ ";
7590    X = FULL.COST(I): GOSUB 3125 'format prompt$
7600    FL = 108: PROMPT$ = X$
7610    GOSUB 1040: IF MOVE.IT THEN 7750
7620    IF VAL(IN$) <> FULL.COST(I) THEN FULL.COST(I) = VAL(IN$):
            LOCATE,67: PRINT USING U6$; FULL.COST(I);
7630 GOTO 7280
7640 '
7650 RETURN 'to main
7660 '
7670 'calculate full cost
7680 IF AR$(I) = "N" THEN AR.BASE = DAYS.PAID - FR.DAYS
        ELSE IF AR$(I) = "G" THEN AR.BASE = DAYS.PAID
            ELSE AR.BASE = 0
7690 DIVISOR = AR.BASE * HOURS.WORKED * APPLIED(I)
7700 IF DIVISOR <> 0 THEN FULL.COST(I) =
            TIME.UNIT * SALARY(I) * FC.MULT / DIVISOR
7710 RETURN
7720 'print full cost
7730 LOCATE ,67: PRINT USING U6$; FULL.COST(I);: RETURN
7740 '
7750 'handle cursor keys
7760 KY = ASC(RIGHT$(N$,1))
7770 IF KY = ESC THEN RETURN
7780 IF KY = PAGE.UP THEN I = 1: R = 4: GOTO 7310
7790 IF KY = PAGE.DN THEN I = 9: R = 20: GOTO 7310
7800 IF KY = CURSOR.LF THEN
            IF Q = 1 THEN KY = CURSOR.UP
            ELSE ON Q - 1 GOTO 7320, 7370, 7420, 7460, 7530
7810 IF KY = CURSOR.UP THEN
            IF I > 1 THEN I = I - 1: R = R - 4: GOTO 7310
7820 IF KY = CURSOR.DN THEN
            IF I < 9 THEN 7630
7830 ON Q GOTO 7320, 7370, 7420, 7460, 7530, 7580
7840 '
7850 '
7860 'look for initials entered
7870 APPL.RATE = 1: FOUND = NO: I = 1
7880 I = 1: FOUND = NO: N$ = LAB.NAME$(S,O,N)
7890 IF INITIALS$(I) = "" THEN 7910
7900    IF INITIALS$(I) = N$ THEN FOUND = YES: LAB.NUMBER(S,O,N) = NUMBER(I):
            LAB.SALARY(S,O,N) = SALARY(I): APPL.RATE = APPLIED(I):
            LAB.COST(S,O,N) = FULL.COST(I)
7910    I = I + 1: IF I > 9 THEN 7930
7920 GOTO 7890
7930 RETURN
7940 '
8000 'error handler for printing
8010 IF ERR = 25 THEN LOCATE 4,1:
        PRINT "Printer is not turned on." SPACE$(20): RESUME
8020 IF ERR = 27 THEN LOCATE 4,1:
        PRINT "Printer is out of paper." SPACE$(20): RESUME
8030 ON ERROR GOTO 0
8040 RESUME
8050 '
8060 'error handler for file I/O
8070 IF ERR = 52 THEN LOCATE 9,1:
        PRINT "File name is invalid, re-enter file name.": RESUME 6050
8080 IF ERR = 53 THEN LOCATE 9,1:
        PRINT "File not found, re-enter file name." SPACE$(6): RESUME 6050
8090 IF ERR = 70 THEN LOCATE 9,1:
        PRINT "Disk is write-protected." SPACE$(20): RESUME 6050
```

```
8100 IF ERR = 71 THEN LOCATE 9,1:
        PRINT "Disk is not ready." SPACE$(30): RESUME 6050
8110 ON ERROR GOTO 0
8120 RESUME
8130 '
8140 'various messages
8150 LOCATE 24,20: PRINT SPACE$(55);
8160 IF KASE = 1 THEN LOCATE ,22:
        PRINT " PRESS [Esc] TO RETURN TO MAIN MENU";: RETURN
8170 IF KASE = 2 THEN LOCATE ,22:
        PRINT "PRESS "; E$; " TO CONTINUE";: RETURN
8180 IF KASE = 3 THEN LOCATE ,22:
        PRINT "PRESS ANY KEY TO CONTINUE";: RETURN
8190 IF KASE = 4 THEN LOCATE ,22:
        PRINT "RECALCULATING ORGANIZATIONAL DATA";: RETURN
8200 IF KASE = 5 THEN LOCATE ,22:
        PRINT "RE-INITIALIZING DATA";: RETURN
8210 IF KASE = 6 THEN LOCATE ,22:
        PRINT "READING DATA FROM DISK";: RETURN
8220 IF KASE = 7 THEN LOCATE ,22:
        PRINT "SAVING DATA TO DISK";: RETURN
8230 RETURN
8240 '
8250 'initialize data
8260 KASE = 5: GOSUB 8150 're-init data
8270 FOR I = 1 TO 9
8280    INITIALS$(I) = "": NUMBER(I) = 0: SALARY(I) = 0: APPLIED(I) = 0:
        AR$(I) = "": FULL.COST(I) = 0
8290 NEXT I
8300 PROJ.NAME$ = "": TIME.UNIT$ = "HOUR"
8310 FOR S = 1 TO STEP.MAX
8320    STEP.COUNT(S) = 0
8330    FOR O = 1 TO 2
8340       STEP.NAME$(S,O) = "": STEP.TOTAL(S,O) = 0: TOTAL.LAB(S,O) = 0:
           TOTAL.EXP(S,O) = 0
8350       FOR N = 1 TO N.MAX
8360          LAB.NAME$(S,O,N) = "": LAB.NUMBER(S,O,N) = 0:LAB.SALARY(S,O,N) = 0:
              LAB.COST(S,O,N) = 0: LAB.TIME(S,O,N) = 0: LAB.TOTAL(S,O,N) = 0
8370          EXP.NAME$(S,O,N) = "": EXP.COST(S,O,N) = 0: EXP.NUMBER(S,O,N) = 0:
              EXP.TOTAL(S,O,N) = 0
8380       NEXT N
8390    NEXT O
8400 NEXT S
8410 RETURN
```

Index